Handbook of Home Rule

by W. E. Gladstone

EDITOR'S NOTE.

Of the articles contained in this volume, those by Mr. Gladstone, Mr. E.L. Godkin on "A Lawyer's Objections to Home Rule," and Mr. Barry O'Brien appear for the first time. The others are reprinted from the Contemporary Review, the Nineteenth Century, and the New Princeton Review, to the proprietors and editors of which periodicals respectively the thanks of the several writers and of the editor are tendered. In most of these reprints some passages of transitory interest have been omitted, and some few additions have been made.

The object of the writers has been to treat the difficult questions connected with the Government of Ireland in a dispassionate spirit; and the volume is offered to the public in the hope that it may, at a time of warm controversy over passing events, help to lead thoughtful men back to the consideration of the principles which underlie those questions, and which it seeks to elucidate by calm discussion and by references to history.

October, 1887.

CONTENTS.

PREFACE. BY THE RIGHT HON. EARL SPENCER, K.G.

AMERICAN HOME RULE. BY E.L. GODKIN

HOW WE BECAME HOME RULERS. BY JAMES BRYCE, M.P.

HOME RULE AND IMPERIAL UNITY. BY LORD THRING

THE IRISH GOVERNMENT BILL AND THE IRISH LAND BILL. BY LORD THRING

THE "UNIONIST" POSITION. BY CANON MACCOLL

A LAWYER'S OBJECTIONS TO HOME RULE. BY E.L. GODKIN

THE "UNIONIST" CASE FOR HOME RULE. BY R. BARRY O'BRIEN

IRELAND'S ALTERNATIVES. BY LORD THRING

THE PAST AND FUTURE OF THE IRISH QUESTION. BY JAMES BRYCE, M.P.

SOME ARGUMENTS CONSIDERED. BY THE RIGHT HON. JOHN MORLEY, M.P.

LESSONS OF IRISH HISTORY IN THE EIGHTEENTH CENTURY. BY THE RIGHT HON. W.E. GLADSTONE, M.P.

PREFACE.

The present seems an excellent moment for bringing forward the arguments in favour of a new policy for Ireland, which are to be found in the articles contained in this volume.

We are realizing the first results of the verdict given at the election of 1886. And this I interpret as saying that the constituencies were not then ready to depart from the lines of policy which, up to last year, nearly all politicians of both parties in Parliament had laid down for their guidance in Irish affairs.

We have had the Session occupied almost wholly with Lord Salisbury's proposals for strengthening the power of the central Government to maintain law and order in Ireland, and for dealing with the most pressing necessities of the Land question in that country.

It is well, before the policy of the Government is practically tested, that the views of thoughtful men holding different opinions should be clearly set forth, not in the shape of polemical speeches, but in measured articles which specially appeal to those who have not hitherto joined the fighting ranks of either side, and who are sure to intervene with great force at the next election, when the Irish question is again submitted to the constituencies.

I feel that I can add little or nothing to the weight of the arguments contained in these papers, but I should like to give some reasons why I earnestly hope that they will receive careful consideration.

The writers have endeavoured to approach their work with impartiality, and to free themselves from those prejudices which make it difficult for Englishmen to discuss Irish questions in a fresh and independent train of thought, and realize how widely Irish customs, laws, traditions, and sentiments differ from our own.

We are apt to think that what has worked well here will work well in Ireland; that Irishmen who differ from us are unreasonable; and that their proposals for change must be mistaken. We do not make allowance for the soreness of feeling prevailing among men who have long objected to the system by which Ireland has been governed, and who find that their earnest appeals for reform have been, until recent times, contemptuously disregarded by English politicians. Time after time moderate counsels have been rejected until too late. Acts of an exceptional character intended to secure law and order have been very numerous, and every one of them has caused fresh irritation; while remedial measures have been given in a manner which has not won the sympathy of the people, because they have not been the work of the Irish themselves, and have not been prepared in their own way.

Parliament seems during the past Session to have fallen into the same error. By the power of an English majority, measures have been passed which are vehemently opposed by the political leaders and the majority of the Irish nation, and which are only agreeable to a small minority in Ireland. This action can only succeed if the Irish can be persuaded to relinquish the national sentiments of Home Rule; and yet this was never stronger or more vigorous than at the present time. It is supported by millions of Irish settled in America and in Australia; and here I would say that it has often struck me that the strong feeling of dissatisfaction, or, I might say, of disaffection, among the Irish is fed and nurtured by the marked contrast existing between the social condition of large numbers of the Irish in the South and West of Ireland and the views and habits of their numerous relatives in the United States.

The social condition of many parts of Ireland is as backward, or perhaps more backward, than the condition of the rural population of England at the end of last or the beginning of this century. The Irish peasantry still live in poor hovels, often in the same room with animals; they have few modern comforts; and yet they are in close communication with those who live at ease in the cities and farms of the United States. They are also imbued with all the advanced political notions of the American Republic, and are sufficiently educated to read the latest political doctrines in the Press which circulates among them. Their social condition at home is a hundred years behind their state of political and mental culture. They naturally contrast the misery of many Irish peasants with the position of their relatives in the New World. This cannot but embitter their views against English rulers, and strengthen their leaning to national sentiments. Their national aspirations have never died out since 1782. They have taken various forms; but if the movements arising from them have been put down, fresh movements have constantly sprung up. The Press has grown into an immense power, and its influences have all been used to strengthen the zeal for Irish nationality, while, at the same time, the success of the national movements in Italy, Hungary, Greece, and Germany have had the same effect. Lastly, the sentiment of Home Rule has gained the sympathy of large bodies of electors in the constituencies of Great Britain, and, under the circumstances, it is difficult to suppose that, even if the country remains quiet, constitutional agitation will vanish or the Irish relinquish their most cherished ambition.

We hear, from men who ought to know something of Ireland, that if the Land question is once settled, and dual ownership practically abolished, the tenants will be satisfied, and the movement for Home Rule will no longer find active support in Ireland. Without going into the whole of this argument, I should like to say two things: first, that I do not know how a large scheme of Land Purchase can be carried through Parliament with safety to Imperial interests without establishing, at the same time, some strong Irish Government in Dublin to act between the Imperial Government and the tenants of Ireland; and, second, that the feeling for Home Rule has a vitality of its own which will survive the Land question, even if independently settled.

Home Rule is an expression of national feeling which cannot be extinguished in Ireland, and the only safe method of dealing with it is to turn its force and power to the support of an Irish Government established for the management of local Irish affairs. There are those who think that this must lead to separation. I cannot believe in this fear, for I know of no English statesman who looks upon complete separation of Ireland from Great Britain as possible. The geographical position of Ireland, the social and commercial connection between the two peoples, renders such a thing impossible. The Irish know this, and they are not so foolish as to think that they could gain their independence by force of arms; but I do not believe that they desire it. They are satisfied to obtain the management of their own local affairs under the 鎔 is of the flag of England. The papers in this volume show how this can be done with due regard to Imperial interests and the rights of minorities.

I shall not enlarge on this part of the subject, but I wish to draw attention to the working of the Irish Government, and the position which it holds in the country, for it is through its administration that the policy of the Cabinet will be carried out. At the outset I feel bound to deprecate the exaggerated condemnation which the "Castle" receives from its opponents. It has its defects. Notwithstanding efforts of various ministers to enlarge the circle from which its officials are drawn, it is still too narrow for the modern development of Irish society, and it has from time to time been recruited from partisans without sufficient regard to the efficiency and requirements of the public service. But, on the whole, its members, taken as individuals, can well bear comparison with those of other branches of the Civil Service. They are diligent; they desire to do their duty with impartiality, and to hold an even balance between many opposing interests in Ireland. Whatever party is in office, they loyally carry out the policy of their chiefs. They are, probably, more plastic to the leadership of the heads of departments than members of some English offices, and they are more quickly moved by the influences around them. Sometimes they may relapse into an attitude of indifference and inertness if their chiefs are not active; but, on the other hand, they will act with vigour and decision if they are led by men who know their own minds and desire to be firm in the government of the country.

When speaking of the chiefs of the Irish Civil Service, who change according to the political party in office, we must not overlook the legal officers, who exercise a most powerful influence on Irish administration. They consist of the Lord Chancellor, the Attorney and Solicitor General, and, until 1883, there was also an officer called the Law Adviser, who was the maid-of-all-work of Castle administration. In England, those who hold similar legal offices take no part in the daily administration of public affairs. The Lord Chancellor, as a member of the Cabinet, takes his share in responsibility for the policy of the Government. The law officers are consulted in special cases, and take their part from time to time in debates in the House of Commons. In Ireland, however, the Chancellor is constantly consulted by the Lord-Lieutenant on any difficult matter of administration, and the Attorney and Solicitor General are in constant communication with the Lord-Lieutenant, if he carries out the daily work of administration, and with the Chief and the Under Secretary.

Governments differ as to the use they make of these officials. Some Governments have endeavoured to confine their work to cases where a mere legal opinion has to be obtained; but, when the country is in a disturbed state, even these limited references become very frequent, and questions of policy as well as of law are often discussed with the law officers. It is needless to say that, with their knowledge of Ireland and the traditions of Castle government (it is rare that all the law officers are new to office, and, consequently, they carry on the traditions from one Government to another), they often exercise a paramount influence over the policy of the Irish Government, and practically control it.

They are connected with the closest and most influential order in Irish society--the legal order, consisting of the judges and Bar of Ireland. This adds to the general weight of their advice, but it has a special bearing when cases of legal reform or administration are under consideration; it then requires unwonted courage and independence for the law officers of the Crown to support changes which the lay members of the Government deem necessary.

I have known conspicuous instances of the exercise of these high qualities by law officers enabling reforms to be carried, but as a rule, particularly when the initiative of legal reform is left to them, the Irish law officers do not care to move against the feeling of the legal world in Dublin. The lawyers, like other bodies, oppose the diminution of offices and honours belonging to them, or of the funds which, in the way of fees and salaries, are distributed among members of the bar; and they become bitterly hostile to any permanent official who is known to be a firm legal reformer. It would be impossible for me not to acknowledge the great service often done to the Government by the able men who have filled the law offices, yet I feel that under certain circumstances, when their influence has been allowed too strongly to prevail, it has tended to narrow the views of the Irish Government, and to keep it within a circle too narrow for the altered circumstances of modern life.

The chief peculiarity of the Irish Administration is its extreme centralization. In this two departments may be mentioned as typical of the whole--the police and administration of local justice.

The police in Dublin and throughout Ireland are under the control of the Lord-Lieutenant, and both these forces are admirable of their kind. They are almost wholly maintained by Imperial funds. The Dublin force costs about ?50,000 a year. The Royal Irish Constabulary costs over a million in quiet, and a million and a half in disturbed times. Local authorities have nothing to do with their action or management. Local justice is administered by unpaid magistrates as in England, but they have been assisted, and gradually are being supplanted, by magistrates appointed by the Lord-Lieutenant and paid by the State.

This state of things arose many years ago from the want of confidence between resident landlords and the bulk of the people. When agrarian or religious differences disturbed a locality the people distrusted the local magistrates, and by degrees the system of stipendiary, or, as they are called, resident magistrates, spread over the country. To maintain the judicial independence and impartiality of these magistrates is of the highest importance. At one time this was in some danger, for the resident magistrates not only heard cases at petty sessions, but, as executive peace officers, to a very great extent took the control of the police in their district, not only at riots, but in following up and discovering offenders. Their position as judicial and executive officers was thus very unfortunately mixed up. Between 1882 and 1883 the Irish Government did their utmost to separate and distinguish between these two functions, and it is to be hoped that the same policy has been and will be now continued, otherwise grave mischief in the administration of justice will arise. The existence of this staff of stipendiary magistrates could not fail to weaken the influence of the gentry in local affairs, and, at the same time, other causes were at work to undermine still further their power. The spread of education, the ballot, the extension of the franchise, communication with America, all tended to strengthen the political leaning of the tenants towards the National party in Ireland, and to widen the political differences between the richer and poorer classes in the country. The result of this has been, that not only have even the best landlords gradually lost their power in Parliamentary elections and on elective boards, but the Government, which greatly relied on them for support, has become isolated.

The system of centralization is felt all over the country. It was the cause of weakness in the disturbed years of 1880 and 1881, and, although the Irish Executive strengthened themselves by placing officers over several counties, on whom they devolved a great deal of responsibility, they did not by these steps meet the real difficulty, which was that everything that went wrong, whether as to police or magisterial decisions, was attributed to the management of the Castle.

In this country, local authorities and benches of magistrates, quite independent of the Home Office, are held responsible for mistakes in police action or irregularities in local justice. The consequence is that there is a strong buffer to protect the character and power of the Home Office.

The absence of such protection in Ireland obviously has a very prejudicial effect on the permanent influence and popularity of the Irish Government. But as long as our system of government from England exists, this centralization cannot be avoided, for it would not be possible to transfer the responsibility of the police to local representative bodies, as they are too much opposed to the landlords and the Government to be trusted when strong party differences arise; nor, for the same reason, would it be possible to fall back on local men to administer justice. The fact is, that, out of the Protestant part of Ulster, the Irish Government receives the cordial support of only the landed proprietors, and a part of the upper middle classes in the towns. The feeling of the mass of the people has been so long against them that no change in the direction of trust in any centralized government of anti-national character can be expected.

It would be difficult, perhaps impossible, to find any Municipal Council, Boards of Guardians, or Local Boards, in Leinster, Munster, or Connaught, whose members do not consist of a majority of Nationalists. At nearly all such assemblies, whenever any important political movement takes place in the country, or when the Irish Government take any action which is displeasing to the Nationalists, resolutions are discussed and carried in a spirit of sharp hostility to the Government.

In Parliamentary elections we also find clear evidence of the strength of the Nationalists, and the extreme weakness of their opponents. This is a test which those who accept popular representative government cannot disregard, particularly at an election when for the first time the new constituencies were called upon to exercise the privileges entrusted to them by Parliament. Such was the election of 1885, followed in 1886 by another General Election. In 1885 contests took place in most of the Irish constituencies. They were between Liberals allied with Conservatives, and Parnellites. In 1886 the contests were between those who called themselves Unionists and Parnellites, and the Irish policy of Mr. Gladstone was specially referred to the electors.

In regard to the number of members returned on the two sides, the result of each election was almost identical, but in 1886 there were fewer contests. We may, then, assume that the relative forces of Parnellites and Unionists were accurately represented at the election of 1885. If we take the votes at the election of 1885 for candidates standing as Nationalists, we shall find, roughly speaking, that they obtained in round numbers about 300,000 votes, and candidates who stood either as Liberals or Conservatives about 143,000. But the case is really stronger than these figures represent it, because in some constituencies the contests were between Liberals and Conservatives, and there can be no doubt that in those constituencies a number of Nationalist votes were given for one or both of such candidates--votes which, therefore, would have to be deducted from the 143,000, leaving a still heavier majority on the Nationalist side.[1]

If we look at individual constituencies, we find that in South Kerry only 133 persons voted for the "Unionist" candidate, while 2742 voted for the Nationalist. In six out of seven constituencies in Cork where contests took place 27,692 votes were given for the Nationalists, and only 1703 for their opponents. In Dublin, in the division which may be considered the West End constituency of the Irish metropolis, the most successful man of commerce in Ireland, a leader of society, whose liberality towards those in his employment is only equalled by his munificence in all public works, was defeated by over 1900 votes. He did not stand in 1886, but his successor was defeated by a still larger majority. These elections show the numbers in Ireland on which the Government and those who oppose Mr. Parnell's policy can count for support.

It is absurd to say that these results are caused by terrorism exercised over the minds of the electors by the agitators in Ireland; the same results occurred in every part of three provinces, and in part of Ulster, and the universality of the feeling proves the dominant feeling of the Irish electors. They show the extreme difficulty, the impossibility, of gaining that support and confidence which a Government needs in a free country. As it is, the Irish Government stands isolated in Ireland, and relies for support solely on England. Is a policy opposed to national feeling, which has been often, and by different Ministers, tried in Ireland, likely to succeed in the hands of a Government such as I have described, and isolated, as I think few will deny it to be? It is impossible in the long run to maintain it. The roots of strength are wanting.

If we turn from Dublin to London, we do not find greater prospects of success. Twice within fourteen months Lord Salisbury has formed a Government. In 1885 his Cabinet, on taking office, deliberately decided to rule Ireland without exceptional laws; after a few months, they announced that they must ask Parliament for fresh powers. They resigned before they had defined their measures. But within six months Lord Salisbury was once more Prime

Minister, and again commenced his administration by governing Ireland under the ordinary law. This attempt did not continue longer than the first, for when Parliament met in 1887, preparations were at once made to carry the Criminal Law Amendment Act, which occupied so large a portion of the late Session.

This is not the action of men who have strong faith in their principles. Nor can it be shown that the continuous support so necessary for success will be given to this policy. No doubt it may be urged that the operation of the Act is not limited in duration; but, notwithstanding that, few politicians believe that the constituencies of Great Britain will long support the application of exceptional criminal laws to any part of the United Kingdom.

This would be wholly inconsistent with past experience In relation to these measures, which points entirely the other way; and the publication in English newspapers and constant discussion on English platforms of the painful incidents which seem, unfortunately, inseparable from a rigid administration of the law in Ireland, together with the prolonged debates, such incidents give rise to, in Parliament, aggravate the difficulties of administration, and lead the Irish people to believe that exceptional legislation will be as short-lived in the future as it has been in the past.

It was this evidence of want of continuity of policy in 1885, and the startling disclosure of the weakness of the anti-national party in Ireland at the election in the autumn of that year, which finally convinced me that the time had come when we could no longer turn to a mixed policy of remedial and exceptional criminal legislation as the means of winning the constituencies of that country in support of our old system of governing Ireland. That system has failed for eighty-six years, and obviously cannot succeed when worked with representative institutions. As the people of Great Britain will not for a moment tolerate the withdrawal of representative government from Ireland, we must adopt some new plan. What I have here written deals with but a fragment of the arguments for Home Rule, some of which are admirably set forth by the able men who have written the articles to which this is the preface. I earnestly wish that they may arrest the attention of many excellent Irishmen who still cling to the old traditions of English rule, and cause them to realize that the only way of relieving their country from the intolerable uncertainty which hangs over her commercial, social, and political interests and paralyzes all efforts for the improvement of her people, will be to form a Constitution supported by all classes of the community. I trust that they will join in this work before it is too late, for they may yet exercise a powerful and salutary influence in the settlement of this great question.

FOOTNOTES:

[Footnote 1: There was one case--North Louth--in which two Nationalists opposed one another, and I have left that case out of the calculation.]

AMERICAN HOME RULE

BY E.L. GODKIN

American experience has been frequently cited, in the course of the controversy now raging in England over the Irish question, both by way of warning and of example. For instance, I have found in the Times as well as in other journals--the Spectator, I think, among the number--very contemptuous dismissals of the plan of offering Ireland a government like that of an American State, on the ground that the Americans are loyal to the central authority, while in Ireland there is a strong feeling of hostility to it, which would probably increase under Home Rule. The Queen's writ, it has been remarked, cannot be said to run in large parts of Ireland, while in every part of the United States the Federal writ is implicitly obeyed, and the ministers of Federal authority find ready aid and sympathy from the people. If I remember rightly, the Duke of Argyll has been very emphatic in pointing out the difference between giving local self-government to a community in which the tendencies of popular feeling are "centrifugal," and giving it to one in which these tendencies are "centripetal." The inference to be drawn was, of course, that as long as Ireland disliked the Imperial government the concession of Home Rule would be unsafe, and would only become safe when the Irish people showed somewhat the same sort of affection for the English connection which the people of the State of New York now feel for the Constitution of the United States.

Among the multitude of those who have taken part in the controversy on one side or the other, no one has, so far as I have observed, pointed out that the state of feeling in America toward the central government with which the state of feeling in Ireland towards the British Government is now compared, did not exist when the American Constitution was set up; that the political tendencies in America at that time were centrifugal, not centripetal, and that the extraordinary love and admiration with which Americans now regard the Federal government are the result of eighty years' experience of its working. The first Confederation was as much as the people could bear in the way of surrendering local powers when the War of Independence came to an end. It was its hopeless failure to provide peace and security which led to the framing of the present Constitution. But even with this experience still fresh, the adoption of the Constitution was no easy matter. I shall not burden this article with historical citations showing the very great difficulty which the framers of the Constitution had in inducing the various States to adopt it, or the magnitude and variety of the fears and suspicions with which, many of the most influential men in all parts of the country regarded it. Any one who wishes to know how numerous and diversified these fears and suspicions were, cannot do better than read the series of papers known as "The Federalist," written mainly by Hamilton and Madison, to commend the new plan to the various States. It was adopted almost as a matter of necessity, that is, as the only way out of the Slough of Despond in which the Confederation had plunged the union of the States; but the objections to it which were felt at the beginning were only removed by actual trial. Hamilton's two colleagues, as delegates from New York, Yates and Lansing, withdrew in disgust from the Convention, as soon as the Constitution was outlined, and did not return. The notion that the Constitution was produced by the craving of the American people for something of that sort to love and revere, and that it was not bestowed on them until they had given ample assurance that they would lavish affection on it, has no foundation whatever in fact. The devotion of Americans to the Union is, indeed, as clear a case of cause and effect as is to be found in political history. They have learned to like the Constitution because the country has prospered under it, and because it has given them all the benefits of national life without interference with local liberties. If they had not set up a central government until the centrifugal sentiment had disappeared from the States, and the feeling of loyalty for a central authority had fully shown itself, they would assuredly never have set it up at all.

Moreover, it has to be borne in mind that the adoption of the Constitution did not involve the surrender of any local franchises, by which the people of the various States set great store. The States preserved fully four-fifths of their autonomy, or in fact nearly all of it which closely concerned the daily lives of individuals. Set aside the post-office, and a citizen of the State of New York, not engaged in foreign trade, might, down to the outbreak of the Civil War, have passed a long and busy life without once coming in contact with a United States official, and without being made aware in any of his doings, by any restriction or regulation, that he was living under any government but that of his own State. If he went abroad he had to apply for a United States passport. If he quarrelled with a foreigner, or with the citizen of another State, he might be sued in the Federal Court. If he imported foreign goods he had to pay duties to the collector of a Federal Custom-house. If he invented something, or wrote a book, he had to apply to the Department of the Interior for a patent or a copyright. But how few there were in the first seventy years of American history who had any of these experiences! No one supposes, or has ever supposed, that had the Federalists demanded any very large sacrifice of local franchises, or attempted to set up even a close approach to a centralized Government, the adoption of the Constitution would have been possible. If, for instance, such a transfer of both administration and legislation to the central authority as took place in Ireland after the Union had been proposed, it would have been rejected with derision. You will get no American to argue with you on this point. If you ask him whether he thinks it likely that a highly centralized government could have been created in 1879--such a one, for example, as Ireland has been under since 1800--or whether if created it would by this time have won the affection of the people, or filled them with centripetal tendencies, he will answer you with a smile.

The truth is that nowhere, any more than in Ireland, do people love their Government from a sense of duty or because they crave an object of political affection, or even because it exalts them in the eyes of foreigners. They love it because they are happy or prosperous under it; because it supplies security in the form best suited to their tastes and habits, or in some manner ministers to their self-love. Loyalty to the king as the Lord's anointed, without any sense either of favours received or expected, has played a great part in European politics, I admit; but, for reasons which I will not here take up space in stating, a political arrangement, whether it be an elected monarch or a constitution, cannot be made, in our day, to reign in men's hearts except as the result of benefits so palpable that common people, as well as political philosophers, can see them and count them.

Many of the opponents of Home Rule, too, point to the vigour with which the

United States Government put down the attempt made by the South to break up the Union as an example of the American love of "imperial unity," and of the spirit in which England should now meet the Irish demands for local autonomy. This again is rather surprising, because you will find no one in America who will maintain for one moment that troops could have been raised in 1860 to undertake the conquest of the South for the purpose of setting up a centralized administration, or, in other words, for the purpose of wiping out State lines, or diminishing State authority. No man or party proposed anything of this kind at the outbreak of the war, or would have dared to propose it. The object for which the North rose in arms, and which Lincoln had in view when he called for troops, was the restoration of the Union just as it was when South Carolina seceded, barring the extension of slavery into the territories. During the first year of the war, certainly, the revolted States might at any time have had peace on the status quo basis, that is, without the smallest diminution of their rights and immunities under the Constitution. It was only when it became evident that the war would have to be fought out to a finish, as the pugilists say--that is, that it would have to end in a complete conquest of the Southern territory--that the question, what would become of the States as a political organization after the struggle was over, began to be debated at all. What did become of them? How did Americans deal with Home Rule, after it had been used to set on foot against the central authority what the newspapers used to delight in calling "the greatest rebellion the world ever saw"? The answer to these questions is, it seems to me, a contribution of some value to the discussion of the Irish problem in its present stage, if American precedents can throw any light whatever on it.

There was a Joint Committee of both Houses of Congress appointed in 1866 to consider the condition of the South with reference to the safety or expediency of admitting the States lately in rebellion to their old relations to the Union, including representation in Congress. It contained, besides such fanatical enemies of the South as Thaddeus Stevens, such very conservative men as Mr. Fessenden, Mr. Grimes, Mr. Morrill, and Mr. Conkling. Here is the account they gave of the condition of Southern feeling one year after Lee's surrender:--

"Examining the evidence taken by your committee still further, in connection with facts too notorious to be disputed, it appears that the Southern press, with few exceptions, and those mostly of newspapers recently established by

Northern men, abounds with weekly and daily abuse of the institutions and people of the loyal States; defends the men who led, and the principles which incited, the rebellion; denounces and reviles Southern men who adhered to the Union; and strives constantly and unscrupulously, by every means in its power, to keep alive the fire of hate and discord between the sections; calling upon the President to violate his oath of office, overturn the Government by force of arms, and drive the representatives of the people from their seats in Congress. The national banner is openly insulted, and the national airs scoffed at, not only by an ignorant populace, but at public meetings, and once, among other notable instances, at a dinner given in honour of a notorious rebel who had violated his oath and abandoned his flag. The same individual is elected to an important office in the leading city of his State, although an unpardoned rebel, and so offensive that the President refuses to allow him to enter upon his official duties. In another State the leading general of the rebel armies is openly nominated for Governor by the Speaker of the House of Delegates, and the nomination is hailed by the people with shouts of satisfaction, and openly endorsed by the press....

"The evidence of an intense hostility to the Federal Union, and an equally intense love of the late Confederacy, nurtured by the war is decisive. While it appears that nearly all are willing to submit, at least for the time being, to the Federal authority, it is equally clear that the ruling motive is a desire to obtain the advantages which will be derived from a representation in Congress. Officers of the Union army on duty, and Northern men who go south to engage in business, are generally detested and proscribed. Southern men who adhered to the Union are bitterly hated and relentlessly persecuted. In some localities prosecutions have been instituted in State courts against Union officers for acts done in the line of official duty, and similar prosecutions are threatened elsewhere as soon as the United States troops are removed. All such demonstrations show a state of feeling against which it is unmistakably necessary to guard.

"The testimony is conclusive that after the collapse of the Confederacy the feeling of the people of the rebellious States was that of abject submission. Having appealed to the tribunal of arms, they had no hope except that by the magnanimity of their conquerors, their lives, and possibly their property, might be preserved. Unfortunately the general issue of pardons to persons who had been prominent in the rebellion, and the feeling of kindliness and conciliation manifested by the Executive, and very generally indicated through the Northern press, had the effect to render whole communities forgetful of the crime they had committed, defiant towards the Federal Government, and regardless of their duties as citizens. The conciliatory measures of the Government do not seem to have been met even half-way. The bitterness and defiance exhibited towards the United States under such circumstances is without a parallel in the history of the world. In return for our leniency we receive only an insulting denial of our authority. In return for our kind desire for the resumption of fraternal relations we receive only an insolent assumption of rights and privileges long since forfeited. The crime we have punished is paraded as a virtue, and the principles of republican government which we have vindicated at so terrible a cost are denounced as unjust and oppressive.

"If we add to this evidence the fact that, although peace has been declared by the President, he has not, to this day, deemed it safe to restore the writ of habeas corpus, to relieve the insurrectionary States of martial law, nor to withdraw the troops from many localities, and that the commanding general deems an increase of the army indispensable to the preservation of order and the protection of loyal and well-disposed people in the South, the proof of a condition of feeling hostile to the Union and dangerous to the Government throughout the insurrectionary States would seem to be overwhelming."

This Committee recommended a series of coercive measures, the first of which was the adoption of the fourteenth amendment to the Constitution, which disqualified for all office, either under the United States or under any State, any person who having in any capacity taken an oath of allegiance to the United States afterwards engaged in rebellion or gave aid and comfort to the rebels. This denied the jus honorum to all the leading men at the South who had survived the war. In addition to it, an Act was passed in March, 1867, which put all the rebel States under military rule until a constitution should have been framed by a Convention elected by all males over twenty-one, except such as would be excluded from office by the above-named constitutional amendment if it were adopted, which at that time it had not been. Another Act was passed three weeks later, prescribing, for voters in the States lately in rebellion, what was known as the "ironclad oath," which excluded from the franchise not only all who had borne arms against the United States, but all who, having ever held any office for which the taking an oath of allegiance to the United States was a qualification, had afterwards ever given "aid or comfort to the enemies thereof." This practically disfranchised all the white men of the South over twenty-five years old.

On this legislation there grew up, as all the world now knows, what was called the "carpet-bag" regime. Swarms of Northern adventurers went down to the Southern States, organized the ignorant negro voters, constructed State constitutions to suit themselves, got themselves elected to all the chief offices, plundered the State treasuries, contracted huge State debts, and stole the proceeds in connivance with legislatures composed mainly of negroes, of whom the most intelligent and instructed had been barbers and hotel-waiters. In some of the States, such as South Carolina and Mississippi, in which the negro population were in the majority, the government became a mere caricature. I was in Columbia, the capital of South Carolina, in 1872, during the session of the legislature, when you could obtain the passage of almost any measure you pleased by a small payment--at that time seven hundred dollars-- to an old negro preacher who controlled the coloured majority. Under the pretence of fitting up committee-rooms, the private lodging-rooms at the boarding-houses of the negro members, in many instances, were extravagantly furnished with Wilton and Brussels carpets, mirrors, and sofas. A thousand dollars were expended for two hundred elegant imported china spittoons. There were only one hundred and twenty-three members in the House of Representatives, but the residue were, perhaps, transferred to the private chambers of the legislators.

Now, how did the Southern whites deal with this state of things? Well, I am sorry to say they manifested their discontent very much in the way in which the Irish have for the last hundred years been manifesting theirs. If, as the English opponents of Home Rule seem to think, readiness to commit outrages, and refusal to sympathize with the victims of outrages, indicate political incapacity, the whites of the South showed, in the period between 1866 and 1876, that they were utterly unfit to be entrusted with the work of self-government. They could not rise openly in revolt because the United States troops were everywhere at the service of the carpet-baggers, for the suppression of armed resistance. They did not send petitions to Congress, or write letters to the Northern newspapers, or hold indignation meetings. They simply formed a huge secret society on the model of the "Molly Maguires" or "Moonlighters," whose special function was to intimidate, flog, mutilate, or murder political opponents in the night time. This society was called the "Ku-Klux Klan." Let me give some account of its operation, and I shall make it as brief as possible. It had become so powerful in 1871 that President Grant in that year, in his message to Congress, declared that "a condition of things existed in some of the States of the Union rendering life and property insecure, and the carrying of the mails and the collecting of the revenue dangerous." A Joint Select Committee of Congress was accordingly appointed, early in 1872, to "inquire into the condition of affairs in the late insurrectionary States, so far as regards the execution of the laws and the safety of the lives and property of the citizens of the United States." Its report now lies before me, and it reads uncommonly like the speech of an Irish Secretary in the House of Commons bringing in a "Suppression of Crime Bill." The Committee say--

"There is a remarkable concurrence of testimony to the effect that, in those of the late rebellious States into whose condition we have examined, the courts and juries administer justice between man and man in all ordinary cases, civil and criminal; and while there is this concurrence on this point, the evidence is equally decisive that redress cannot be obtained against those who commit crimes in disguise and at night. The reasons assigned are that identification is difficult, almost impossible; that, when this is attempted, the combinations and oaths of the order come in and release the culprit by perjury, either upon the witness-stand or in the jury-box; and that the terror inspired by their acts, as well as the public sentiment in their favour in many localities, paralyzes the arm of civil power.

* * * * *

"The murders and outrages which have been perpetrated in many counties of Middle and West Tennessee, during the past few months, have been so numerous, and of such an aggravated character, as almost baffles investigation. In these counties a reign of terror exists which is so absolute in its nature that the best of citizens are unable or unwilling to give free expression to their opinions. The terror inspired by the secret organization known as the Ku-Klux Klan is so great, that the officers of the law are powerless to execute its provisions, to discharge their duties, or to bring the guilty perpetrators of these outrages to the punishment they deserve. Their stealthy movements are generally made under cover of night, and under masks and disguises, which render their identification difficult, if not impossible. To add to the secrecy which envelops their operations, is the fact that no information of their murderous acts can be obtained without the greatest difficulty and danger in the localities where they are committed. No one dares to inform upon them, or take any measures to bring them to punishment, because no one can tell but that he may be the next victim of their hostility or animosity. The members of this organization, with their friends, aiders, and abettors, take especial pains to conceal all their operations.

* * * * *

"Your committee believe that during the past six months, the murders--to say nothing of other outrages--would average one a day, or one for every twenty-four hours; that in the great majority of these cases they have been perpetrated by the Ku-Klux above referred to, and few, if any, have been brought to punishment. A number of the counties of this State (Tennessee) are entirely at the mercy of this organization, and roving bands of nightly marauders bid defiance to the civil authorities, and threaten to drive out every man, white or black, who does not submit to their arbitrary dictation. To add to the general lawlessness of these communities, bad men of every description take advantage of the circumstances surrounding them, and perpetrate acts of violence, from personal or pecuniary motives, under the plea of political necessity."

Here is some of the evidence on which the report was based.

A complaint of outrages committed in Georgia was referred by the general of the army, in June, 1869, to the general of the Department of the South for thorough investigation and report. General Terry, in his report, made August 14, 1869, says[2]--

"In many parts of the State there is practically no government. The worst of crimes are committed, and no attempt is made to punish those who commit them. Murders have been and are frequent; the abuse, in various ways, of the blacks is too common to excite notice. There can be no doubt of the existence of numerous insurrectionary organizations known as 'Ku-Klux Klans,' who, shielded by their disguise, by the secrecy of their movements, and by the terror which they inspire, perpetrate crime with impunity. There is great reason to believe that in some cases local magistrates are in sympathy with the members of these organizations. In many places they are overawed by them and dare not attempt to punish them. To punish such offenders by civil proceedings would be a difficult task, even were magistrates in all cases disposed and had they the courage to do their duty, for the same influences which govern them equally affect juries and witnesses."

Lieutenant-Colonel Lewis Merrill, who assumed command (in Louisiana) on the 26th of March, and commenced investigation into the state of affairs, says (p. 1465)--

"From the best information I can get, I estimate the number of cases of whipping, beating, and personal violence of various grades, in this county, since the first of last November, at between three and four hundred, excluding numerous minor cases of threats, intimidation, abuse, and small personal violence, as knocking down with a pistol or gun, etc. The more serious outrages, exclusive of murders and whippings, noted hereafter, have been the following:--"

He then proceeds with the details of sixty-eight cases, giving the names of the parties injured, white and black, and including the tearing up of the railway, on the night before a raid was made by the Ku-Klux on the county treasury building. The rails were taken up, to prevent the arrival of the United States troops, who, it was known, were to come on Sunday morning. The raid was made on that Sunday night while the troops were lying at Chester, twenty-two miles distant, unable to reach Yorkville, because of the rails being torn up.

Another witness said: "To give the details of the whipping of men to compel them to change their mode of voting, the tearing of them away from their families at night, accompanied with insults and outrage, and followed by their murder, would be but repeating what has been described in other States, showing that it is the same organization in all, working by the same means for the same end. Five murders are shown to have been committed in Monroe County, fifteen in Noxubee, one in Lowndes, by the testimony taken in the city of Washington; but the extent to which school-houses were burnt, teachers whipped, and outrages committed in this State, cannot be fully given until the testimony taken by the sub-committee shall have been printed and made ready to report."

There are about eighty, closely printed, large octavo pages of this kind of testimony given by sufferers from the outrages.

Something was done to suppress the Ku-Klux by a Federal Act passed in 1871, which made offences of this kind punishable in the Federal Courts. Considerable numbers of them were arrested, tried, and convicted, and sent to undergo their punishment in the Northern jails. But there was no complete pacification of the South until the carpet-bag governments were refused the support of the Federal troops by President Hayes, on his accession to power in 1876. Then the carpet-bag r 間 ime disappeared like a house of cards. The chief carpet-baggers fled, and the government passed at once into the hands of the native whites. I do not propose to defend or explain the way in which they have since then kept it in their hands, by suppressing or controlling the negro vote. This is not necessary to my purpose.

What I seek to show is that the Irish are not peculiar in their manner of expressing their discontent with a government directed or controlled by the public opinion of another indifferent or semi-hostile community which it is impossible to resist in open warfare; that Anglo-Saxons resort to somewhat the same methods under similar circumstances, and that lawlessness and cruelty, considered as expressions of political animosity, do not necessarily argue any incapacity for the conduct of an orderly and efficient government, although I admit freely that they do argue a low state of civilization.

I will add one more illustration which, although more remote than those which I have taken from the Southern States during the reconstruction period, is not too remote for my purpose, and is in some respects stronger than any of them. I do not know a more orderly community in the world, or one which, down to the outbreak of the Civil War, when manufactures began to multiply, and the Irish immigration began to pour in, had a higher average of intelligence than the State of Connecticut. Down to 1818 all voters in that State had to be members of the Congregational Church. It had no large cities, and this, with the aid of its seat of learning, Yale College, preserved in it, I think, in greater purity than even Massachusetts, the old Puritan simplicity of manners, the Puritan spirit of order and thrift, and the business-like view of government which grew out of the practice of town government. A less sentimental community, I do not think, exists anywhere, or one in which the expression of strong feeling on any subject but religion is less cultivated or viewed with less favour. In the matter of managing their own political affairs in peace or war, I do not expect the Irish to equal the Connecticut people for a hundred years to come, no matter how much practice they may have in the interval, and I think that fifty years ago it was only picked bodies of Englishmen who could do so. Yet, in 1833, in the town of Canterbury, one of the most orderly and intelligent in the State, an estimable and much-esteemed lady, Miss Prudence Crandall, was carrying on a girls' school, when something happened to touch her conscience about the condition of the free negroes of the North. She resolved, in a moment of enthusiasm, to undertake the education of negro girls only. What follows forms one of the most famous episodes in the anti-slavery struggle in America, and is possibly familiar to many of the older readers of this article. I shall extract the account of it as given briefly in the lately published life of William Lloyd Garrison, by his sons. Some of the details are much worse than is here described.

"The story of this remarkable case cannot be pursued here except in brief.... It will be enough to say that the struggle between the modest and heroic young Quaker woman and the town lasted for nearly two years; that the school was opened in April; that attempts were immediately made under the law to frighten the pupils away and to fine Miss Crandall for harbouring them; that in May an Act prohibiting private schools for non-resident coloured persons, and providing for the expulsion of the latter, was procured from the legislature, amid the greatest rejoicing in Canterbury (even to the ringing of church bells); that, under this Act, Miss Crandall was in June arrested and temporarily imprisoned in the county jail, twice tried (August and October) and convicted; that her case was carried up to the Supreme Court of Errors, and her persecutors defeated on a technicality (July, 1834), and that pending this litigation the most vindictive and inhuman measures were taken to isolate the school from the countenance and even the physical support of the townspeople. The shops and the meeting-house were closed against teacher and pupils, carriage in the public conveyances was denied them, physicians would not wait upon them, Miss Crandall's own family and friends were forbidden, under penalty of heavy fines, to visit her, the well was filled with manure and water from other sources refused, the house itself was smeared with filth, assailed with rotten eggs and stones, and finally set on fire" (vol. i. p. 321).

Miss Crandall is still living in the West, in extreme old age, and the Connecticut legislature voted her a small pension two years ago, as a slight expiation of the ignominy and injustice from which she had suffered at the hands of a past generation.

The Spectator frequently refers to the ferocious hatred displayed toward the widow of Curtin, the man who was cruelly murdered by moonlighters somewhere in Kerry, as an evidence of barbarism which almost, if not quite, justifies the denial of self-government to a people capable of producing such monsters in one spot and on one occasion. Let me match this from Mississippi with a case which I produce, not because it was singular, but because it was notorious at the North, where it occurred, in 1877. One Chisholm, a native of the State, and a man of good standing and character, became a Republican after the war, and was somewhat active in organizing the negro voters in his district. He was repeatedly warned by some of his neighbours to desist and abandon politics, but continued resolutely on his course. A mob, composed of many of the leading men in the town, then attacked him in his house. He made his escape, with his wife and young daughter and son, a lad of fourteen, to the jail. His assailants broke the jail open, and killed him and his son, and desperately wounded the daughter. The poor lad received such a volley of bullets, that his blood went in one rush to the floor, and traced the outlines of his trunk on the ceiling of the room below, where it remained months afterwards, an eye-witness told me, as an illustration of the callousness of the jailer. The leading murderers were tried. They had no defence. The facts were not disputed. The judge and the bar did their duty, but the jury acquitted the prisoners without leaving their seats. Mrs. Chisholm, the widow, found neither sympathy nor friends at the scene of the tragedy. She had to leave the State, and found refuge in Washington, where she now holds a clerkship in the Treasury department.

Let me cite as another illustration the violent ways in which popular discontent may find expression in communities whose political capacity and general respect for the law and its officers, as well as for the sanctity of contracts, have never been questioned. Large tracts of land were formerly held along the Hudson river in the State of New York, by a few families, of which the Van Rensselaers and the Livingstons were the chief, either under grants from the Dutch at the first settlement of the colony, or from the English Crown after the conquest. That known as the "Manor of Rensselaerwick," held by the Van Rensselaers, comprised a tract of country extending twenty-four miles north and south, and forty-eight miles east and west, lying on each side of the

Hudson river. It was held by the tenants for perpetual leases. The rents were, on the Van Rensselaer estate, fourteen bushels of wheat for each hundred acres, and four fat hens, and one day's service with a carriage and horses, to each farm of one hundred and sixty acres. Besides this, there was a fine on alienation amounting to about half a year's rent. The Livingston estates were let in much the same way.

In 1839, Stephen Van Rensselaer, the proprietor, or "Patroon" as he was called, died, with $400,000 due to him as arrears from the tenants, for which, being a man of easy temper, he had forborne to press them. But he left the amount in trust by his will for the payment of his debts, and his heirs proceeded to collect it, and persisted in the attempt during the ensuing seven years. What then happened I shall describe in the words of Mr. John Bigelow. Mr. Tilden was a member of the State Legislature in 1846, and was appointed Chairman of a Committee to investigate the rent troubles, and make the report which furnished the basis for the legislation by which they were subsequently settled. Mr. Bigelow, who has edited Mr. Tilden's Public Writings and Speeches, prefaces the report with the following explanatory note:--

"Attempts were made to enforce the collection of these rents. The tenants resisted. They established armed patrols, and, by the adoption of various disguises, were enabled successfully to defy the civil authorities. Eventually it became necessary to call out the military, but the result was only partially satisfactory. These demonstrations of authority provoked the formation of 'anti-rent clubs' throughout the manorial district, with a view of acquiring a controlling influence in the legislature. Small bands, armed and disguised as Indians, were also formed to hold themselves in readiness at all times to resist the officers of the law whenever and wherever they attempted to serve legal process upon the tenants. The principal roads throughout the infected district were guarded by the bands so carefully, and the animosity between the tenants and the civil authorities was so intense, that at last it became dangerous for any one not an anti renter to be found in these neighbourhoods. It was equally dangerous for the landlords to make any appeal to the law or for the collection of rents or for protection of their persons. When Governor Wright entered upon his duties in Albany in 1845, he found that the anti-rent party had a formidable representation in the legislature, and that the questions involved were assuming an almost national importance."

The sheriff made gallant attempts to enforce the law, but his deputies were killed, and a legal investigation in which two hundred persons were examined, failed to reveal the perpetrators of the crime. The militia were called out, but they were no more successful than the sheriff. In the case of one murder committed in Delaware County in 1845, however, two persons were convicted, but their sentence was commuted to imprisonment for life. Various others concerned in the disturbances were convicted of minor offences, but when Governor Young succeeded Governor Seward after an election in which the anti-renters showed considerable voting strength, he pardoned them all on the ground that their crimes were political. The dispute was finally settled by a compromise--that is, the Van Rensselaers and the Livingstons both sold their estates, giving quit-claim deeds to the tenants for what they chose to pay, and the granting of agricultural leases for a longer term than twelve years was forbidden by the State Constitution of 1846.

This anti-rent agitation is described by Professor Johnston of Princeton, in the Cyclop錳ia of Political Science, as "a reign of terror which for ten years practically suspended the operations of law and the payment of rent throughout the district." Suppose all the land of the State had been held under similar tenures; that the controversy had lasted one hundred years; that the rents had been high; and that the Van Rensselaers and the Livingstons had had the aid of the Federal army in enforcing distraints and evictions, and in enabling them to set local opinion at defiance, what do you suppose the state of morals and manners would have been in New York by this time? What would have been the feelings of the people towards the Federal authority had the matter been finally adjusted with the strong hand, in accordance, not with the views of the people of the State, but of the landholders of South Carolina or of the district of Columbia? I am afraid they would have been terribly Irish.

I know very well the risk I run, in citing all these precedents and parallels, of seeming to justify, or at all events to palliate, Irish lawlessness. But I am not doing anything of the kind. I am trying to illustrate a somewhat trite remark which I recently made: "that government is a very practical business, and that those succeed best in it who bring least sentiment or enthusiasm to the conduct of their affairs." The government of Ireland, like the government of all other countries, is a piece of business--a very difficult piece of business, I admit-- and therefore horror over Irish doings, and the natural and human desire to "get even with" murderers and moonlighters, by denying the community which produces them something it would like much to possess, should have no influence with those who are charged with Irish government. It is only in nurseries and kindergartens that we can give offenders their exact due and withhold their toffee until they have furnished satisfactory proofs of repentance. Rulers of men have to occupy themselves mainly with the question of drying up the sources of crime, and often, in order to accomplish this, to let much crime and disorder go unwhipped of justice.

With the state of mind which cannot bear to see any concessions made to the Irish Nationalists because they are such wicked men, in which so many excellent Englishmen, whom we used to think genuine political philosophers, are now living, we are very familiar in the United States. It is a state of mind which prevailed in the Republican party with regard to the South, down to the election of 1884, and found constant expression on the stump and in the newspapers in what is described, in political slang, as "waving the bloody shirt." It showed itself after the war in unwillingness to release the South from military rule; then in unwillingness to remove the disfranchisement of the whites or to withdraw from the carpet-bag State governments the military support without which they could not have existed for a day; and, last of all, in dread of the advent of a Democratic Federal Administration in which Southerners or "ex-rebels" would be likely to hold office. At first the whole Republican party was more or less permeated by these ideas; but the number of those who held them gradually diminished, until in 1884 it was at last possible to elect a Democratic President. Nevertheless a great multitude witnessed the entrance into the White House of a President who is indebted for his election mainly to the States formerly in rebellion, with genuine alarm. They feared from it something dreadful, in the shape either of a violation of the rights of the freedmen, or of an assault on the credit and stability of the Federal Government. Nothing but actual experiment would have disabused them.

I am very familiar with the controversy with them, for I have taken some part in it ever since the passage of the reconstruction Acts, and I know very well how they felt, and am sometimes greatly impressed by the similarity between their arguments and those of the opponents of Irish Home Rule. One of their fixed beliefs for many years, though it is now extinct, was that Southerners were so bent on rebelling again, and were generally so prone to rebellion, that the awful consequences of their last attempt in the loss of life and property, had made absolutely no impression on them. The Southerner was, in fact, in their eyes, what Mr. Gladstone says the Irishman is in the eyes of some Englishmen: "A lusus natur? that justice, common sense, moderation, national prosperity had no meaning for him; that all he could appreciate was strife and perpetual dissension. It was for many years useless to point out to them the severity of the lesson taught by the Civil War as to the physical superiority of the North, or the necessity of peace and quiet to enable the new generation of Southerners to restore their fortunes, or even gain a livelihood. Nor was it easy to impress them with the inconsistency of arguing that it was slavery which made Southerners what they were before they went to war, and maintaining at the same time that the disappearance of slavery would produce no change in their manners, ideas, or opinions. All this they answered by pointing to speeches delivered by some fiery adorer of "the lost cause," to the Ku-Klux outrages, to political murders, like that of Chisholm, to the building of monuments to the Confederate dead, or to some newspaper expression of reverence for Confederate nationality. In fact, for fully ten years after the close of the war the collection of Southern "outrages" and their display before Northern audiences, was the chief work of Republican politicians. In 1876, during the Hayes-Tilden canvass, the opening speech which furnished what is called "the key-note of the campaign" was made by Mr. Wheeler, the Republican candidate for the Vice-Presidency, and his advice to the Vermonters, to whom it was delivered, was "to vote as they shot," that is, to go to the polls with the same feelings and aims as those with which they enlisted in the war.

I need hardly tell English readers how all this has ended. The withdrawal of the Federal troops from the South by President Hayes, and the consequent complete restoration of the State governments to the discontented whites, have fully justified the expectations of those who maintained that it is no less true in politics than in physics, that if you remove what you see to be the cause, the effect will surely disappear. It is true, at least in the Western world, that if you give communities in a reasonable degree the management of their own affairs, the love of material comfort and prosperity which is now so strong among all civilized, and even partially civilized men, is sure in the long run to do the work of creating and maintaining order; or, as Mr. Gladstone has expressed it, in setting up a government, "the best and surest foundation we can find to build on is the foundation afforded by the affections, the convictions, and the will of men."

FOOTNOTES:

[Footnote 2: Report of Secretary of War, 1869-70, vol. i. p. 89.]

HOW WE BECAME HOME RULERS.

BY JAMES BRYCE, M.P.

In the Home Rule contest of the last eighteen months no argument has been more frequently used against the Liberal party than the charge of sudden, and therefore, it would seem, dishonest change of view. "You were opposed to an Irish Parliament at the election of 1880 and for some time afterward; you are not entitled to advocate it in 1886." "You passed a Coercion Bill in 1881, your Ministry (though against the protests of an active section of its supporters) passed another Coercion Bill in 1882; you have no right to resist a third such Bill in 1887, and, if you do, your conduct can be due to nothing but party spite and revenge at your own exclusion from office." Reproaches of this kind are now the stock-in-trade, not merely of the ordinary politician, who, for want of a case, abuses the plaintiff's attorney, but of leading men, and, still more, of leading newspapers, who might be thought bound to produce from recent events and an examination of the condition of Ireland some better grounds for the passion they display. It is noticeable that such reproaches come more often from the so-called Liberal Unionists than from the present Ministry. Perhaps, with their belief that all Liberals are unprincipled revolutionaries, the Tories deem a sin more or less to be of small account. Perhaps a recollection of their own remarkable gyrations, before and after the General Election of 1885, may suggest that the less said about the past the better for everybody. Be the cause what it may, it is surprising to find that a section commanding so much ability as the group of Dissentient Liberals does, should rely rather on the charge of inconsistency than on the advocacy of any counter-policy of their own. It is not large and elevated, but petty, minds that rejoice to say to an opponent (and all the more so if he was once a friend), "You must either be wrong now, or have been wrong then, because you have changed your opinion. I have not changed; I was right then, and I am right now." Such an argument not only dispenses with the necessity of sifting the facts, but it fosters the satisfaction of the person who employs it. Consistency is the pet virtue of the self-righteous, and the man who values himself on his consistency can seldom be induced to see that to shut one's eyes to the facts which time develops, to refuse to reconsider one's position by the light they shed, to cling to an old solution when the problem is substantially new, is a proof, not of fortitude and wisdom, but rather of folly and conceit.

Such persons may be left to the contemplation of their own virtues. But there are many fair-minded men of both political parties, or of neither, who, while acquitting those Liberal members who supported Home Rule in 1886 and opposed Coercion in 1887 of the sordid or spiteful motives with which the virulence of journalism credits them, have nevertheless been surprised at the apparent swiftness and completeness of the change in their opinions. It would be idle to deny that, in startling the minds of steady-going people, this change did, for the moment, weaken the influence and weight of those who had changed. This must be so. A man who says now what he denied six years ago cannot expect to be believed on his ipse dixit. He must set forth the grounds of his conviction. He must explain how his views altered, and why reasons which formerly satisfied him satisfy him no longer. It may be that the Liberal party have omitted to do this as they ought. Occupied by warm and incessant discussions, and conscious, I venture to believe, of their own honesty, few of its members have been at the trouble of showing what were the causes which modified their views, and what the stages of the process which carried them from the position of 1880 to that of 1886.

Of that process I shall attempt in the following pages to give a sketch. Such a sketch, though mainly retrospective, is pertinent to the issues which now divide the country. It will indicate the origin and the strength of the chief reasons by which Liberals are now governed. And, if executed with proper fairness and truth, it may, as a study in contemporary history, be of some little interest to those who in future will attempt to understand our present conflict. The causes which underlie changes of opinion are among the most obscure phenomena in history, because those who undergo, these changes are often only half conscious of them, and do not think of recording that which is imperceptible in its growth, and whose importance is not realized till it already belongs to the past.

The account which follows is based primarily on my own recollection of the phases of opinion and feeling through which I myself, and the friends whom I knew most intimately in the House of Commons, passed during the Parliament which sat from 1880 till 1885. But I should not think of giving it to the public if I did not believe that what happened to our minds happened to many others also, and that the record of our own slow movement from the position of 1880 to that of 1886 is substantially a record of the movement of the Liberal party at large. We were fairly typical members of that party, loyal to our leaders, but placing the principles for which the Liberal party exists above the success of the party itself; with our share of prepossessions and prejudices, yet with reasonably open minds, and (as we believed) inferior to no other section of the House of Commons in patriotism and in attachment to the Constitution. I admit frankly that when we entered Parliament we knew less about the Irish question than we ought to have known, and that even after knowledge had been forced upon us, we were more deferential to our leaders than was good either for us or for them. But these are faults always chargeable on the great majority of members. It is because those of whom I speak were in these respects fairly typical, that it seems worth while to trace the history of their opinions. If any one should accuse me of attributing to an earlier year sentiments which began to appear in a later one, I can only reply that I am aware of this danger, as one which always besets those who recall their past states of mind, and that I have done my utmost to avoid it.

The change I have to describe was slow and gradual. It was reluctant--that is to say, it seemed rather forced upon us by the teaching of events than the work of our own minds. Each session marked a further stage in it; and I therefore propose to examine its progress session by session.

Session of 1880.--The General Election of 1880 turned mainly on the foreign policy of Lord Beaconsfield's Government. Few Liberal candidates said much about Ireland. Absorbed in the Eastern and Afghan questions, they had not watched the progress of events in Ireland with the requisite care, nor realized the gravity of the crisis which was approaching. They were anxious to do justice to Ireland, in the way of amending both the land laws and local government, but saw no reason for going further. Nearly all of them refused, even when pressed by Irish electors in their constituencies, to promise to vote for that "parliamentary inquiry into the demand for Home Rule," which was then propounded by those electors as a sort of test question. We (i.e. the Liberal candidates of 1880) then declared that we thought an Irish Parliament would involve serious constitutional difficulties, and that we saw no reason why the Imperial Parliament should not do full justice to Ireland. Little was said about Coercion. Hopes were expressed that it would not be resorted to, but very few (if any) pledged themselves against it.

When Mr. Forster was appointed Irish Secretary in Mr. Gladstone's Government which the General Election brought into power, we (by which I mean throughout the new Liberal members) were delighted. We knew him to be conscientious, industrious, kind-hearted. We believed him to be penetrating and judicious. We applauded his conduct in not renewing the Coercion Act which Lord Beaconsfield's Government had failed to renew before dissolving Parliament, and which indeed there was scarcely time left after the election to renew, a fact which did not save Mr. Forster from severe censure on the part of the Tories.

The chief business of the session was the Compensation for Disturbance Bill, which Mr. Forster brought in for the sake of saving from immediate eviction tenants whom a succession of bad seasons had rendered utterly unable to pay their rents. This Bill was pressed through the House of Commons with the utmost difficulty, and at an expenditure of time which damaged the other work of the session, though the House continued to sit into September. The Executive Government declared it to be necessary, in order not only to relieve the misery of the people, but to secure the tranquillity of the country. Nevertheless, the whole Tory party, and a considerable section of the Liberal party, opposed it in the interests of the Irish landlords, and of economic principles in general, principles which (as commonly understood in England) it certainly trenched on. When it reached the House of Lords it was contemptuously rejected, and the unhappy Irish Secretary left to face as he best might the cries of a wretched peasantry and the rising tide of outrage. What was even more remarkable, was the coolness with which the Liberal party took the defeat of a Bill their leaders had pronounced absolutely needed. Had it been an English Bill of the same consequence to England as it was to Ireland, the country would have been up in arms against the House of Lords, demanding the reform or the abolition of a Chamber which dared to disregard the will of the people. But nothing of the kind happened. It was only an Irish measure. We relieved ourselves by a few strong words, and the matter dropped.

It was in this session that the Liberal party first learnt what sort of a spirit was burning in the hearts of Irish members. There had been obstruction in the last years of the previous Parliament, but, as the Tories were in power, they had to bear the brunt of it. Now that a Liberal Ministry reigned, it fell on the Liberals. At first it incensed us. Full of our own good intentions towards Ireland, we thought it contrary to nature that Irish members should worry us, their friends, as they had worried Tories, their hereditary enemies. Presently we came to understand how matters stood. The Irish members made little difference between the two great English parties. Both represented to them a hostile domination. Both were ignorant of the condition of their country. Both cared so little about Irish questions that nothing less than deeds of violence out of doors or obstruction within doors could secure their attention. Concessions had to be extorted from both by the same devices; Coercion might be feared at the hands of both. Hence the Irish party was resolved to treat both parties alike, and play off the one against the other in the interests of Ireland alone, using the questions which divide Englishmen and Scotchmen merely as levers whereby to effect their own purposes, because themselves quite indifferent to the substantial merits of those questions. To us new members this was an alarming revelation. We found that the House of Commons consisted of two distinct and dissimilar bodies: a large British body (including some few Tories and Liberals from Ireland), which, though it was distracted by party quarrels, really cared for the welfare of the country and the dignity of the House, and would set aside its quarrels in the presence of a great emergency; and a small Irish body, which, though it spoke the English language, was practically foreign, felt no interest in, no responsibility for, the business of Britain or the Empire, and valued its place in the House only as a means of making itself so disagreeable as to obtain its release. When we had grasped this fact, we began to reflect on its causes and conjecture its effects. We had read of the same things in the newspapers, but what a difference there is between reading a drama in your study and seeing it acted on the stage! We realized what Irish feeling was when we heard these angry cries, and noted how appeals that would have affected English partisans fell on deaf ears. I remember how one night in the summer of 1880, when the Irish members kept us up very late over some trivial Bill of theirs, refusing to adjourn till they had extorted terms, a friend, sitting beside me, said, "See how things come round. They keep us out of bed till five o'clock in the morning because our ancestors bullied theirs for six centuries." And we saw that the natural relations of an Executive, even a Liberal Executive, to the Irish members were those of strife. Whose fault it was we were unable to decide. Perhaps the Government was too stiff; perhaps the members were vexatious. Anyhow, this strife was evidently the normal state of things, wholly unlike that which existed between Scotch members, to whichever party they belonged, and the executive authorities of Scotland.

Thus the session of 1880, though it did not bring us consciously nearer to Home Rule, impressed three facts upon us: first, that the House of Lords regarded Ireland solely from the point of view of English landlords, sympathizing with Irish landlords; secondly, that the House of Commons knew so little or cared so little about Ireland that when the Executive declared a measure essential to the peace of Ireland, it scarcely resented the rejection of that measure by the House of Lords; thirdly, that the Irish Nationalists in the House of Commons were a foreign body, foreign in the sense in which a needle which a man swallows is foreign, not helping the organism to discharge its functions, but impeding them, and setting up irritation. We did not yet draw from these facts all the conclusions we should now draw. But the facts were there, and they began to tell upon our minds.

SESSION OF 1881.--The winter of 1880-81 was a terrible one in Ireland. The rejection of the Compensation for Disturbance Bill had borne the fruit which Mr. Forster had predicted, and which the House of Lords had ignored. Outrages were numerous and serious. The cry in England for repressive measures had gone on rising from November, when it occasioned a demonstration at the Guildhall banquet. Several Liberal members (of whom I was one) went to Ireland at Christmas, to see with our own eyes how things stood. We were struck by the difficulty of obtaining trustworthy information in Dublin, where the richer classes, with whom we chiefly came in contact, merely abused the Land League, while the Land Leaguers declared that the accounts of outrages were grossly exaggerated. The most prominent, Mr. Michael Davitt, assured me, and I believe with perfect truth, that he had exerted himself to discountenance outrage, and that if, as he expected, he was locked up by the Government, outrages would increase. When one reached the disturbed districts, where, of course, one talked to members as well of the landlord class as of the peasantry, the general conclusion which emerged from the medley of contradictions was that, though there was much agrarian crime, and a pervading sense of insecurity, the disorders were not so bad as people in England believed, and might have been dealt with by a vigorous administration of the existing law. Unfortunately, the so-called "better classes," full of bitterness against the Liberal Ministry and Mr. Forster (whom they did not praise till it was too late), had not assisted the Executive, and had allowed things to reach a pass at which it found the work of governing very difficult.

When the Coercion Bill of 1881 was introduced, many English Liberals were inclined to resist it. The great majority voted for it, but within two years they bitterly repented their votes. Our motives, which I mention by way of extenuation, not of defence, were these. The Executive Government declared that it could not deal with crime by the ordinary law. If its followers refused exceptional powers, they must displace the Ministry, and let in the Tories, who would doubtless obtain such powers, and probably use them worse. We had still confidence in Mr. Forster's judgment, and a deference to Irish Executive Governments generally which Parliamentary experience is well fitted to dissipate. The violence with which the Nationalist members resisted the introduction of the Bill had roused our blood, and the foolish attempts which the Radical and Irish electors in some constituencies had made to deter their members from supporting it had told the other way, and disposed these members to vote for it, in order to show that they were not to be cowed by threats. Finally, we were assured that votes given for the Coercion Bill would purchase a thorough-going Land Bill, and our anxiety for the latter induced us, naturally, but erringly, to acquiesce in the former.

When that Land Bill went into Committee we perceived how much harm the Coercion Bill had done in intensifying the bitterness of Irish members. Although the Ministry was fighting for their interests against the Tory party and the so-called Whiggish section of its own supporters, who were seeking to cut down the benefits which the measure offered to Irish tenants, the Nationalist members regarded it, and in particular Mr. Forster, as their foe. They resented what they deemed the insult put upon their country. They saw those who had been fighting, often, no doubt, by unlawful methods, for the national cause, thrown into prison and kept there without trial. They anticipated (not without reason) the same fortune for themselves. Hence the friendliness which the Liberal party sought to show them met with no response, and Mr. Forster was worried with undiminished vehemence. In the discussions on the Bill we found the Ministry generally resisting all amendments which came from Irish members. When these amendments seemed to us right, we voted for them, but they were almost always defeated by the union of the Tories with the steady Ministerialists. Subsequent events have proved that many were right, but, whether they were right or wrong, the fact which impressed us was that in matters which concerned Ireland only, and lay within the exclusive knowledge of Irishmen, Irish members were constantly outvoted by English and Scotch members, who knew nothing at all of the merits of the case, but simply obeyed the party whip. This happened even when the Irish members who sat on the Liberal side (such as Mr. Dickson and his Liberal colleagues from Ulster) joined the Nationalist section in demanding some extension of the Bill which the Ministry refused. And we perceived that nothing incensed the Irish members more than the feeling that their arguments were addressed to deaf ears; that they were overborne, not by reason, but by sheer weight of numbers. Even if they convinced the Ministry, they could seldom hope to obtain its assent, because the Ministry had to consider the House of Lords, sure to reject amendments which favoured the tenant, while to detach a number of Ministerialists sufficient to carry an amendment against the Treasury Bench, the Moderate Liberals, and the Tories, was evidently hopeless.

At the end of the session the House of Lords came again upon the scene. It seriously damaged the Bill by its amendments, and would have destroyed it but for the skill with which the head of the Government handled these amendments, accepting the least pernicious, so as to enable the Upper House without loss of dignity to recede from those which were wholly inadmissible. Several times it seemed as if the conflict would have to pass from Westminster to the country, and, in contemplating the chances of a popular agitation or a dissolution, we were regretfully obliged to own that the English people cared too little and knew too little about Irish questions to give us much hope of defeating the House of Lords and the Tories upon these issues.

An incident which occurred towards the end of the session seems, though trifling in itself, so illustrative of the illogical position in which we stood towards Ireland, as to deserve mention. Mr. Forster, still Chief Secretary, had brought in a Bill for extinguishing the Queen's University in Ireland, and creating in place of it a body to be called the Royal University, which, however, was not to be a real university at all, but only a set of examiners plus some salaried fellowships, to be held at various places of instruction. Regarding this as a gross educational blunder, which would destroy a useful existing body, and create a sham university in its place, and finding several Parliamentary friends on whose judgment I could rely to be of the same opinion, I gave notice of opposition to the Bill. Mr. Forster came to me, and pressed with great warmth that the opposition should be withdrawn. The Bill, he said, would satisfy the Roman Catholic hierarchy, and complete the work of the Land Bill in pacifying Ireland. The Irish members wanted it: what business had an English member to interfere to defeat their wishes, and thwart the Executive? The reply was obvious. Not to speak of the simplicity of expecting the hierarchy to be satisfied by this small concession, what were such arguments but the admission of Home Rule in its worst form? "You resist the demand of the Irish members to legislate for Ireland; you have just been demanding, and obtaining, the support of English members against those amendments of the Land Bill which Irish members declare to be necessary. Now you bid us surrender our own judgment, ignore our own responsibility, and blindly pass a Bill which we, who have studied these university questions as they affect both Ireland and England, believe to be thoroughly mischievous to the prospects of higher education in Ireland, only because the Irish members, as you say, desire it. Do one thing or the other. Either give them the power and the responsibility, or leave both with the Imperial Parliament. You are now asking us to surrender the power, but to remain still subject to the responsibility. We will not bear the latter without the former. We shall prefer Home Rule." Needless to add that this device--a sample of the petty sops by which successive generations of English statesmen, Whigs and Tories alike, have sought to win over a priesthood which uses and laughs at them--failed as completely as its predecessors to settle the University question or to range the bishops on the side of the Government.

The autumn and winter of 1881 revealed the magnitude of the mischief done by making a Coercion Bill precede a Relief Bill. The Land Bill was the largest concession made to the demands of the people since Catholic Emancipation. It was a departure, justified by necessity, but still a departure from our established principles of legislation. It ought to have brought satisfaction and confidence, if not gratitude, with it; ought to have led Ireland to believe in the sincere friendliness of England, and produced a new cordiality between the islands. It did nothing of the kind. It was held to have been extorted from our fears; its grace and sweetness were destroyed by the concomitant severities which the Coercion Act had brought into force, as wholesome food becomes distasteful when some bitter compound has been sprinkled over it. We were deeply mortified at this result of our efforts. What was the malign power which made the boons we had conferred shrivel up, "like fairy gifts fading away"? We still believed the Coercion Act to have been justified, but lamented the fate which baffled the main object of our efforts, the winning over Ireland to trust the justice and the capacity of the Imperial Parliament. And thus the two facts which stood out from the history of this eventful session were, first, that even in legislating for the good of Ireland we were legislating against the wishes of Ireland, imposing on her enactments which her representatives opposed, and which we supported only at the bidding of the Ministry; and, secondly, that at the end of a long session, entirely devoted to her needs, we found her more hostile and not less disturbed than she had been at its beginning. We began to wonder whether we should ever succeed better on our present lines. But we still mostly regarded Home Rule as a disagreeable solution.

SESSION OF 1882.--Still graver were the lessons of the first four months of this year. Mr. Forster went on filling the prisons of Ireland with persons whom he arrested under the Habeas Corpus Suspension Act, and never brought to trial. But the country grew no more quiet. At last he had nine hundred and forty men under lock and key, many of them not "village ruffians," whose power a few weeks' detention was to break, but political offenders, and even popular leaders. How long could this go on? Where was it to stop? It became plain that the Act was a failure, and that the people, trained to combination by a century and a half's practice, were too strong for the Executive. Either the scheme and plan of the Act had been wrong, or its administration had been incompetent. Whichever was the source of the failure (most people will now blame both), the fault must be laid at the door of the Irish Executive; not of Mr. Forster himself, but of those on whom he relied. It had been a Dublin Castle Bill, conceived and carried out by the incompetent bureaucracy which has so long pretended to govern Ireland. Such a proof of incompetence destroyed whatever confidence in that bureaucracy then remained to us, and the disclosures which the Phoenix Park murders and the subsequent proceedings against the Invincibles brought out, proved beyond question that the Irish Executive had only succeeded in giving a more dark and dangerous form, the form of ruthless conspiracy, to the agitation it was combating.

When therefore the Prevention of Crime Bill of 1882 was brought in, some of us felt unable to support it, and specially bound to resist those of its provisions which related to trials without a jury, and to boycotting. It was impossible, on the morrow of the Phoenix Park murders, to deny that some coercive measure might be needed; but we had so far lost faith in repression, and in the officials who were to administer it, as to desire to limit it to what was absolutely necessary, and we protested against enacting for Ireland a criminal code which was not to be applied to Great Britain. Our resistance might have been more successful but for the manner in which the Nationalist members conducted their opposition. When they began to obstruct--not that under the circumstances we felt entitled to censure them for obstructing a Bill dealing so harshly with their countrymen--we were obliged to desist, and our experience of the stormy scenes of the summer of 1882 deepened our sense of the passionate bitterness with which they regarded English members, scarcely making an exception in favour of those who were most disposed to sympathize with them. Many and many a time when we listened to their fierce cries, we seemed to hear in them the battle-cries of the centuries of strife between Celt and Englishman from Athenry to Vinegar Hill; many a time we felt that this rage and mistrust were chiefly of England's making; and yet not of England's, but rather of the overmastering fate which had prolonged to our own days the hatreds and the methods of barbarous times.

So much of the session as the Crime Bill had spared was consumed by the Arrears Bill, over which we had again a "crisis" with the House of Lords. This was the third session that had been practically given up to Irishmen. The freshness and force of the Parliament of 1880--a Parliament full of zeal and ability--had now been almost spent, yet few of the plans of domestic legislation spread before the constituencies of 1880 had been realized. The Government had been anxious to legislate, their majority had been ready to support them, but Ireland had blocked the way; and now the only expedient for improving the procedure of the House was to summon Parliament in an extra autumn session. Here was another cause for reflection. England and Scotland were calling for measures promised years ago, but no time could be found to discuss them. Nothing was done to reorganize local government, to reform the liquor laws, to improve secondary education, to deal with the housing of the poor, or a dozen other urgent questions, because we were busy with Ireland; and yet how little more loyal or contented did Ireland seem to be for all we had done. We began to ask whether Home Rule might not be as much an English and Scotch question as an Irish question. It was, at any rate, clear that to allow Ireland to manage her own affairs would open a prospect for England and Scotland to obtain time to attend to theirs.[3]

This feeling was strengthened by the result of the attempts made in the autumn session of 1882, to improve the procedure of the House of Commons.

We had cherished the hope that more drastic remedies against obstruction and better arrangements for the conduct of business, might relieve much of the pressure Irish members had made us suffer. The passing of the New Rules shattered this hope, for it was plain they would not accomplish what was needed. Some blamed the Government for not framing a more stringent code. Some blamed the Tory and the Irish Oppositions (now beginning to work in concert) for cutting down the proposals of the Government. But most of us saw, and came to see still more clearly in the three succeeding sessions, that the evil was too deep-rooted to be cured by any changes of procedure, unless they went so far as to destroy freedom of debate for English members also. The presence in a deliberative assembly of a section numbering (or likely soon to number) one-seventh of the whole--a section seeking to lower the character of the assembly, and to derange its mechanism, with no further interest in the greater part of its business except that of preventing it from conducting that business--this was the phenomenon which confronted us, and we felt that no rules of debate would overcome the dangers it threatened.

It is from this year 1882 that I date the impression which we formed, that Home Rule was sure to come. "It may be a bold experiment," we said to one another in the lobbies; "there are serious difficulties in the way, though the case for it is stronger than we thought two years ago. But if the Irishmen persist as they are doing now, they will get it. It is only a question of their tenacity."

It was impossible not to be struck during the conflicts of 1881 and 1882 with the small amount of real bitterness which the conduct of the Irish members, irritating as it often was, provoked among the Liberals, who of course bore the brunt of the conflict. The Nationalists did their best to injure a Government which was at the same time being denounced by the Tories as too favourable to Irish claims; they lowered the character of Parliament by scenes far more painful than those of the session of 1887, on which so much indignation has been lately expended; they said the hardest things they could think of against us in the House; they attacked us in our constituencies. Their partisans (for I do not charge this on the leaders) interrupted and broke up our meetings. Nevertheless, all this did not provoke responsive hatred from the Liberals. There could not be a greater contrast than that between the way in which the great bulk of the Liberal members all through the Parliament of 1880 behaved towards their Irish antagonists, and the violence with which the Tory members, under much slighter provocation, conduct themselves towards those antagonists now. I say this not to the credit of our temper, which was no better than that of other men heated by the struggles of a crowded assembly. It was due entirely to our feeling that there was a great balance of wrong standing to the debit of England; that if the Irish were turbulent, it was the ill-treatment of former days that had made them so; and that, whatever might be their methods, they were fighting for their country. Although, therefore, there was little social intercourse between us and them, there was always a hope and a wish that the day might come when the Liberal party should resume its natural position of joining the representatives of the Irish people in obtaining radical reforms in Irish government. And the remarkable speech of February 9, 1882, in which Mr. Gladstone declared his mind to be open on the subject, and invited the Nationalists to propound a practicable scheme of self-government, had encouraged us to hope that this day might soon arrive.

SESSION OF 1883.--Three facts stood out in the history of this comparatively quiet session, each of which brought us further along the road we had entered.

One was the omission of Parliament to complete the work begun by the Land Bill of 1881, of improving the condition of the Irish peasantry and reorganizing Irish administration. The Nationalist members brought in Bills for these purposes, including one for amending the Land Act by admitting leaseholders to its benefits and securing tenants against having their improvements reckoned against them in the fixing of rents. Though we could not approve all the contents of these Bills, we desired to see the Government either take them up and amend them, or introduce Bills of its own to do what was needed. Some of us spoke strongly in this sense, nor will any one now deny that we were right. Sound policy called aloud for the completion of the undertaking of 1881. The Government however refused, alleging, no doubt with some truth, that Ireland could not have all the time of Parliament, but must let England and Scotland have their turn. Nor was anything done towards the creation of new local institutions in Ireland, or the reform of the Castle bureaucracy. We were profoundly disheartened. We saw golden opportunities slipping away, and doubted more than ever whether Westminster was the place in which to legislate for Irish grievances.

Another momentous fact was the steady increase in the number of Nationalist members. Every seat that fell vacant in Ireland was filled by them. The moderate Irish party, most of whom had by this time crossed the floor of the House, and were sitting among us, had evidently no future. They were estimable, and, in some cases, able men, from whom we had hoped much, as a link between the Liberal party and the Irish people. But they seemed to have lost their hold on the people, nor were they able to give us much practical counsel as to Irish problems. It was clear that they would vanish at the next General Election, and Parliament be left to settle accounts with the extreme men, whose spirits rose as those of our friends steadily sank.

Lastly: it was in this session that the alliance of the Nationalists and the Tory Opposition became a potent factor in politics. Its first conspicuous manifestation was in the defeat of the Government by the allied forces on the Affirmation Bill, when the least respectable privates in both armies vied with one another in boisterous rejoicings over the announcement of numbers in the division. I do not refer to this as ground for complaint. It was in the course of our usual political warfare that two groups, each hating and fearing the Ministry, should unite to displace it. But we now saw what power the Irish section must exert when it came to hold the balance of numbers in the House. Till this division, the Government had commanded a majority of the whole House. This would probably not outlast a dissolution. What then? Could the two English parties, differing so profoundly from one another, combine against the third party? Evidently not. We must, therefore, look forward to unstable Governments, if not to a total dislocation of our Parliamentary system.

Session of 1884.--I pass over the minor incidents of this year, including the continued neglect of remedial legislation for Ireland to dwell on its dominant and most impressive lesson. It was the year of the Franchise Bill, which, as regards Ireland, worked an extension, not merely of the county but also of the borough franchise, and produced, owing to the economic condition of the humbler classes in that country, a far more extensive change than in England or Scotland. When the Bill was introduced the question at once arose--Should Ireland be included?

There were two ways of treating Ireland between which Parliament had to choose.

One was to leave her out of the Bill, on the ground that the masses of her population could not be trusted with the franchise, as being ignorant, sympathetic to crime, hostile to the English Government. This course was the logical concomitant of exceptional coercive legislation, such as had been passed in 1881 and 1882. It was quite compatible with generous remedial legislation. But it placed Ireland in an unequal and lower position, treating her, as the Coercion Acts did, as a dependent country, inhabited by a population unfit for the same measure of power which the inhabitants of Britain might receive.

The other course was to bestow on Ireland the same extended franchise which the English county occupiers were to receive, applying the principle of equality, and disregarding the obvious consequences. These consequences were both practical and logical. The practical consequence was the increase in numbers and weight of the Irish party in Parliament hostile to Parliament itself. The logical consequence was the duty of complying with the wishes of the enfranchised nation. Whatever reasons were good for giving this enlarged suffrage to the Irish masses, were good for respecting the will which they might use to express it. If the Irish were deemed fit to exercise the same full constitutional rights in legislation as the English, must they not be fit for the same rights of trial by jury, a free press, and all the privileges of personal freedom?

Of these two courses the Cabinet chose the latter, those of its members whom we must suppose, from the language they now hold, to have then hesitated, either stifling their fears or not apprehending the consequences of their boldness. It might have been expected, and indeed was generally expected, that the Tory party would refuse to follow. They talked largely about the danger of an extended Irish suffrage, and pointed out that it would be a weapon in the hands of disloyalty. But when the moment for resistance came, they swerved, and never divided in either House against the application of the Bill to Ireland. They might have failed to defeat the measure; but they would have immensely strengthened their position, logically and morally, had they given effect by their votes to the sentiments they were known to entertain, and which not a few Liberals shared.

The effect of this uncontested grant to Ireland of a suffrage practically universal was immense upon our minds, and the longer we reflected on it the more significant did it become. It meant to us that the old methods were abandoned, and, as we supposed, for ever. We had deliberately given the Home Rule party arms against English control far more powerful than they previously possessed. We had deliberately asserted our faith in the Irish people. Impossible after this to fall back on Coercion Bills. Impossible to refuse any request compatible with the general safety of the United Kingdom, which Ireland as a nation might prefer. Impossible to establish that system of Crown Colony Government which we had come to perceive was the only real and solid alternative to self-government. To those of us who had been feeling that the Irish difficulty was much the greatest of all England's difficulties, this stood out beyond the agitation of the autumn and the compromise of the winter as the great political event of 1884.[4]

Although this sketch is in the main a record of Parliamentary opinion, I ought not to pass over the influence which the study of their constituents' ideas exerted upon members for the larger towns. We found the vast bulk of our supporters--English supporters, for after 1882 it was understood that the Irish voters were our enemies--sympathetic with the Irish people. They knew and thought little about Home Rule, believing that their member understood that question better than they did, and willing, so long as he was sound on English issues, to trust him. But they pitied Irish tenants, and condemned Irish landlords. Though they acquiesced in a Coercion Bill when proposed by a Liberal Cabinet, because they concluded that nothing less than necessity would lead such a Cabinet to propose one, they so much disliked any exceptional or repressive legislation that it was plain they would not long tolerate it. Any popular leader denouncing coercion was certain to have the sentiment of the English masses with him, while as to suspending Irish representation or carrying out consistently the policy of treating Ireland as a subject country, there was no chance in the world of their approval. Those of us, therefore, who represented large working-class constituencies became convinced that the solution of the Irish problem must be sought in conciliation and self-government, if only because the other solution, Crown Colony Government, was utterly repugnant to the English masses, in whom the Franchise Bill of 1884, completing that of 1867, had vested political supremacy.[5]

Session of 1885.--The allied powers of Toryism and Nationalism gained in this year the victory they had so long striven for. In February they reduced the Ministerial majority to fourteen; in June they overthrew the Ministry. No one supposed that on either occasion the merits of the issue had anything to do with the Nationalist vote: that vote was given simply and solely against the Government, as the Government which had passed the Coercion Acts of 1881 and 1882--Acts demanded by the Tory party, and which had not conceded an Irish Parliament. At last the Irish party had attained its position as the arbiter of power and office. Some of us said, as we walked away from the House, under the dawning light of that memorable 9th of June, "This means Home Rule." Our forecast was soon to be confirmed. Lord Salisbury's Cabinet, formed upon the resignation of Mr. Gladstone's, announced that it would not propose to renew any part of the Coercion Act of 1882, which was to expire in August. Here was a surrender indeed! But the Tory leaders went further. They did not excuse themselves on the ground of want of time. They took credit for their benevolence towards Ireland; they discovered excellent reasons why the Act should be dropped. They even turned upon Lord Spencer, whose administration they had hitherto blamed for its leniency, and attacked him in Parliament, among the cheers of his Irish enemies. From that time till the close of the General Election in December everything was done, short of giving public pledges, to keep the Irish leaders and the Irish voters in good humour. The Tory party in fact posed as the true friends of Ireland, averse from coercion, and with minds perfectly open on the subject of self-government.

This change of front, so sudden, so unblushing, completed the process which had been going on in our minds. By 1882 we had come to feel that Home Rule was inevitable, though probably undesirable. Before long we had asked ourselves whether it was really undesirable, whether it might not be a good thing both for England, whose Parliament and Cabinet system it would relieve from impending dangers, while leaving free scope for domestic legislation, and for Ireland, which could hardly manage her affairs worse than we were managing them for her, and might manage them better. And thus, by the spring of 1885, many of us were prepared for a large scheme of local self-government in Ireland, including a central legislative body in Dublin.[6]

Now when it was plain that the English party which had hitherto called for repression, and had professed itself anxious for a patriotic union of all parties to maintain order and a continuity of policy in Ireland, was ready to bid for Irish help at the polls by throwing over repression and reversing the policy it had advocated, we felt that the sooner Ireland was taken out of English party politics the better. What prospect was there of improving Ireland by the superior wisdom and fairness of the British Parliament, if British leaders were to make their Irish policy turn on interested bargains with Nationalist leaders? Repression, which we clearly saw to be the only alternative to self-government, seemed to be by common consent abandoned. I remember how, at a party of members in the beginning of July, some one said, "Well, there's an end for ever of coercion at any rate," and every one assented as to an obvious truth. Accordingly the result of the new departure of the Salisbury Cabinet in 1885 was to convince even doubters that Home Rule must come, and to make those already convinced anxious to see it come quickly, and to find the best form that could be given it. Many of us expected the Tory Government to propose it. Rumour declared the new Lord Lieutenant to be in favour of it. His government was extremely conciliatory in Ireland, even to the recalcitrant corporation of Limerick. Not to mention less serious and less respected Tory Ministers, Lord Salisbury talked at Newport about the dualism of the Austro-Hungarian Monarchy with the air of a man who desired to have a workable scheme, analogous, if not similar, suggested for Ireland and Great Britain. The Irish Nationalists appeared to place their hopes in this quarter, for they attacked the Liberal party with unexampled bitterness, and threw all their voting strength into the Tory scale.

As it has lately been attempted to blacken the character of the Irish leaders, it deserves to be remarked that whatever has been charged against them was said or done by them before the spring of 1885, and was, practically, perfectly well known to the Tory leaders when they accepted the alliance of the Irish party in the House of Commons, and courted their support in the election of 1885. To those who remember what went on in the House in the sessions of 1884 and 1885, the horror now professed by the Tory leaders for the conduct and words of the Irish party would be matter for laughter if it were not also matter for just indignation.

Why, it may be asked, if the persuasion that Home Rule was certain, and even desirable, had become general among the Liberals who had sat through the Parliament of 1880, was it not more fully expressed at the election of 1885? This is a fair question, which I shall try to answer.

In the first place, the electors made few inquiries about Ireland. They disliked the subject; they had not realized its supreme importance. Those of us who felt anxious to explain our views (as was my own case) had to volunteer to do so, for we were not asked about them. The Irish party in the constituencies was in violent opposition to Liberal candidates; it did not interrogate, but denounced. Further, it was felt that the issue was mainly one to be decided in Ireland itself. The question of Home Rule was being submitted, not, as heretofore, to a limited constituency, but to the whole Irish people. Till their will had been constitutionally declared at the polls it was not proper that Englishmen or Scotchmen should anticipate its tenour. We should even have been accused, had we volunteered our opinions, of seeking to affect the result in Ireland, and, not only of playing for the Irish vote in Great Britain, as we saw the Tories doing, but of prejudicing the chances of those Liberal candidates who, in Irish constituencies, were competing with extreme Nationalists. A third reason was that most English and Scotch Liberals did not know how far their own dispositions towards Home Rule were shared by their leaders. Mr. Gladstone's declaration in his Midlothian address was no doubt a decided intimation of his views, and was certainly understood by some (as by myself) to imply the grant to Ireland of a Parliament; but, strong as its words were, its importance does not seem to have been fully appreciated at the moment. And the opinions of a statesman whose unequalled Irish experience and elevated character gave him a weight only second to that of Mr. Gladstone--I mean Lord Spencer--had not been made known. We had consequently no certainty that there were leaders prepared to give prompt effect to the views we entertained. Lastly, we were not prepared with a practical scheme of self-government for Ireland. The Nationalist members had propounded none which we could either adopt or criticize. Convinced as we were that Home Rule would come and must come, we felt the difficulties surrounding every suggestion that had yet been made, and had not hammered out any plan which we could lay before the electors as approved by Liberal opinion.[7] We were forced to confine ourselves to generalities.

Whether it would have been better for us to have done our thinking and scheme-making in public, and thereby have sooner forced the details of the problem upon the attention of the country, need not now be inquired. Any one can now see that something was lost by the omission. But those who censure a course that has actually been taken usually fail to estimate the evils that would have followed from the taking of the opposite course. Such evils might in this instance have been as great as those we have encountered.

I have spoken of the importance we attached to the decision of Ireland itself, and of the attitude of expectancy which, while that decision was uncertain, Englishmen were forced to maintain. We had not long to wait. Early in December it was known that five-sixths of the members returned from Ireland were Nationalists, and that the majorities which had returned them were crushing. If ever a people spoke its will, the Irish people spoke theirs at the election of 1885. The last link in the chain of conviction, which events had been forging since 1880, was now supplied. In passing the Franchise Bill of 1884, we had asked Ireland to declare her mind. She had now answered. If the question was not a mockery, and representative government a sham, we were bound to accept the answer, subject only, but subject always, to the interests of the whole United Kingdom. In other words, we were bound to devise such a scheme of self-government for Ireland as would give full satisfaction to her wishes, while maintaining the ultimate supremacy of the Imperial Parliament and the unity of the British Empire.

Very few words are needed to summarize the outline which, omitting many details which would have illustrated and confirmed its truth, I have attempted to present of the progress of opinion among Liberal members of the Parliament of 1880.

1. Our experience of the Coercion Bills of 1881 and 1882 disclosed the enormous mischief which such measures do in alienating the minds of Irishmen, and the difficulty of enlisting Irish sentiment on behalf of the law. The results of the Act of 1881 taught us that the repression of open agitation means the growth of far more dangerous conspiracy; those of the Act of 1882 proved that even under an administration like Lord Spencer's repression works no change for the better in the habits and ideas of the people.

2. The conduct of the House of Lords in 1880 and 1881, and the malign influence which its existence exerted whenever remedial legislation for Ireland came in question, convinced us that full and complete justice will never be done to Ireland by the British Parliament while the Upper House (as at present constituted) remains a part of that Parliament.

3. The break-down of the procedure of the House of Commons, and the failure of the efforts to amend it, proved that Parliament cannot work so long as a considerable section of its members seek to impede its working. To enable it to do its duty by England and Scotland, it was evidently necessary, either to

make the Irish members as loyal to Parliament as English and Scotch members usually are, or else to exclude them.

4. The discussions of Irish Bills in the House of Commons made us realize how little English members knew about Ireland; how utterly different were their competence for, and their attitude towards, Irish questions and English questions. We perceived that we were legislating in the dark for a country whose economic and social condition we did not understand--a country to which we could not apply our English ideas of policy; a country whose very temper and feeling were strange to us. We were really fitter to pass laws for Canada or Australia than for this isle within sight of our shores.

5. I have said that we were legislating in the dark. But there were two quarters from which light was proffered, the Irish members and the Irish Executive. We rejected the first, and could hardly help doing so, for to accept it would have been to displace our own leaders. We followed the light which the Executive gave. But in some cases (as notably in the case of the Coercion Bill of 1881) it proved to be a "wandering fire," leading us into dangerous morasses. And we perceived that at all times legislation at the bidding of the Executive, against the wishes of Irish members, was not self-government or free government. It was despotism. The rule of Ireland by the British Parliament was really "the rule of a dependency through an official, responsible no doubt, but responsible not to the ruled, but to an assembly of which they form less than a sixth part."[8] As this assembly closed its ears to the one-sixth, and gave effect to the will of the official, this was essentially arbitrary government, and wanted those elements of success which free government contains.

This experience had, by 1884, convinced us that the present relations of the British Parliament to Ireland were bad, and could not last; that the discontent of Ireland was justified; that the existing system, in alienating the mind of Ireland, tended, not merely to Repeal, but to Separation; that the simplest, and probably the only effective, remedy for the increasing dangers was the grant of an Irish Legislature. Two events clinched these conclusions. One was the Tory surrender of June, 1885. Self-government, we had come to see, was the only alternative to Coercion, and now Coercion was gone. The other was the General Election of December, 1885, when newly-enfranchised Ireland, through five-sixths of her representatives, demanded a Parliament of her own.

These were not, as is sometimes alleged, conclusions of despair. We were mostly persons of a cautious and conservative turn of mind, as men imbued with the spirit of the British Constitution ought to be. The first thing was to convince us that the existing relations of the islands were faulty, and could not be maintained. This was a negative result, and while we remained in that stage we were despondent. Many Liberal members will remember the gloom that fell on us in 1882 and 1883 whenever we thought or spoke of Ireland. But presently the clouds lifted. We still felt the old objections to any Home Rule scheme, though we now saw that they were less formidable than the evils of the present system. But we came to feel that the grant of self-government was a right thing in itself. It was not merely a means of ridding ourselves of our difficulties, not merely a boon yielded because long demanded. It was a return to broad and deep principles, a conformity to those natural laws which govern human society as well as the inanimate world--an effort to enlist the better and higher feelings of mankind in the creation of a truer union between the two nations than had ever yet existed. When we perceived this, hope returned. It is strong with us now, for, though we see troubles, perhaps even dangers, in the immediate future, we are confident that the principles on which Liberal policy towards Ireland is based will in the long run work out a happy issue for her, as they have in and for every other country that has trusted to them.

One last word as to Consistency. We learnt in the Parliament of 1880 many facts about Ireland we had not known before; we felt the force and bearing of other facts previously accepted on hearsay, but not realized. We saw the Irish problem change from what it had been in 1880 into the new phase which stood apparent at the end of 1885, Coercion abandoned by its former advocates, Self-government demanded by the nation. Were we to disregard all these new facts, ignore all these new conditions, and cling to old ideas, some of which we perceived to be mistaken, while others, still true in themselves, were out-weighed by arguments of far wider import? We did not so estimate our duty. We foresaw the taunts of foes and the reproaches of friends. But we resolved to give effect to the opinions we slowly, painfully, even reluctantly formed, opinions all the stronger because not suddenly adopted, and founded upon evidence whose strength no one can appreciate till he has studied the causes of Irish discontent in Irish history, and been forced (as we were) to face in Parliament the practical difficulties of the government of Ireland by the British House of Commons.

FOOTNOTES:

[Footnote 3: I may mention here another fact whose significance impressed some among us. Parliament, which usually sinned in not doing for Ireland what Ireland asked, occasionally passed bills for Ireland which were regarded as setting very bad precedents for England. By some bargain between the Irish Office and the Nationalist members, measures were put through which may have been right as respects Ireland, but which embodied principles mischievous as respects Great Britain. We felt that if it was necessary to enact such statutes, it would be better that they should proceed from an Irish Legislature rather than from the Imperial Parliament, which might be embarrassed by its own acts when asked to extend the same principles to England. The Labourers' Act of July, 1885, is the most conspicuous example.]

[Footnote 4: At Easter, 1885, I met a number of leading Ulster Liberals in Belfast, told them that Home Rule was certainly coming, and urged them to prepare some plan under which any special interests they conceived the Protestant part of Ulster to have, would be effectually safe-guarded. They were startled, and at first discomposed, but presently told me I was mistaken; to which I could only reply that time would show, and perhaps sooner then even English Liberals expected.]

[Footnote 5: My recollection of a conversation with a distinguished public man in July, 1882, enables me to say that this fact had impressed itself upon us as early as that year. He doubted the fact, but admitted that, if true, it was momentous. The passing of the Franchise Bill made it, in our view, more momentous than ever.]

[Footnote 6: Some thought that its functions should be very limited, while large powers were granted to county boards or provincial councils. But most had, I think, already perceived that the grant of a merely local self-government, while retaining an irresponsible central bureaucracy, would do more harm than good. It seemed at first sight a safer experiment than the creation of a central legislative body. But, like many middle courses, it combined the demerits and wanted the merits of each of the extreme courses. It would not make the country tranquil, as firm and long-continued repression might possibly do. Neither would it satisfy the people's demands, and divert them from struggles against England to disputes and discussions among themselves, as the gift of genuine self-government might do.]

[Footnote 7: Some of us had tried to do so. I prepared such a scheme in the autumn of 1885, and submitted it to some specially competent friends. Their objections, made from what would now be called the Unionist point of view, were weighty. But their effect was to convince me that the scheme erred on the side of caution; and I believe the experience of other Liberals who worked at the problem to have been the same as my own--viz. that a small and timid scheme is more dangerous than a large and bold one. Thus the result of our thinking from July, 1885, till April, 1886, was to make us more and more disposed to reject half-and-half solutions. Some of us (of whom I was one) expressed this feeling by saying in our election addresses in 1885, "the further we go in giving the Irish people the management of their own affairs (subject to the maintenance of the unity of the empire) the better."]

[Footnote 8: Quoted from an article contributed by myself to the American Century Magazine, which I refer to because, written in the spring of 1883, it expresses the ideas here stated.]

HOME RULE AND IMPERIAL UNITY

BY LORD THRING

The principal charge made against the scheme of Home Rule contained in the Irish Government Bill, 1886, is that it is incompatible with the maintenance of the unity of the Empire and the supremacy of the Imperial Parliament. A further allegation states that the Bill is useless, as agrarian exasperation lies at the root of Irish discontent and Irish disloyalty, and that no place would be found for a Home Rule Bill even in Irish aspirations if an effective Land Bill were first passed. An endeavour will be made in the following pages to secure a verdict of acquittal on both counts--as to the charge relating to Imperial unity and the supremacy of the Imperial Parliament, by proving that the accusation is absolutely unfounded, and based partly on a misconception of the nature of Imperial ties, and partly on a misapprehension of the effect of the provisions of the Home Rule Bill as bearing on Imperial questions; and as to the inutility of the Home Rule Bill in view of the necessity of Land Reform, by showing that without a Home Rule Bill no Land Bill worth consideration as a means of pacifying Ireland can be passed.

The complete partisan spirit in which Home Rule has been treated is the more to be deplored as the subject is one which does not lend itself readily to the trivialities of party debates. It raises questions of principle, not of detail. It ascends at once into the highest region of politics. It is conversant with the great questions of constitutional and international law, and leads to an inquiry into the very nature of governments and the various modes in which communities of men are associated together either as simple or composite nations. To describe those modes in detail would be to give a history of the various despotic, monarchical, oligarchical, and democratic systems of government which have oppressed or made happy the children of men. Such a description is calculated to perplex and mislead from its very extent; not so an inquiry into the powers of government, and a classification of those powers. They are limited in extent, and, if we confine ourselves to English names and English necessities, we shall readily attain to an apprehension of the mode in which empires, nations, and political societies are bound together, at least in so far as such knowledge is required for the understanding of the nature of Imperial supremacy, and the mode in which Home Rule in Ireland is calculated to affect that supremacy.

The powers of government are divisible into two great classes--1. Imperial powers; 2. State powers, using "State" in the American sense of a political community subordinated to some other power, and not in the sense of an independent nation. The Imperial powers are in English law described as the prerogatives of the Crown, and consist in the main of the powers of making peace and war, of maintaining armies and fleets and regulating commerce, and making treaties with foreign nations. State powers are complete powers of local self-government, described in our colonial Constitutions as powers to make laws "for the peace, order, and good government of the Colony or State" in which such powers are to be exercised.

Intermediate between the Imperial and State powers are a class of powers required to prevent disputes and facilitate intercourse between the various parts of an empire or other composite system of States--for example, the coinage of money, and other regulations relating to the currency; the laws relating to copyright, or other exclusive rights to the use and profits of any works or inventions; and so forth. These powers may be described as quasi-

Imperial powers.

Having arrived at a competent knowledge of the materials out of which governments are formed, it may be well to proceed to a consideration of the manner in which those materials have been worked up in building the two great Anglo-Saxon composite nations--namely, the American Union and the British Empire--for, if we find that the arrangements proposed by the Irish Home Rule Bill are strictly in accordance with the principles on which the unity of the American Union was based and on which the Imperial power of Great Britain has rested for centuries, the conclusion must be that the Irish Home Rule Bill is not antagonistic to the unity of the Empire or to the supremacy of the British Parliament.

In discussing these matters it will be convenient to begin with the American Union, as it is less extensive in area and more homogeneous in its construction than the British Empire. The thirteen revolted American colonies, on the conclusion of their war with England, found themselves in the position of thirteen independent States having no connection with each other. The common tie of supremacy exercised by the mother country was broken, and each State was an independent nation, possessed both of Imperial and Local rights.

The impossibility of a cluster of thirteen small independent nations maintaining their independence against foreign aggression became immediately apparent, and, to remedy this evil, the thirteen States appointed delegates to form a convention authorized to weld them into one body as respected Imperial powers. This was attempted to be done by the establishment of a central body called a Congress, consisting of delegates from the component States, and invested with all the powers designated above as Imperial and quasi-Imperial powers. The expenses incurred by the confederacy were to be defrayed out of a common fund, to be supplied by requisitions made on the several States. In effect, the confederacy of the thirteen States amounted to little more than an offensive and defensive alliance between thirteen independent nations, as the central power had States for its subjects and not individuals, and could only enforce the law against any disobedient State by calling on the twelve other States to make war on the refractory member of the union. A system dependent for its efficacy on the concurrence of so many separate communities contained in itself the seeds of dissolution, and it soon became apparent that one of two things must occur--either the American States must cease as such to be a nation, or the component members of that union must each be prepared to relinquish a further portion of the sovereign or quasi-sovereign powers which it possessed. Under those circumstances, what was the course taken by the thirteen States? They perceived that it was quite possible to maintain complete unity and compactness as a nation if, in addition to investing the Supreme Government with Imperial and quasi-Imperial powers, they added full power to impose federal taxes on the component States and established an Executive furnished with ample means to carry all federal powers into effect through the medium of federal officers. The government so formed consisted of a President and two elected Houses called Congress, and, as a balance-wheel of the Constitution, a Supreme Court was established, to which was confided the task of deciding in case of dispute all questions arising under the Constitution of the United States or relating to international law. The Executive of the United States, with the President as its source and head, was furnished with full authority and power to enforce the federal laws. The army and navy were under its command, and it was provided with courts of justice, and subordinate officers to enforce the decrees of those courts throughout the length and breadth of the Union. Above all, a complete system of federal taxation supplied the Central Government with the necessary funds to perform effectually all the functions of a supreme national government.

The nature of the Constitution of the United States will be best understood by considering the position in which its subjects stand to the Central Government and their own State Governments. In effect, every inhabitant of the United States has a double nationality. He belongs to one great nation called the United States, or, as it would be more aptly called to show its absolute unity, the American Republic, having jurisdiction over the whole surface of ground comprised in the area of the United States. He is also a citizen of a smaller local and partially self-governing body--more important than a county, but not approaching the position of a nation--called a State.

It is no part of the object of this article to enter into the details of the American government, its advantages or defects. This much, however, is clear--the American Constitution has lasted nearly one hundred years, and shows no signs of decay or disruption. It has stood the strain of the greatest war of modern times, and has emerged from the conflict stronger than before. Even during the war the antagonism of the rebels was directed, not against the Union, but against the efforts of the Northern States to suppress slavery, or, in other words, to destroy, as the Southern States believed (not unjustly as the event showed), their property in slaves, and consequently the only means they had of making their estates profitable. One conclusion, then, we may draw, that a nation in which the Imperial powers and the State powers are vested in different authorities is no less compact and powerful, as respects all national capacities, than a nation in which both classes of powers are wielded by the same functionaries; and one lesson more may be learnt from the American War of Secession--namely, that in a nation having such a division of powers, any conflict between the two classes results in the Supreme or Imperial powers prevailing over the Local governmental powers, and not in the latter invading or driving a wedge into the Supreme powers. In fact, the tendency in case of a struggle is towards an undue centralization of the nation by reason of the encroachment by the Supreme authority, rather than towards a weakening of the national unity by separatist action on the part of the constituent members of the nation.

In comparing the Constitution of the United States with the Constitution of the British Empire, we find an apparent resemblance in form as respects the Anglo-Saxon colonies, but underlying the surface a total difference of principle. The United States is an aggregate of homogeneous and contiguous States which, in order to weld themselves into a nation, gave up a portion of their rights to a central authority, reserving to themselves all powers of government which they did not expressly relinquish.

The British Empire is an aggregate of many communities under one common head, and is thus described by Mr. Burke in 1774, in language which may seem to have been somewhat too enthusiastic at the time when it was spoken, but at the present day does not more than do justice to an Empire which comprises one-sixth of the habitable globe in extent and population:--

"I look, I say, on the Imperial rights of Great Britain, and the privileges which the colonies ought to enjoy under those rights, to be just the most reconcilable things in the world. The Parliament of Great Britain sits at the head of her extensive Empire in two capacities: one as the local legislature of this island, providing for all things at home immediately and by no other instrument than the executive power; the other, and I think her nobler capacity, is what I call her Imperial character, in which, as from the throne of heaven, she superintends all the several Legislatures, and guides and controls them all without annihilating any. As all these provincial Legislatures are only co-ordinate with each other, they ought all to be subordinate to her, else they can neither preserve mutual peace, nor hope for mutual justice, nor effectually afford mutual assistance."[9]

The means by which the possessions of Great Britain were acquired have been as various as the possessions themselves. The European, Asiatic, and African possessions became ours by conquest and cession; the American by conquest, treaty, and settlement; the Australasian by settlement, and by that dubious system of settlement known by the name of annexation. Now, what is the link which fastens each of these possessions to the mother country? Surely it is the inherent and indestructible right of the British Crown to exercise Imperial powers--in other words, the supremacy of the Queen and the British Parliament? What, again, is the common bond of union between these vast colonial possessions, differing in laws, in religion, and in the character of the population? The same answer must be given: the joint and several tie, so to speak, is the same--namely, the sovereignty of Great Britain. It is true that the mode in which the materials composing the British Empire have been cemented together is exactly the reverse of the manner of the construction of the American Union. In the case of the Union, independent States voluntarily relinquished a portion of their sovereignty to secure national unity, and entrusted the guardianship of that unity to a representative body chosen by themselves. Such a union was based on contract, and could only be constructed by communities which claimed to be independent. Far different have been the circumstances under which England has developed itself into the British Empire. England began as a sovereign power, having its sovereignty vested at first solely in the Sovereign, but gradually in the Sovereign and Parliament. This sovereignty neither the Crown nor the Parliament can, jointly or severally, get rid of, for it is of the very essence of a sovereign power that it cannot, by Act of Parliament or otherwise, bind its successors.[10] This principle of supremacy has never been lost sight of by the British Parliament. Their right to alter or suspend a colonial Constitution has never been disputed. Contract never enters into the question. The dominant authority delegates to its subordinate communities as much or as little power as it deems advantageous for each body, and, if it sees fit, resumes a portion or the whole of the delegated authority. The last point of difference to be noted between the American Constitution and the Constitution of the British Empire is the fact that as Minerva sprang from the brain of Jupiter fully equipped, so the American Constitution came forth from the hands of its framers complete and, what is of more importance, practically in material matters unchangeable except by the agony of an internecine war or some overwhelming passions. The British Empire, on the other hand, is, as respects its component members, ever in progress and flux. An Anglo-Saxon colony, no less than a human being, has its infancy under the maternal care of a governor, its boyhood subject to the government of a representative council and an Executive appointed by the Crown, its manhood under Home Rule and responsible government, in which the Executive are bound to vacate their offices whenever they are out-voted in the Legislature. Changes are ever taking place in the growth, so to speak, of the several British possessions, but what is the result? Nobody ever dreams of these changes injuring the Imperial tie or the supremacy of the British Parliament, that alone towers above all, unchangeable and unimpaired; and, what is most notable, loyalty and devotion to the Crown--that is to say, the Imperial tie--so far from being weakened by the transition of a colony from a state of dependence in local affairs to the higher degree of a self-governing colony, are, on the contrary, strengthened almost in direct proportion as the central interference with local affairs is diminished. On this point an unimpeachable witness--Mr. Merivale--says: "What, then, are the lessons to be learnt from a consideration of the American Constitution and of our colonial system? Surely these: that Imperial unity and Imperial supremacy are in no degree dependent on the control exercised by the central power on its dependent members." Facts, however, are more conclusive than any arguments; and we have only to look back to the state some forty years ago of Canada, New Zealand, and the various colonies of Australia, and compare that state with their condition to-day, to come to the conclusion that the fullest power of local government is perfectly consistent with the unity of the Empire and the supremacy of the British Parliament. Under the old colonial Constitutions the Executive of those colonies was under the control of the Crown; and Mr. Merivale says "that the political existence consisted of a series of quarrels and reconciliations between the two opposing authorities--the colonial legislative body and the Executive nominated by the Crown." England resolved to give up the control of the Executive, and to grant complete responsible government--that is to say, the Governor of each colony was instructed that his Executive Council (or Ministry, as we should call it) must resign whenever they were out-voted by the legislative body. The effect of this change, this relaxing, as would be supposed, of the Imperial tie, was magical, and is thus described by Mr. Merivale:[11]

"The magnitude of that change--the extraordinary rapidity of its beneficial effects--it is scarcely possible to exaggerate. None but those who have traced it can realize the sudden spring made by a young community under its first release from the old tie of subjection, moderate as that tie really was. The cessation, as if by magic, of the old irritant sores between colony and mother country is the first result. Not only are they at concord, but they seem to leave hardly any traces in the public mind behind them. Confidence and affection towards the home, still fondly so termed by the colonist as well as the emigrant, seem to supersede at once distrust and hostility. Loyalty, which was before the badge of a class suspected by the rest of the community, became the common watchword of all, and, with some extravagance in the sentiment, there arises no small share of its nobleness and devotion. Communities, which but a few years ago would have wrangled over the smallest item of public expenditure to which they were invited by the Executive to contribute, have vied with each other in their subscriptions to purposes of British interests in response to calls of humanity, or munificence for objects but indistinctly heard of at the distance of half the world."

The Dominion of Canada has been so much talked about that it may be well to give a summary of its Constitution, though, in so far as regards its relations to the mother country, it differs in no material respect from any other self-governing colony. The Dominion consists of seven provinces, each of which has a Legislature of its own, but is at the same time subject to the Legislature of the Dominion, in the same manner as each State in the American Union has a Legislature of its own, and is at the same time subject to the control of Congress. The distinguishing feature between the system of the American States and the associated colonies of the Dominion of Canada is this--that all Imperial powers, everything that constitutes a people a nation as respects foreigners, are reserved to the mother country. The division, then, of the Dominion and its provinces consists only in a division of Local powers. It is impossible to mark accurately the line between Dominion and Provincial powers, but, speaking generally, Dominion powers relate to such matters--for example, the regulation of trade and commerce, postal service, currency, and so forth--as require to be dealt with on a uniform principle throughout the whole area of a country; while the Provincial powers relate to provincial and municipal institutions, provincial licensing, and other subjects restricted to the limits of the province. As a general rule, the Legislature of the Dominion and the Legislature of each province have respectively exclusive jurisdiction within the limits of the subjects entrusted to them; but, as respects agriculture and immigration, the Dominion Parliament have power to overrule any Act of the provincial Legislatures, and, as respects property and civil rights in Ontario, Nova Scotia, and New Brunswick, the Dominion Parliament may legislate with a view to uniformity, but their legislation is not valid unless it is accepted by the Legislature of each province to which it applies.

The executive authority in the Dominion Government, as in all the self-governing colonies, is carried on by the Governor in the name of the Queen, but with the advice of a Council: that is to say, as to all Imperial matters, he is under the control of the mother country; as to all local matters, he acts on the advice of his local Council. The result of the whole is that the citizenship of an inhabitant of the Dominion of Canada is a triple tie. Suppose him to reside in the province of Quebec. First, he is a citizen of that province, and bound to obey all the laws which it is within the competence of the provincial Legislature to pass. Next, he is a citizen of the Dominion of Canada, and acknowledges its jurisdiction in all matters outside the legitimate sphere of the province. Lastly, and above all, he is a subject of her Majesty. He is to all intents and purposes, as respects the vast company of nations, an Englishman, entitled to all the privileges as he is to all the glory of the mother country so far as such privileges can be enjoyed and glory participated in without actual residence in England. One startling point of likeness in events and unlikeness in consequences is to be found in the history of Ireland and Canada. In 1798 Ireland rebelled. Protestant and Catholic were arrayed in arms against each other. The rebellion was quenched in blood, and measures of repression have been in force, with slight intervals of suspension, ever since, with this result-- that the Ireland of 1886 is scarcely less disloyal and discontented than the Ireland of 1798. In 1837 and 1838 Canada rebelled. Protestants and Catholics, differing in nationality as well as in religion, were arrayed in arms against each other. The rebellion was quelled with the least possible violence, a free Constitution was given, and the Canada of 1886 is the largest, most loyal, and most contented colony in her Majesty's dominions.

Assuming, then, thus much to be proved by the Constitution of the United States that national unity of the closest description is consistent with complete

Home Rule in the component members of the nation, and by the history of Canada and the British colonial empire that an Imperial tie is sufficient to bind together for centuries dependencies differing in situation, in nationality, in religion, in laws, in everything that distinguishes peoples one from another, and further and more particularly that emancipation of the Anglo-Saxon colonies from control in their internal affairs strengthens instead of weakening Imperial unity, let us turn to Ireland and inquire whether there is anything in the circumstances under which Home Rule was proposed to be granted to Ireland, or in the measures intended to establish that Home Rule, fairly leading to the inference that disruption of the Empire or an impairment of Imperial powers would probably be a consequence of passing the Irish Government Bill and the Irish Land Bill. And, first, as to the circumstances which would seem to recommend the Irish Home Rule Bill.

Ireland, from the very commencement of her connection with England, has chafed under the restraints which that connection imposed. The closer the apparent union between the two countries the greater the real disunion. The Act of 1800, in words and in law, effected not a union merely, but a consolidation of the two countries. The effect of those words and that law was to give rise to a restless discontent, which has constantly found expression in efforts to procure the repeal of the Act of Union and the reestablishment of a National Parliament in Dublin. How futile have been the efforts of the British Parliament to diminish by concession or repress by coercion Irish aspirations or Irish discontent it is unnecessary to discuss here. All men admit the facts, however different the conclusions which they draw from those facts. What Burke said of America on moving in 1775 his resolution on conciliation with the colonies was true in 1885 with respect to Ireland:--

"The fact is undoubted, that under former Parliaments the state of America [read for America, Ireland] has been kept in continual agitation. Everything administered as remedy to the public complaint, if it did not produce, was at least followed by an heightening of the distemper, until, by a variety of experiments, that important country has been brought into her present situation--a situation which I will not miscall, which I dare not name, which I scarcely know how to comprehend in the terms of any description."[12]

At length, after the election of 1885, Mr. Gladstone and the majority of his followers came to the conclusion that an opportunity had presented itself for providing Ireland with a Constitution conferring on the people of that country the largest measure of self-government consistent with the absolute supremacy of the Crown and the Imperial Parliament and the entire unity of the Empire. A scheme was proposed which was accepted in principle by the representatives of the National party in Ireland as a fair and sufficient adjustment of the Imperial claims of Great Britain and the Local claims of Ireland. The scheme was shortly this. A Legislative Assembly was proposed to be established in Ireland with power to make all laws necessary for the good government of Ireland--in other words, invested with the same powers of local self-government as a colonial Assembly. The Irish Assembly was in one respect unlike a colonial Legislature. It consisted of one House only, but this House was divided into two orders, each of which, in case of differences on any important legislative matter, voted separately. This form was adopted in order to minimize the chances of collision between the two orders, by making it imperative on each order to hear the arguments of the other before proceeding to a division, thus throwing on the dissentient order the full responsibility of its dissent, with a complete knowledge of the consequences likely to ensue therefrom. The clause conferring on the Irish Legislature full powers of local self-government was immediately followed by a provision excepting, by enumeration, from any interference on the part of the Irish Legislature, all Imperial powers, and declaring any enactment void which infringed on that provision. This exception (as is well known) is not found in colonial Constitutional Acts. In them the restriction of the words of the grant to Local powers only has been held sufficient to safeguard the supremacy of the British Parliament and the unity of the Empire. The reason for making a difference in the case of the Home Rule Bill was political, not legal. Separation was declared by the enemies of the Bill to be the real intention of its supporters, and destruction of the unity of the Empire to be its certain consequence. It seemed well that Ireland, by her representatives, should accept as a satisfactory charter of Irish liberty a document which contained an express submission to Imperial power and a direct acknowledgment of Imperial unity. Similarly with respect to the supremacy of the British Parliament. In the colonial Constitutions all reference to this supremacy is omitted as being too clear to require notice. In the case of the Irish Home Rule Bill instructions were given to preserve in express words the supremacy of the British Parliament in order to pledge Ireland to an express admission of that supremacy by the same vote which accepted Local powers. It is true that the wording by the draftsman of the sentence reserving the supremacy of

Parliament was justly found fault with as inaccurate and doubtful, but that defect would have been cured by an amendment in Committee; and, even if there had not been any such clause in the Bill, it is clear, from what has been said above, that the Imperial Legislature could not, if it would, renounce its supremacy or abdicate its sovereign powers. The executive government in Ireland was continued in the Queen, to be carried on by the Lord Lieutenant on behalf of her Majesty, with the aid of such officers and Council as to her Majesty might from time to time seem fit. Her Majesty was also a constituent part of the Legislature, with power to delegate to the Lord Lieutenant the prerogative of assenting to or dissenting from Bills, and of summoning, proroguing, and dissolving Parliament. Under these provisions the Lord Lieutenant resembled the Governor of a colony with responsible government. He was invested with a double authority--first, Imperial; secondly, Local. As an Imperial officer, he was bound to veto any Bill injuriously affecting Imperial interests or inconsistent with general Imperial policy; as a Local officer, it was his duty to act in all local matters according to the advice of his Council, whose tenure of office depended on their being in harmony with, and supported by, a majority of the Legislative Assembly. Questions relating to the constitutionality of any particular law were not left altogether to the decision of the Governor. If a Bill containing a provision infringing Imperial rights passed the Legislature, its validity might be decided in the first instance by the ordinary courts of law, but the ultimate appeal lay to the Judicial Committee of the Privy Council, and, with a view to secure absolute impartiality in the Committee, it was provided that Ireland should be represented on that body by persons who either were or had been Irish judges. Not the least important provision of the Bill, as respects the maintenance of Imperial interests, was the continuance of Imperial taxation. The Customs and Excise duties were directed to be levied, as heretofore, in pursuance of the enactments of the Imperial Parliament, and were excepted from the control of the Irish Legislature, which had full power, with that exception, to impose such taxes in Ireland as they might think expedient. The Bill further provided that neither the Imperial taxes of Excise nor any Local taxes that might be imposed by the Irish Legislature should be paid into the Irish Exchequer. An Imperial officer, called the Receiver-General, was appointed, into whose hands the produce of every tax, both Imperial and Local, was required to be paid, and it was the duty of the Receiver-General to take care that all claims of the English Exchequer, including especially the contribution payable by Ireland for Imperial purposes, were satisfied before a farthing found its way into the Irish

Exchequer for Irish purposes. The Receiver-General was provided with an Imperial Court to enforce his rights of Imperial taxation, and adequate means for enforcing all Imperial powers by Imperial civil officers. The Bill did not provide for the representation of Ireland in the Imperial Parliament on all Imperial questions, including questions relating to Imperial taxation, but it is fully understood that in any Bill which might hereafter be brought forward relating to Home Rule those defects would be remedied.

An examination, then, of the Home Rule Bill, that "child of revolution and parent of separation," appears to lead irresistibly to two conclusions. First, that Imperial rights and Imperial powers, representation for Imperial purposes, Imperial taxation--in short, every link that binds a subordinate member of an Empire to its supreme head--have been maintained unimpaired and unchanged. Secondly, that, in granting Home Rule to discontented Ireland, that form of responsible government has been adopted which, as Mr. Merivale declares-- and his declaration subsequent events have more than verified--when conferred on the discontented colonies, changed restless aspirations for separation into quiet loyalty.

That such a Bill as the Home Rule Bill should be treated as an invasion of Imperial rights is a proof of one, or perhaps of both, the following axioms-- that Bills are never read by their accusers, and that party spirit will distort the plainest facts. The union of Great Britain and Ireland was not, so far as Imperial powers were concerned, disturbed by the Bill, and an Irishman remains a citizen of the British Empire under the Home Rule Bill, with the same obligations and the same privileges, on the same terms as before. All the Bill did was to make his Irish citizenship distinct from his Imperial citizenship, in the same manner as the citizenship of a native of the State of New York is distinct from his citizenship as a member of the United States. Now it has been found that the Central power in the United States has been more than a match for the State powers, and can it be conceived for a moment that the Imperial power of Great Britain should not be a match for the Local power of Ireland--a State which has not one-seventh of the population or one-twentieth part of the income of the dominant community?

One argument remains to be noticed which the opponents of Home Rule urge as absolutely condemnatory of the measure, whereas, if properly weighed, it is conclusive in its favour. Home Rule, they say, is a mere question of sentiment.

"National aspirations" are the twaddle of English enthusiasts who know nothing of Ireland. What is really wanted is the reform of the Land Law. Settle the agrarian problem, and Home Rule may be relegated to the place supposed to be paved with good intentions. The Irish will straightway change their character, and become a law-abiding, contented, loyal people. Be it so. But suppose it to be proved that the establishment of an Irish Government, or, in other words, Home Rule, is an essential condition of agrarian reform--that the latter cannot be had without the former--surely Home Rule should stand none the worse in the estimation of its opponents if it not only secures a safe basis for putting an end to agrarian exasperation, but also gratifies the feeling of the Irish people as expressed by the majority of its representatives in Parliament? Now, what is the nature of the Irish Land Question? This we must understand before considering the remedy. In Ireland (meaning by Ireland that part of the country which is in the hands of tenants, and falls within the compass of a Land Bill) the tenure of land is wholly unlike that which is found in the greater part of England. Instead of large farms in which the landlord makes all the improvements and the tenant pays rent for the privilege of cultivating the land and receives the produce, small holdings are found in which the tenant does the improvements (if any) and pays a fixed rent-charge to the owner. In England the tenant does not perform the obligations or in any way aspire to the character of owner. If he thinks he can get a cheaper farm, he quits his former one, regarding his interest in the land as a mere matter of pounds, shillings, and pence. Not so the Irish tenant. He has made what he calls improvements, he claims a quasi-ownership in the land, and has the characteristic Celtic attachment for the patch of ground forming his holding, however squalid it may be, however inadequate for his support. In short, in Ireland there is a dual ownership--that of the proprietor, who has no interest in the soil so long as the tenant pays his rent and fulfils the conditions of his tenancy; and that of the tenant, who, subject to the payment of his rent and performance of the fixed conditions, acts, thinks, and carries himself as the owner of his holding. A system, then, of agrarian reform in Ireland resolves itself into an inquiry as to the best mode of putting an end to this dual ownership--that is to say, of making the tenant the sole proprietor of his holding, and compensating the landlord for his interest in the ownership. The problem is further narrowed by the circumstance that the tenant cannot be expected to advance any capital or pay an increased rent, so that the means of compensating the landlord must be found out of the existing rent.

The plan adopted in Mr. Gladstone's Land Bill was to commute the rent-charges, offering the landlord, as a general rule, twenty years' purchase on the net rental of the estate (that is to say, the rent received by him after deducting all outgoings), and paying him the purchase-money in ? per cent. stock taken at par. The stock was to be advanced by the English Government to an Irish State department at 3-1/8 per cent. interest, and the Bill provided that the tenant, instead of rent, was to pay an annuity of ? per cent. on a capital sum equal in amount to twenty times the gross rental.

The notable feature which distinguished this plan from all other schemes was the security given for the repayment of the purchase-money: hitherto the English Government has lent the money directly to the landlord or tenant, and has become the mortgagee of the land--in other words, has become in effect the landlord of the land sold to the tenant until the repayment of the loan has been completed. To carry into effect under such a system any extensive scheme of agrarian reform (and if not extensive such a reform would be of no value in pacifying Ireland) presupposes a readiness on the part of the English Government to become virtually the landlord of a large portion of Ireland, with the attendant odium of absenteeism and alien domination. Under a land scheme such as that of 1886, all these difficulties would be overcome. The Irish, not the English, Government would be the virtual landlord. It would be the interest of Ireland that the annuities due from the tenants should be regularly paid, as, subject to the prior charge of the English Exchequer, they would form part of the Irish revenues. The cardinal difference, then, between Mr. Gladstone's scheme and any other land scheme that has seen the light is this--that in Mr. Gladstone's scheme the English loans would have been lent to the Irish Government on the security of the whole Irish revenues, whereas in every other scheme they have been lent by the English Government to the Irish creditors on the security of individual patches of land.

The whole question, then, of the relation between Home Rule and agrarian reform may be summed up as follows:--Agrarian reform is necessary for the pacification of Ireland; agrarian reform cannot be efficiently carried into effect without an Irish Government; an Irish Government can only be established by a Home Rule Bill: therefore a Home Rule Bill is necessary for the pacification of Ireland. It is idle to say, as has been said on numerous platforms, that plans no doubt can be devised for agrarian reform without Home Rule. The Irish revenues are the only collateral security that can be obtained for loans of

English money, and Irish revenues are only available for the purpose on the establishment of an Irish Government. Baronial guarantees, union guarantees, county guarantees, debenture schemes, have all been tried and found wanting, and vague assertions as to possibilities are idle unless they are based on intelligible working plans.

The foregoing arguments will be equally valid if, instead of making the tenants peasant-proprietors, it were thought desirable that the Irish State should be the proprietor and the tenants be the holders of the land at perpetual rents and subject to fixed conditions. Again, it might be possible to pay the landlords by annual sums instead of capital sums. Such matters are really questions of detail. The substance is to interpose the Irish Government between the tenant and the English mortgagee, and to make the loans general charges on the whole of the Irish Government revenues as paid into the hands of an Imperial Receiver instead of placing them as special charges, each fixed on its own small estate or holding. The fact that Mr. Gladstone's land scheme was denounced as confiscation of ?00,000,000 of the English taxpayers' property, while Lord Ashbourne's Act is pronounced by the same party wise and prudent, shows the political blindness of party spirit in its most absurd form. Lord Ashbourne's Act requires precisely the same expenditure to do the same work as Mr. Gladstone's Bill requires, but in Mr. Gladstone's scheme the whole Irish revenue was pledged as collateral security, and the Irish Government was interposed between the ultimate creditor and the Irish tenant, while under Lord Ashbourne's Act the English Government figures without disguise as the landlord of each tenant, exacting a debt which the tenant is unwilling to pay as being due to what he calls an alien Government.

An endeavour has been made in the preceding pages to prove that Home Rule in no respect infringes on Imperial rights or Imperial unity, for the simple reason that the Imperial power remains exactly in the same position as it was before, the Home Rule Bill dealing only with Local matters. At all events, Burke thought that the Imperial supremacy alone constituted a real union between England and Ireland. He says--

"My poor opinion is, that the closest connection between Great Britain and Ireland is essential to the well-being--I had almost said to the very being--of the three kingdoms; for that purpose I humbly conceive that the whole of the superior, and what I should call Imperial politics, ought to have its residence here, and that Ireland, locally, civilly, and commercially independent, ought politically to look up to Great Britain in all matters of peace and war. In all these points to be joined with her, and, in a word, with her to live and to die."[13]

How strange to Burke would have seemed the doctrine that the restoration of a limited power of self-government to Ireland, excluding commerce, and excluding all matters not only Imperial, but those in which uniformity is required, should be denounced as a disruption of the Empire!

It remains to notice one other charge made against the Gladstonian Home Rule Bill, namely, that of impairing the supremacy of the British Parliament. That allegation has been shown also to be founded on a mistake. Next, it is said that the Gladstonian scheme does not provide securities against executive and legislative oppression. The answer is complete. The executive authority being vested in the Queen, it will be the duty of the Governor not to allow executive oppression; still more will it be his duty to veto any act of legislative oppression. Further, it is stated that difficulties will arise with respect to the power of the Privy Council to nullify unconstitutional Acts. But it is hard to see why a power which is exercised with success in the United States, where all the States are equal, and without dispute in our colonies, which are all dependent, should not be carried into effect with equal ease in Ireland, which is more closely bound to us and more completely under our power than the colonies are, or than the several States are under the power of the Central Government.

To conclude: the cause of Irish discontent is the conjoint operation of the passion for nationality and the vicious system of land tenure, and the scheme of the Irish Home Rule Bill and the Land Bill removes the whole fabric on which Irish discontent is raised. The Irish, by the great majority of their representatives, have accepted the Home Rule Bill as a satisfactory settlement of the nationality question. The British Parliament can, through the medium of the Home Rule Bill and the establishment of an Irish Legislature, carry through a final settlement of agrarian disputes with less injustice to individuals than could a Parliament sitting in Dublin, and, be it added, with scarcely any appreciable risk to the British taxpayer. Of course it may be said that an Irish Parliament will go farther--that Home Rule is a step to separation, and a reform of the Land Laws a spoliation of the landlords. To those who urge such arguments I would recommend the perusal of the speech of Burke on Conciliation with America, and especially the following sentences, substituting "Ireland" for "the colonies:"--

"But [the Colonies] Ireland will go further. Alas! alas! when will this speculating against fact and reason end? What will quiet these panic fears which we entertain of the hostile effect of a conciliatory conduct? Is it true that no case can exist in which it is proper for the Sovereign to accede to the desires of his discontented subjects? Is there anything peculiar in this case to make it a rule for itself? Is all authority of course lost when it is not pushed to the extreme? Is it a certain maxim that the fewer causes of discontentment are left by Government the more the subject will be inclined to resist and rebel?"

FOOTNOTES:

[Footnote 9: Burke's Speech on American Taxation, vol. i. p. 174]

[Footnote 10: This is the opinion of both English and American lawyers. See Blackstone's Comm., i. 90; Austin on Jurisprudence, i. 226. As to American cases, see Corley on Constitutional Limitations, pp. 2-149.]

[Footnote 11: "Lectures on the Colonies," p, 641.]

[Footnote 12: Burke, vol. i. p. 181.]

[Footnote 13: "Letter on Affairs of Ireland," i. 462.]

THE IRISH GOVERNMENT BILL AND THE IRISH LAND BILL

BY LORD THRING

A mere enumeration or analysis of the contents of the Irish Government Bill, 1886, and the Land (Ireland) Bill, 1886, would convey scarcely any intelligible idea to the mind of an ordinary reader. It is, therefore, proposed in the following pages, before entering on the details of each Bill, to give a summary of the reasons which led to its introduction, and of the principles on which it is founded. To begin with the Irish Government Bill--

The object of the Irish Government Bill is to confer on the Irish people the largest measure of self-government consistent with the absolute supremacy of the Crown and Imperial Parliament and the entire unity of the Empire. To carry into effect this object it was essential to create a separate though subordinate legislature; thus occasion was given to opponents to apply the name of Separatists to the supporters of the Bill--a term true in so far only as it denoted the intention to create a separate legislature, but false and calumnious when used in the sense in which it was intended to be understood--of imputing to the promoters of the Bill the intention to disunite or in any way to disintegrate the Empire. Indeed, the very object of the measure was, by relaxing a little the legal bonds of union, to draw closer the actual ties between England and Ireland, in fact, to do as we have done in our Colonies, by decentralizing the subordinate functions of government to strengthen the central supremacy of natural affection and Imperial unity. The example of the effects of giving complete self-government to our Colonies would seem not unfavourable to trying the same experiment in Ireland. Some forty years ago, Canada, New Zealand, and the various colonies of Australia were discontented and uneasy at the control exercised by the Government of England over their local affairs. What did England do? She gave to each of those communities the fullest power of local government consistent with the unity of the Empire. The result was that the real union was established in the same degree as the apparent tie of control over local affairs was loosened. Are there any reasons to suppose that the condition of Ireland is such as to render the example of the Colonies applicable? Let us look a little at the past history of that country. Up to 1760 Ireland was governed practically as a conquered country. The result was that in 1782, in order to save Imperial unity, we altogether relaxed the local tie and made Ireland legislatively independent. The Empire was thus saved, but difficulties naturally arose between two independent legislatures. The true remedy would have been to have imposed on Grattan's Parliament the conditions imposed by the Irish Government Bill on the statutory Parliament created by that Bill; the course actually taken was that, instead of leaving the Irish with their local government, and arranging for the due supremacy of England, the Irish Legislature was destroyed under the guise of Union, and Irish representatives were transferred to an assembly in which they had little weight, and in which they found no sympathy. The result was that from the date of the Union to the present day Ireland has been constantly working for the reinstatement of its National Legislature, and has been governed by a continuous system of extraordinary legislature called coercion; the fact being that between 1800, the date of the Act of Union, and 1832, the date of the great Reform Act, there were only eleven years free from coercion, while in the fifty-three years since that period there have been only two years entirely free from special repressive legislation. So much, therefore, is clear, that Irish discontent at not being allowed to manage their own affairs has gradually increased instead of diminishing. The conclusion then would seem irresistible, that if coercion has failed, the only practical mode of governing Ireland satisfactorily is to give the people power to manage their local affairs. Coming, then, to the principle of the Bill, the first step is to reconcile local government with Imperial supremacy, in other words, to divide Imperial from local powers; for if this division be accurately made, and the former class of powers be reserved to the British Crown and British Parliament, while the latter only are intrusted to the Irish Parliament, it becomes a contradiction in terms to say that Imperial unity is dissolved by reserving to the Imperial authority all its powers, or that Home Rule is a sundering of the Imperial tie when that tie is preserved inviolable. Imperial powers, then, are the prerogatives of the Crown with respect to peace and war, and making treaties with foreign nations; in short, the power of regulating the relations of the Empire towards foreign nations. These are the jura summi imperii, the very insignia of supremacy; the attributes of sovereign authority in every form of government, be it despotism, limited monarchy, or republic; the only difference is that in a system of government under one supreme head, they are vested in that head alone, in a federal government, as in America or Switzerland, they reside in the composite body forming the federal supreme authority. Various subsidiary powers necessarily attend the above supreme powers; for example, the power of maintaining armies and navies, of commanding the militia, and other incidental powers. Closely connected with the power of making peace and war is the power of regulating commerce with foreign nations. Next in importance to the reservations necessary to constitute the Empire a Unity with regard to foreign nations, are the powers required to prevent disputes and to facilitate intercourse between the various parts of the Empire. These are the coinage of money and other regulations relating to currency, to copyright or other exclusive rights to the use or profit of any works or inventions. The above subjects must be altogether excluded from the powers of the subordinate legislature; it ceases to be subordinate as soon as it is invested with these Imperial, or quasi-Imperial, powers.

Assuming, however, the division between Imperial and local powers to be accurately determined, how is the subordinate legislative body to be kept within its due limits? The answer is very plain,--an Imperial court must be established to decide in the last resort whether the subordinate legislature has or has not infringed Imperial rights. Such a court has been in action in the United States of America ever since their union, and no serious conflict has arisen in carrying its decisions into effect, and the Privy Council, acting as the Supreme Court in respect to Colonial appeals, has been accepted by all the self-governing colonies as a just and impartial expositor of the meaning of their several constitutions.

Next in importance to the right division of Imperial and local powers is a correct understanding of the relation borne by the executive of an autonomous country to the mother country. In every part of the British Empire which enjoys home rule the legislature consists of the Queen and the two local legislative bodies. The administrative power resides in the Queen alone. The Queen has the appointment of all the officers of the government; money bills can be introduced into the legislature only with the consent of the Queen. The initiative power of taxation then is vested in the Queen, the executive head, in practice represented by the Governor. But such a power of initiation is of course useless unless the legislative body is willing to support the executive, and grants it the necessary funds for carrying on the government. What, then, is the contrivance by which the governmental machine is prevented from being stopped by a difference between the executive and legislative authorities? It is the same in the mother country, and in every British home-rule country, with this difference only--that beyond the limits of the mother country the Queen is represented by a governor to whom are delegated such a measure of powers as is necessary for the supreme head of a local self-governing community. The contrivance is this in the mother country:--the Queen acts upon the advice of a cabinet council; in home-rule dependencies the Governor acts on the advice of a local council. If this cabinet council in the mother country, or local council in a dependency, ceases to command a majority in the popular legislative body, it resigns, and the Governor is obliged to select a council which, by commanding such a majority, can obtain the supplies necessary to carry on the government. The consequence then is, that in a home-rule community, if a serious difficulty arises between the legislative and executive authority, the head of the executive, the governor, refers the ultimate decision of the question to the general body of electors by dissolving the popular legislative body. It has been urged in the discussion on the Irish Government Bill that the powers of the executive in relation to the legislative body ought to be expressed in the Bill itself; but it is clear to anybody acquainted with the rudiments of legislation that the details of such a system (in other words, the mode in which a governor ought to act under the endless variety of circumstances which may occur in governing a dependency) never have been and never can be expressed in an Act of Parliament. But how little difficulty this absence of definition has caused may be judged from the fact that neither in England nor in any of her home-rule dependencies has any vital collision arisen between the executive and legislative authorities, and that all the home-rule colonies have managed to surmount the obstacles which the opponents of Home Rule argued would be fatal to their existence. The main principles have now been stated on which the Irish Government Bill is framed, and it remains to give a summary of the provisions of the Bill, the objects and bearing of which will be readily understood from the foregoing observations. The first clause provides that--

"On and after the appointed day there shall be established in Ireland a Legislature consisting of Her Majesty the Queen and an Irish legislative body."

This is the first step in all English constitutional systems, to vest the power of legislation in the Queen and the legislative body. Such a legislature might have had conferred on it the independent powers vested in Grattan's Parliament: but the second clause at once puts an end to any doubt as to the subordination of the Irish legislative body; for while on the one hand it confers full powers of local self-government, by declaring that the Legislature may make any laws for the peace, order, and good government of Ireland, it subjects that power to numerous exceptions and restrictions. The exceptions are contained in the third clause, and the restrictions in the fourth. The exceptions are as follows:--

"The Legislature of Ireland shall not make laws relating to the following matters or any of them:--

"(1.) The status or dignity of the Crown, or the succession to the Crown, or a Regency;

"(2.) The making of peace or war;

"(3.) The army, navy, militia, volunteers, or other military or naval forces, or the defence of the realm;

"(4.) Treaties and other relations with foreign States, or the relations between the various parts of Her Majesty's dominions;

"(5.) Dignities or titles of honour;

"(6.) Prize or booty of war;

"(7.) Offences against the law of nations; or offences committed in violation of any treaty made, or hereafter to be made, between Her Majesty and any foreign State; or offences committed on the high seas;

"(8.) Treason, alienage, or naturalization;

"(9.) Trade, navigation, or quarantine;

"(10.) The postal and telegraph service, except as hereafter in this Act mentioned with respect to the transmission of letters and telegrams in Ireland;

"(11.) Beacons, lighthouses, or sea-marks;

"(12.) The coinage; the value of foreign money; legal tender; or weights and measures; or

"(13.) Copyright, patent rights, or other exclusive rights to the use or profits of any works or inventions."

Of these exceptions the first four preserve the imperial rights which have been insisted on above, and maintain the position of Ireland as an integral portion of that Empire of which Great Britain is the head. The remaining exceptions are either subsidiary to the first four, or relate, as is the case with exceptions 10 to 13, to matters on which it is desirable that uniformity should exist throughout the whole Empire. The restrictions in clause 4 are:--

"The Irish Legislature shall not make any law--

"(1.) Respecting the establishment or endowment of religion, or prohibiting the free exercise thereof; or

"(2.) Imposing any disability, or conferring any privilege, on account of religious belief; or

"(3.) Abrogating or derogating from the right to establish or maintain any place of denominational education or any denominational institution or charity; or

"(4.) Prejudicially affecting the right of any child to attend a school receiving public money without attending the religious instruction at that school; or

"(5.) Impairing, without either the leave of Her Majesty in Council first obtained on an address presented by the legislative body of Ireland, or the consent of the corporation interested, the rights, property, or privileges of any existing corporation incorporated by royal charter or local and general Act of Parliament; or

"(6.) Imposing or relating to duties of customs and duties of excise, as defined by this Act, or either of such duties, or affecting any Act relating to such duties or either of them; or

"(7.) Affecting this Act, except in so far as it is declared to be alterable by the Irish Legislature."

These restrictions differ from the exceptions, inasmuch as they do not prevent the Legislature of Ireland from dealing with the subjects to which they refer, but merely impose on it an obligation not to handle the specified matters in a manner detrimental to the interests of certain classes of Her Majesty's subjects. For example, restrictions 1 to 4 are practically concerned in securing religious freedom; restriction 5 protects existing charters; restriction 6 is necessary, as will be seen hereinafter, to carrying into effect the financial scheme of the bill; restriction 7 is a consequence of the very framework of the Bill: it provides for the stability of the Irish constitution, by declaring that the Irish Legislature is not competent to alter the constitutional act to which it owes its existence, except on those points on which it is expressly permitted to make alterations.

Clause 5 is an exposition, so to speak, of the consequence which would seem to flow from the fact of the Queen being a constitutional part of the Legislature.

It states that the royal prerogatives with respect to the summoning, prorogation, and dissolution of the Irish legislative body are to be the same as the royal prerogatives in relation to the Imperial Parliament. The next clause (6) is comparatively immaterial; it merely provides that the duration of the Irish legislative body is to be quinquennial. As it deals with a matter of detail, it perhaps would have more aptly found a place in a subsequent part of the Bill. Clause 7 passes from the legislative to the executive authority; it declares:--

(1.) The executive government of Ireland shall continue vested in Her Majesty, and shall be carried on by the Lord Lieutenant on behalf of Her Majesty with the aid of such officers and such council as to Her Majesty may from time to time seem fit.

(2.) Subject to any instructions which may from time to time be given by Her Majesty, the Lord Lieutenant shall give or withhold the assent of Her Majesty to bills passed by the Irish legislative body, and shall exercise the prerogatives of Her Majesty in respect of the summoning, proroguing, and dissolving of the Irish legislative body, and any prerogatives the exercise of which may be delegated to him by Her Majesty.

Bearing in mind what has been said in the preliminary observations in respect of the relation between the executive and the legislative authority, it will be at once understood how much this clause implies, according to constitutional maxims, of the dependence on the one hand of the Irish executive in respect of imperial matters, and of its independence in respect of local matters. The clause is practically co-ordinate and correlative with the clause conferring complete local powers on the Irish Legislature, while it preserves all imperial powers to the Imperial Legislature. The governor is an imperial officer, and will be bound to watch over imperial interests with a jealous scrutiny, and to veto any bill which may be injurious to those interests. On the other hand, as respects all local matters, he will act on and be guided by the advice of the Irish executive council. The system is, as has been shown above, self-acting. The governor, for local purposes, must have a council which is in harmony with the legislative body. If a council, supported by the legislative body and the governor do not agree, the governor must give way unless he can, by dismissing his council and dissolving the legislative body, obtain both a council and a legislative body which will support his views. As respects imperial questions, the case is different; here the last word rests with the mother country, and in the last resort a determination of the executive council, backed by the legislative body, to resist imperial rights, must be deemed an act of rebellion on the part of the Irish people, and be dealt with accordingly.

The above clauses contain the pith and marrow of the whole scheme. The exact constitution of the legislative body, and the orders into which it should be divided, the exclusion or non-exclusion of the Irish members from the Imperial Parliament, indeed, the whole of the provisions found in the remainder of this Bill, are matters which might be altered without destroying, or even violently disarranging, the Home-rule scheme as above described.

Clauses 9, 10, and 11 provide for the constitution of the legislative body; it differs materially from the colonial legislative bodies, and from the Legislature of the United States. For the purpose of deliberation it consists of one House only; for the purpose of voting on all questions (except interlocutory applications and questions of order), it is divided into two classes, called in the Bill "Orders," each of which votes separately, with the result that a question on which the two orders disagree is deemed to be decided in the negative. The object of this arrangement is to diminish the chances of collision between the two branches of the Legislature, which have given rise to so much difficulty both in England and the colonies. Each order will have ample opportunity of learning the strength and hearing the arguments of the other order. They will therefore, each of them, proceed to a division with a full sense of the responsibility attaching to their action. A further safeguard is provided against a final conflict between the first and second orders. If the first order negative a proposition, that negative is in force only for a period of three years, unless a dissolution takes place sooner, in which case it is terminated at once; the lost bill or clause may then be submitted to the whole House, and if decided in the affirmative, and assented to by the Queen, becomes law. The first order of the Irish legislative body comprises 103 members. It is intended to consist ultimately wholly of elective members; but for the next immediate period of thirty years the rights of the Irish representative peers are, as will be seen, scrupulously reserved. The plan is this: of the 103 members composing the first order, seventy-five are elective, and twenty-eight peerage members. The qualification of the elective members is an annual income of ?00, or the possession of a capital sum of ?000 free from all charges. The elections are to be conducted in the electoral districts set out in the schedule to the Bill. The electors must possess land or tenements within the district of the annual value of ?5. The twenty-eight peerage members consist of the existing twenty-eight representative peers, and any vacancies in their body during the next thirty years are to be filled up in the manner at present in use respecting the election of Irish representative peers. The Irish representative peers cease to sit in the English Parliament; but a member of that body is not required to sit in the Irish Parliament without his assent, and the place of any existing peer refusing to sit in the Irish Parliament will be filled up as in the case of an ordinary vacancy. The elective members of the first order sit for ten years; every five years one half their number will retire. The members of the first order do not vacate their seats on a dissolution of the legislative body. At the expiration of thirty years, that is to say, upon the exhaustion of all the existing Irish representative peers, the whole of the upper order will consist of elective members. The second order consists of 204 members, that is to say, of the 103 existing Irish members (who are transferred to the Irish Parliament), and of 101 additional members to be elected by the county districts and the represented towns, in the same manner as that in which the present 101 members for counties and towns are elected--each constituency returning two instead of one member. If an existing member does not assent to his transfer, his seat is vacated.

A power is given to the Legislature of Ireland to enable the Royal University of Ireland to return two members.

The provisions with respect to this second order fall within the class of enactments which are alterable by the Irish Legislature. After the first dissolution of parliament the Irish Legislature may deal with the second order in any manner they think fit, with the important restrictions:--(1) That in the distribution of members they must have due regard to population; (2) that they must not increase or diminish the number of members.

The transfer to the Irish legislative body of the Irish representative peers, and of the Irish members, involves their exclusion under ordinary circumstances from the Imperial Parliament, with this great exception, that whenever an alteration is proposed to be made in the fundamental provisions of the Irish Government Bill, a mode of procedure is devised for recalling both orders of the Irish legislative body to the Imperial Parliament for the purpose of obtaining their consent to such alteration (clause 39).

Further, it is right to state here that Mr. Gladstone in his speech on the second reading of the Bill proposed to provide, "that when any proposal for taxation was made affecting the condition of Ireland, Irish members should have an opportunity of appearing in the House to take a share in the transaction of that business."

Questions arising as to whether the Irish Parliament has or not exceeded its constitutional powers may be determined by the ordinary courts of law in the first instance; the ultimate appeal lies to the Judicial Committee of the Privy Council. An additional safeguard is provided by declaring that before a provision in a Bill becomes law, the Lord Lieutenant may take the opinion of the Judicial Committee of the Privy Council as to its legality, and further, that without subjecting private litigants to the expense of trying the constitutionality of an Act, the Lord Lieutenant may, of his own motion, move the judicial committee to determine the question. With a view to secure absolute impartiality in the committee, Ireland will be represented on that body by persons who are or have been Irish judges (clause 25).

The question of finance forms a separate portion of the Bill, the provisions of which are contained in clauses twelve to twenty, while the machinery for carrying those enactments into effect will be found in Part III. of the Land Bill. The first point to be determined was the amount to be contributed by Ireland to imperial expenses. Under the Act of Union it was intended that Ireland should pay 2/17ths, or in the proportion of 1 to 7-1/2 of the total expenditure of the United Kingdom. This amount being found exorbitant, it was gradually reduced, until at the present moment it amounts to something under the proportion of 1 to 11-1/2. The bill fixes the proportion at 1/15th, or 1 to 14, this sum being arrived at by a comparison between the amount of the income-tax, death-duties, and valuation of property in Great Britain, and the amount of the same particulars in Ireland. The amount to be contributed by Ireland to the imperial expenditure being thus ascertained, the more difficult part of the problem remained to provide the fund out of which the contribution should be payable, and the mode in which its payment should be secured. The plan which commended itself to the framers of the Bill, as combining the advantage of insuring the fiscal unity of Great Britain and Ireland, with absolute security to the British exchequer, was to continue the customs and excise duties under imperial control, and to pay them into the hands of an imperial officer. This plan is carried into effect by the conjoint operation of the clauses of the Irish Government Bill and the Irish Land Bill above referred to. The customs and excise duties are directed to be levied as heretofore in pursuance of the enactments of the Imperial Parliament, and are excepted from the control of the Irish Legislature, which may, with that exception, impose any taxes in Ireland it may think expedient. The imperial officer who is appointed under the Land Bill bears the title of Receiver-General, and into his hands not only the imperial taxes (the customs and excise duties), but also all local taxes imposed by the Irish Parliament are in the first instance paid. (See Clauses 25-27 of the Land Bill.) The Receiver-General having thus in his hands all imperial and local funds levied in Ireland, his duty is to satisfy all imperial claims before paying over any moneys to the Irish Exchequer. Further, an Imperial Court of Exchequer is established in Ireland to watch over the interests of the Receiver-General, and all revenue cases are to be tried, and all defaults punished in that court. Any neglect of the local authorities to carry into effect the decrees of the Imperial Court will amount to treason, and it will be the duty of the Imperial Government to deal with it accordingly.

Supposing the Bill to have passed, the account of the Exchequer in Ireland would have stood thus:--

RECEIPTS.

1. Imperial Taxes: (1) Customs . . . . ?,880,000 (2) Excise . . . . 4,300,000 --------- ?,180,000

2. Local Taxes: (1) Stamps . . . . ?00,000 (2) Income-Tax at 6d. in ?. . 550,000 --------- ?,150,000

3. Non-Tax Revenue: (Post Office, Telegraph, etc.) . . . . . ?,020,000 ---------- ?,350,000

EXPENDITURE.

1. Contribution to Imperial Exchequer on basis of 1/15th of Imperial Expenditure, viz.: (1) Debt Charge . . . . ?,466,000 (2) Army and Navy . . . . 1,666,000 (3) Civil Charges . . . . 110,000 --------- ?,242,000 2. Sinking Fund on 1/15th of Capital of Debt . . . . 360,000 3. Charge for Constabulary[14] . . . . 1,000,000 4. Local Civil Charges other than Constabulary . . . . 2,510,000 5. Collection of Revenue: (1) Imperial

Taxes . . . . . . ?70,000 (2) Local Taxes . . . . 60,000 (3) Non-Tax Revenue . . . . . .
604,000 ------- 834,000 6. Balance or Surplus . . . . 404,000 --------
?,350,000

The Imperial contribution payable by Ireland to Great Britain cannot be increased for thirty years, though it may be diminished if the charges for the army and navy and Imperial civil expenditure for any year be less than fifteen times the contribution paid by Ireland, in which case 1/15th of the diminution will be deducted from the annual Imperial contribution. Apart from the Imperial charges there are other charges strictly Irish, for the security of the payment of which the Bill provides. This it does by imposing an obligation on the Irish legislative body to enact sufficient taxes to meet such charges, and by directing them to be paid by the Imperial Receiver-General, who is required to keep an imperial and an Irish account, carrying the customs and excise duties, in the first instance, to the imperial account, and the local taxes to the Irish account, transferring to the Irish account the surplus remaining after paying the imperial charges on the imperial account. On this Irish account are charged debts due from the Government of Ireland, pensions, and other sums due to the civil servants, and the salaries of the judges of the supreme courts in Ireland.

Some provisions of importance remain to be noticed. Judges of the superior and county courts in Ireland are to be removable from office only on address to the Crown, presented by both orders of the Legislative body voting separately. Existing Civil servants are retained in their offices at their existing salaries; if the Irish Government desire their retirement, they will be entitled to pensions; on the other hand, if at the end of two years the officers themselves wish to retire, they can do so, and will be entitled to the same pensions as if their office had been abolished. The pensions are payable by the Receiver-General out of the Irish account above mentioned.

The supremacy of the Imperial Parliament over all parts of the Empire is an inherent quality of which Parliament cannot divest itself, inasmuch as it cannot bind its successors or prevent them from repealing any prior Act. In order, however, to prevent any misapprehension on this point clause 37 was inserted, the efficacy of which, owing in great measure to a misprint, has been doubted. It is enough to state here that it was intended by express legislation to reserve all powers to the Imperial Parliament, and had the Bill gone into Committee the question would have been placed beyond the reach of cavil by a slight alteration in the wording of the clause. This summary may be concluded by the statement that the appellate jurisdiction of the House of Lords over actions and suits arising in Ireland (except in respect of constitutional questions reserved for the determination of the Judicial Committee of the Privy Council as explained above), and with respect to claims for Irish Peerages, is preserved intact.

The object of the Land Bill was a political one: to promote the contentment of the people, and the cause of good government in Ireland, by settling once and for ever the vexed question relating to land. To do this effectually it was necessary to devise a system under which the tenants, as a class, should become interested in the maintenance of social order, and be furnished with substantial inducements to rally round the institutions of their country. On the other hand, it was just and right that the landlords should participate in the benefits of any measure proposed for remedying the evils attendant upon the tenure of land in Ireland; and should be enabled to rid themselves, on fair terms, of their estates in cases where, from apprehension of impending changes, or for pecuniary reasons, they were desirous of relieving themselves from the responsibilities of ownership. Further, it was felt by the framers of the Bill that a moral obligation rested on the Imperial Government to remove, if possible, "the fearful exasperations attending the agrarian relations in Ireland," rather than leave a question so fraught with danger, and so involved in difficulty, to be determined by the Irish Government on its first entry on official existence. Such were the governing motives for bringing in the Land Bill.

To understand an Irish Land Bill it is necessary to dismiss at once all ideas of the ordinary relations between landlord and tenant in England, and to grasp a true conception of the condition of an Irish tenanted estate. In England the relation between the landlord and tenant of a farm resembles, with a difference in the subject-matter, the relation between the landlord and tenant of a furnished house. In the case of the house, the landlord keeps it in a state fit for habitation, and the tenant pays rent for the privilege of living in another man's house. In the case of the farm, the landlord provides the farm with house, farm-buildings, gates, and other permanent improvements required to fit it for cultivation by the tenant, and the tenant pays rent for the privilege of cultivating the farm, receiving the proceeds of that cultivation. The characters of owner and tenant, however long the connection between them may subsist, are quite distinct. The tenant does no acts of ownership, and never regards the land as belonging to himself, quitting it without hesitation if he can make more money by taking another farm. In Ireland the whole situation is different: instead of a farm of some one hundred or two hundred acres, the tenant has a holding varying, say, from five to fifty acres, for which he pays an annual rent-charge to the landlord. He, or his ancestors have, in the opinion of the tenant, acquired a quasi-ownership in the land by making all the improvements, and he is only removable on non-payment of the fixed rent, or non-fulfilment of certain specified conditions. In short, in Ireland the ownership is dual: the landlord is merely the lord of a quasi-copyhold manor, consisting of numerous small tenements held by quasi-copyholders who, so long as they pay what may be called the manorial rents, and fulfil the manorial conditions, regard themselves as independent owners of their holdings. An Irish Land Bill, then, dealing with tenanted estates, is, in fact, merely a Bill for converting the small holders of tenements held at a fixed rent into fee-simple owners by redemption of the rent due to the landlord and a transfer of the land to the holders. Every scheme, therefore, for settling the Land question in Ireland resolves itself into an inquiry as to the best mode of paying off the rent-charges due to the landlord. The tenant cannot, of course, raise the capital sufficient for paying off the redemption money; some State authority must, therefore, intervene and advance the whole or the greater part of that money, and recoup itself for the advance by the creation in its own favour of an annual charge on the holding sufficient to repay in a certain number of years both the principal and interest due in respect of the advance.

The first problem, then, in an Irish Land Bill, is to settle the conditions of this annuity in such a manner as to satisfy the landlord and tenant; the first, as to the price of his estate; the second, as to the amount of the annuity to be paid by him, at the same time to provide the State authority with adequate security for the repayment of the advance, or, in other words, for the punctual payments of the annuity which is to discharge the advance. Next in importance to the financial question of the adjustment of the annuity comes the administrative difficulty of investigating the title, and thus securing to the tenant the possession of the fee simple, and to the State authority the position of a mortgagee. Under ordinary circumstances the investigation of the title to an estate involves the examination of every document relating thereto for a period of forty years, and the distribution of the purchase-money amongst the head renters, mortgagees, and other encumbrancers, who, in addition to the landlord, are found to be interested in the ownership of almost every Irish estate. Such a process is costly, even in the case of large estates, and involves an expense almost, and, indeed, speaking generally, absolutely prohibitory in the case of small properties. Some mode, then, must be devised for reducing this expense within manageable limits, or any scheme for dealing with Irish land, however well devised from a financial point of view, will sink under the burden imposed by the expense attending the transfer of the land to the new proprietors. Having thus stated the two principal difficulties attending the Land question in Ireland, it may be well before entering on the details of the Sale and Purchase of Land (Ireland) Bill, to mention the efforts which have been made during the last fifteen years to surmount those difficulties. The Acts having this object in view are the Land Acts of 1870, 1872, and 1881, brought in by Mr. Gladstone, and the Land Purchase Act of 1885, brought in by the Conservative Lord Chancellor of Ireland (Lord Ashbourne). The Act of 1870, as amended by the Act of 1872, provided that the State authority might advance two-thirds of the purchase-money. An attempt was made to get over the difficulties of title by providing that the Landed Estates Court or Board of Works shall undertake the investigation of the title and the transfer and distribution of the purchase-money at a fixed price. The Act of 1881 increased the advance to three-quarters, leaving the same machinery to deal with the title. Both under the Acts of 1870 and 1881 the advance was secured by an annuity of 5 per cent., payable for the period of thirty-five years, and based on the loan of the money by the English Exchequer at 3-1/2 per cent. interest. These Acts produced very little effect. The expense of dealing with the titles in the Landed Estates Court proved overwhelming, and neither the Board of Works, under the Act of 1872, nor the Land Commission, under the Act of 1881, found themselves equal to the task of completing inexpensively the transfer of the land; further, the tenants had no means of providing even the quarter of the purchase-money required by the Act of 1881. In 1885 Lord Ashbourne determined to remove all obstacles at the expense of the English Exchequer. By the Land Act of that year he authorized the whole of the purchase-money to be advanced by the State, with a guarantee by the landlord, to be carried into effect by his allowing one-fifth of the purchase-money to remain in the hands of the agents of the State Authority until one-fifth of the purchase-money had been repaid by the annual payments of the tenants. The principal was to be recouped by an annuity of 4 per cent., extending over a period of forty-nine years, instead of an annuity of 5 per cent. extending over a period of thirty-five years. The English Exchequer was to advance the money on the basis of interest at 3-1/8 per cent., instead of at 3-1/2 per cent. Though sufficient time has not yet elapsed to show whether the great bribe offered by the Act of 1885, at the expense of the British taxpayer, will succeed in overcoming the apathy of the tenants, it cannot escape notice that if the Act of 1885 succeeds better than the previous Acts, it will owe that success solely to the greater amount of risk which it imposes on the English Exchequer, and not to any improvement in the scheme in respect of securing greater certainty of sale to the Irish landlord, or of diminishing the danger of loss to the English taxpayer.

Such being the state of legislation, and such the circumstances of the land question in Ireland in the year 1886, the Irish Government Bill afforded Mr. Gladstone the means and the opportunity of bringing in a Land Bill which would secure to the Irish landlord the certainty of selling his land at a fair price, without imposing any practical liability on the English Exchequer, and would, at the same time, diminish the annual sums payable by the tenant; while it also conferred a benefit on the Irish Exchequer. These advantages were, as will be seen, gained, firstly, by the pledge of English credit on good security, instead of advancing money on a mere mortgage on Irish holdings, made directly to the English Government; and, secondly, by the interposition of the Irish Government, as the immediate creditor of the Irish tenant. The scheme of the Land Purchase Bill is as follows:--The landlord of an agricultural estate occupied by tenants may apply to a department of the new Irish Government to purchase his estate. The tenants need not be consulted, as the purchase, if completed, will necessarily better their condition, and thus at the very outset the difficulty of procuring the assent of the tenants, which has hitherto proved so formidable an obstacle to all Irish land schemes, disappears. The landlord may require the department to which he applies (called in the Bill the State Authority) to pay him the statutory price of his estate, not in cash, but in consols valued at par. This price, except in certain unusual cases of great goodness or of great badness of the land, is twenty years' purchase of the net rental. The net rental is the gross rental after deducting from that rent tithe rent-charge, the average percentage for expenses in respect of bad debts, any rates paid by the landlord, and any like outgoings. The gross rental of an estate is the gross rent of all the holdings on the estate, payable in the year ending in November, 1885. Where a judicial rent has been fixed, it is the judicial rent; where no judicial rent has been fixed, it is the rent to be determined in the manner provided by the Bill.

To state this shortly, the Bill provides that an Irish landlord may require the State Authority to pay him for his estate, in consols valued at par, a capital sum equal to twenty times the amount of the annual sum which he has actually put into his pocket out of the proceeds of the estate. The determination of the statutory price is, so far as the landlord is concerned, the cardinal point of the Bill, and in order that no injustice may be done the landlord, an Imperial Commission--called the Land Commission--is appointed by the Bill, whose duty it is to fix the statutory price, and, where there is no judicial rent, to determine the amount of rent which, in the character of gross rental, is to form the basis of the statutory price. The Commission also pay the purchase-money to the landlord, or distribute it amongst the parties entitled, and generally the Commission act as intermediaries between the landlord and the Irish State Authority, which has no power of varying the terms to which the landlord is entitled under the Bill, or of judging of the conditions which affect the statutory price. If the landlord thinks the price fixed by the Land Commission, as the statutory price inequitable, he may reject their offer and keep his estate.

Supposing, however, the landlord to be satisfied with the statutory price offered by the Land Commission, the sale is concluded, and the Land Commission make an order carrying the required sum of consols (which is for convenience hereinafter called the purchase-money, although it consists of stock and not of cash) to the account of the estate in their books after deducting 1 per cent. for the cost of investigation of title and distribution of the purchase-money, and upon the purchase-money being thus credited to the estate, the landlord ceases to have any interest in the estate, and the tenants, by virtue of the order of the Land Commission, become owners in fee simple of their holdings, subject to the payment to the Irish State Authority of an annuity. The amount of the annuity is stated in the Bill. It is a sum equal to ? per cent. on a capital sum equal to twenty times the amount of the gross rental of the holding. The illustration given by Mr. Gladstone in his speech will at once explain these apparently intricate matters of finance. A landlord is entitled to the Hendon estate, producing ?200 a year gross rental; to find the net rental, the Land Commission deduct from this gross rental outgoings estimated at about 20 per cent., or ?40 a year. This makes the net rental ?60 a year, and the price payable to the landlord is ?9,200 (twenty years' purchase of ?60, or ?60 multiplied by 20), which, as above stated, will be paid in consols. The tenants will pay, as the maximum amount for their holdings, ? per cent. for forty-nine years on the capitalized value of twenty years' purchase of the gross rent. This will amount to ?60 instead of ?,200, which they have hitherto paid; a saving of ?40 a year will thus be effected, from which, however, must be deducted the half rates to which they will become liable, formerly paid by the landlord. This ? per cent. charge payable by the tenants will continue for forty-nine years, but at the end of that time each tenant will become a free owner of his estate without any annual payment. Next, as to the position of the State Authority. The State Authority receives ?60 from the tenants; it pays out of that sum ? per cent., not upon the gross rental, but upon the net rental capitalized, that is to say, ?68 to the Imperial Exchequer. The State Authority, therefore, receives,?60, and assuming that the charge of collecting the rental is 2 per cent., that is to say, ?9 4s., the State Authority will, out of ?60, have to disburse only ?87 4s., leaving it a gainer of ?72 16s., or nearly 18 per cent. The result then between the several parties is, the landlord receives ?9,200; the tenantry pay ?40 a year less than they have hitherto paid, and at the end of forty-nine years are exempt altogether from payment; the gain of Irish State Authority is ?72 16s. a year. Another mode of putting the case shortly is as follows: The English Exchequer lends the money to the Irish State Authority at 3-1/8 per cent. and an annuity of 4 per cent. paid during forty-nine years will, as has been stated above, repay both principal and interest for every ?00 lent at 3-1/8 per cent. On the sale of an estate under the Bill, the landlord receives twenty years' purchase; the tenant pays ? per cent. on twenty years' purchase of the gross rental; the Irish State Authority receives ? per cent. on the gross rental; the English Exchequer receives 4 per cent. on the net rental only. The repayment of the interest due by the Irish Authority to the English Exchequer is in no wise dependent on the punctual payment of their annuities by the Irish tenants, nor does the English Government in any way figure as the landlord or creditor of the Irish tenants. The annuities payable by the tenants are due to the Irish Government, and collected by them, while the interest due to the English Government is a charge on the whole of the Irish Government funds; and further, these funds themselves are paid into the hands of the Imperial officer, whose duty it is to liquidate the debt due to his master, the Imperial Exchequer, before a sixpence can be touched by the Irish Government. It is not, then, any exaggeration to say that the Land Purchase Bill of 1886 provides for the settlement of the Irish Land question without any appreciable risk to the English Exchequer, and with the advantage of securing a fair price for the landlord, a diminution of annual payments to the tenant with the ultimate acquisition of the fee simple, also a gain of no inconsiderable sum to the Irish

Exchequer. In order to obviate the difficulties attending the investigation of title and transfer of the property, the Bill provides, as stated above, that on the completion of the agreement for the sale between the landlord and the Commission, the holding shall vest at once in the tenants: it then proceeds to declare that the claims of all persons interested in the land shall attach to the purchase-money in the same manner as though it were land. The duty of ascertaining these claims and distributing the purchase-money is vested in the Land Commission, who undertake the task in exchange for the 1 per cent. which they have, as above stated, deducted from the purchase-money as the cost of conducting the complete transfer of the estate from the landlord to the tenants. The difficulty of the process of dealing with the purchase-money depends, of course, on the intricacy of the title. If the vendor is the sole unencumbered owner, he is put in immediate possession of the stock constituting the price of the estate. If there are encumbrances, as is usually the case, they are paid off by the Land Commission. Capital sums are paid in full; jointures and other life charges are valued according to the usual tables. Drainage and other temporary charges are estimated at their present value, permanent rent-charges are valued by agreement, or in case of disagreement, by the Land Commission; a certain minimum number of years' purchase being assigned by the Bill to any permanent rent-charge which amounts only to one-fifth part of the rental of the estate on which it is charged, this provision being made to prevent injustice being done to the holders of rent-charges which are amply secured.

It remains to notice certain other points of some importance. The landlord entitled to require the State to purchase his property is the immediate landlord, that is to say, the person entitled to the receipt of the rent of the estate; no encumbrancer can avail himself of the privilege, the reason being that the Bill is intended to assist solvent landlords, and not to create a new Encumbered Estates Court. The landlord may sell this privilege, and possibly by means of this power of sale may be able to put pressure on his encumbrancers to reduce their claims in order to obtain immediate payment. The Land Commission, in their character of quasi-arbitrators between the landlord and the Irish State Authority, have ample powers given to enable them to do justice. If the statutory price, as settled according to the Act, is too low, they may raise it to twenty-two years' purchase instead of twenty years' purchase. If it is too high, they may refuse to buy unless the landlord will reduce it to a proper price. In the congested districts scheduled in the Bill the land, on a sale, passes to the

Irish State Authority, as landlords, and not to the tenants; the reason being that it is considered that the tenants would be worsened, rather than bettered, by having their small plots vested in them in fee simple. For the same cause it is provided that in any part of Ireland tenants of holdings under ? a year may object to become the owners of their holdings, which will thereupon vest, on a sale, in the Irish State Authority. Lastly, the opportunity is taken of establishing a registry of title in respect of all property dealt with under the Bill. The result of such a registry would be that any property entered therein would ever thereafter be capable of being transferred with the same facility, and at as little expense, as stock in the public funds.

FOOTNOTES:

[Footnote 14: Any charge in excess of one million was to be borne by Imperial Exchequer.]

THE "UNIONIST" POSITION.

BY CANON MACCOLL

Is it not time that the opponents of Home Rule for Ireland should define their position? They defeated Mr. Gladstone's scheme last year in Parliament and in the constituencies; and they defeated it by the promise of a counter policy which was to consist, in brief, of placing Ireland on the same footing as Great Britain in respect to Local Government; or, if there was to be any difference, it was to be in the direction of a larger and more generous measure for Ireland than for the rest of the United Kingdom. This certainly was the policy propounded by the distinguished leader of the Liberal Unionists in his speech at Belfast, in November, 1885, and repeated in his electoral speeches last year. In the Belfast speech Lord Hartington said: "My opinion is that it is desirable for Irishmen that institutions of local self-government such as are possessed by England and Scotland, and such as we hope to give in the next session in greater extent to England and Scotland, should also be extended to Ireland." But this extension of local self-government to Ireland would require, in Lord Hartington's opinion, a fundamental change in the fabric of Irish Government. "I would not shrink," he says, "from a great and bold reconstruction of the Irish Government," a reconstruction leading up gradually to some real and substantial form of Home Rule. His Lordship's words are: "I submit with some confidence to you these principles, which I have endeavoured to lay down, and upon which, I think, the extension of Local Government in Ireland must proceed. First, you must have some adequate guarantees both for the maintenance of the essential unity of the Empire and for the protection of the minority in Ireland. And, secondly, you must also admit this principle: the work of complete self-government of Ireland, the grant of full control over the management of its own affairs, is not a grant that can be made by any Parliament of this country in a day. It must be the work of continuous and careful effort." Elsewhere in the same speech Lord Hartington says: "Certainly I am of opinion that nothing can be done in the direction of giving Ireland anything like complete control over her own affairs either in a day, or a session, or probably in a Parliament." "Complete control over her own affairs," "the work of complete self-government of Ireland, the grant of full control over the management of its own affairs:" this is the policy which Lord Hartington proclaimed in Ulster, the promise which he, the proximate Liberal leader, held out to Ireland on the eve of the General Election of 1885. It was a policy to be begun "in the next session," though not likely to be completed "in a day, or a session, or probably in a Parliament."

Next to Mr. Gladstone and Lord Hartington the most important member of the Liberal party at that time was undoubtedly Mr. Chamberlain, and Mr. Chamberlain's Irish policy was proclaimed in the Radical Programme, which was published before the General Election as the Radical leader's manifesto to the constituencies. This scheme, which Mr. Chamberlain had submitted as a responsible minister to the Cabinet of Mr. Gladstone in June, 1885, culminated in a National Council which was to control a series of local bodies and govern the whole of Ireland. "His National Council was to consist of two orders; one-third of its members were to be elected by the owners of property, and two-thirds by ratepayers. The National Council also was to be a single one, and Ulster was not to have a separate Council. As the Council was to be charged with the supervision and legislation about education, which is the burning question between Catholics and Protestants, it is clear that Mr. Chamberlain at that time contemplated no special protection for Ulster."[15] Moreover, in a letter dated April 23rd, 1886, and published in the Daily News of May 17th, 1886, Mr. Chamberlain declared that he "had not changed his opinion in the least" since his first public declaration on Irish policy in 1874. "I then said that I was in favour of the principles of Home Rule, as defined by Mr. Butt, but that I would do nothing which would weaken in any way Imperial unity, and that I did not agree with all the details of his plan.... Mr. Butt's proposals were in the nature of a federal scheme, and differ entirely from Mr. Gladstone's, which are on the lines of Colonial independence. Mr. Butt did not propose to give up Irish representation at Westminster." It is true that Mr. Butt did not propose to give up Irish representation at Westminster; but it is also true that he proposed to give it up in the sense in which Mr. Chamberlain wishes to retain it. Mr. Butt's words, in the debate to which Mr. Chamberlain refers, are, "that the House should meet without Irish members for the discussion of English and Scotch business; and when there was any question affecting the Empire at large, Irish members might be summoned to attend. He saw no difficulty in the matter."[16]

There is no need to quote Mr. Gladstone's declarations on the Irish question at the General Election of 1885, and previously. He has been accused of springing a surprise on the country when he proposed Home Rule in the beginning of 1886. That is not, at all events, the opinion of Lord Hartington. In a speech delivered at the Eighty Club in March, 1886, his Lordship, with his usual manly candour, declared as follows: "I am not going to say one word of complaint or charge against Mr. Gladstone for the attitude which he has taken on this question. I think no one who has read or heard, during a long series of years, the declarations of Mr. Gladstone on the question of self-government for Ireland, can be surprised at the tone of his present declarations.... When I look back to those declarations that Mr. Gladstone made in Parliament, which have not been unfrequent; when I look back to the increased definiteness given to those declarations in his address to the electors of Midlothian, and in his Midlothian speeches; I say, when I consider all these things, I feel that I have not, and that no one has, any right to complain of the tone of the declarations which Mr. Gladstone has recently made upon this subject."

So much as to the state of Liberal opinion on the Irish question at the General Election of 1885. The leaders of all sections of the party put the Irish question in the foreground of their programme for the session of 1886. We all remember Sir Charles Dilke's public announcement that he and Mr. Chamberlain were going to visit Ireland in the autumn of 1885, to study the Irish question on the spot, with a view to maturing a plan for the first session of the new Parliament.

What about the Conservative party? Lord Salisbury's Newport speech was avowedly the programme of his Cabinet. It was the Conservative answer to Mr. Gladstone's Midlothian manifesto. He dealt with the Irish question in guarded language; but it was language which plainly showed that he recognized, not less clearly than the Liberal leaders, the crucial change which the assimilation of the Irish franchise to that of Great Britain had wrought in Irish policy. His keen eye saw at once the important bearing which that enfranchisement had on the traditional policy of coercion: "You had passed an Act of Parliament, giving in unexampled abundance, and with unexampled freedom, supreme power to the great mass of the Irish people--supreme power as regards their own locality.... To my mind the renewal of exceptional legislation against a population whom you had treated legislatively to this marked confidence was so gross in its inconsistency that you could not possibly hope, during the few remaining months that were at your disposal before the present Parliament expired, to renew any legislation which expressed on one side a distrust of what on the other side your former legislation had so strongly emphasized. The only result of your doing it would have been, not that you would have passed the Act, but that you would have promoted by the very inconsistency of the position that you were occupying--by the untenable character of the arguments that you were advancing--you would have produced so intense an exasperation amongst the Irish people, that you would have caused ten times more evil, ten times more resistance to law than your Crimes Act, even if it had been renewed, would possibly have been able to check." Lord Salisbury went on to say that "the effect of the Crimes Act had been very much exaggerated," and that "boycotting is of that character which legislation has very great difficulty in reaching." "Boycotting does not operate through outrage. Boycotting is the act of a large majority of a community resolving to do a number of things which are themselves legal, and which are only illegal by the intention with which they are done."

Next to Lord Salisbury the most prominent member of the Conservative party at that date was Lord Randolph Churchill. On the 3rd of January, 1885, when it was rumoured that Mr. Gladstone's Government, then in office, intended to renew a few of the clauses of the Crimes Act, Lord Randolph Churchill made a speech at Bow against any such policy. The following quotation will suffice as a specimen of his opinion: "It comes to this, that the policy of the Government in Ireland is to declare on the one hand, by the passing of the Reform Bill, that the Irish people are perfectly capable of exercising for the advantage of the Empire the highest rights and privileges of citizenship; and by the proposal to renew the Crimes Act they simultaneously declare, on the other hand, that the Irish people are perfectly incapable of performing for the advantage of society the lowest and most ordinary duties of citizenship.... All I can say is that, if such an incoherent, such a ridiculous, such a dangerously ridiculous combination of acts can be called a policy, then, thank God, the Conservative party have no policy."

Within a few months of the delivery of that speech a Conservative Government was in office, with Lord Randolph Churchill as its leader in the House of Commons; and one of the first acts of the new leader was to separate himself ostentatiously from the Irish policy of Lord Spencer and from the policy of coercion in general. Lord Randolph Churchill, as the organ of the Government in the House of Commons, repudiated in scornful language any atom of sympathy with the policy pursued by Lord Spencer in Ireland; and Lord Carnarvon, the new Viceroy, declared that "the era of coercion" was past, and that the Conservative Government intended to govern Ireland by the ordinary law. Lord Carnarvon, in addition, and very much to his credit, sought and obtained an interview with Mr. Parnell, and discussed with him, in sympathetic language, the question of Home Rule. In his own explanation of this interview Lord Carnarvon admitted that he desired to see established in Ireland some form of self-government which would satisfy "the national sentiment."

It is idle, therefore, to assert that the question of Home Rule for Ireland, in some form or other, was sprung on the country as a surprise by Mr. Gladstone in the beginning of 1886. The question was brought prominently before the public in the General Election of 1885 as one that must be faced in the new Parliament. All parties were committed to that policy, and the only difference was as to the character and limits of the measure of self-government to be granted to Ireland; whether it was to be large enough to satisfy "the national sentiment," as Lord Carnarvon, Mr. Chamberlain, Mr. Gladstone, and others desired; or whether it was to consist only of a system of county boards under the control of a reformed Dublin Castle. There was a general agreement that the grant to Ireland of electoral equality with England necessitated equality of political treatment, and that, above all things, there was to be no renewal of the stale policy of Coercion until the Irish people had got an opportunity of proving or disproving their fitness for self-government, unless, indeed, there should happen to be a recrudescence of crime which would render exceptional legislation necessary. The election of 1886 turned almost entirely on the question of Irish government, and it is not too much to say that Conservatives and Liberal Unionists vied with Home Rulers in repudiating a return to the policy of coercion until the effect of some kind of self-government had been tried. Of course, there were the usual platitudes about the necessity of maintaining law and order; but there was a consensus of profession that coercion should not be resorted to unless there was a fresh outbreak of crime and disorder in Ireland.

Such were the professions of the opponents of Home Rule in 1885 and in 1886. They have now been in office for eighteen months, and what do we behold? They have passed a perpetual Coercion Bill for Ireland, and the question of any kind of self-government has been relegated to an uncertain future. In his recent speech at Birmingham (Sept. 29), Mr. Chamberlain has declared that the question is not ripe for solution, and that the question of disestablishment, in Wales, Scotland, and England successively, as well as the questions of Local Option, local government for Great Britain, and of the safety of life at sea, must take precedence of it. That means the postponement of the reform of Irish Government to the Greek Kalends. What justification can be made for this change of front? No valid justification has been offered. So far from there having been any increase of crime in the interval, there has been a very marked decrease. When the Coercion Bill received the royal assent last August, Ireland was more free from crime than it had been for many years past. Nothing had happened to account for the return to the policy of coercion in violation of the promise to try the experiment of conciliation. The National League was in full vigour in 1885-1886, when the policy of coercion was abandoned; boycotting was just as prevalent, and outrages were much more numerous.

Under these circumstances it is the opponents of Home Rule, not its advocates, who owe an explanation to the public. They defeated Mr. Gladstone's Bill, but promised a Bill of their own. Where is their Bill? We hear nothing of it. They have made a complete change of front. They now tell us that the grievance of Ireland is entirely economic, and that the true solution of the Irish question is the abolition of dual ownership in land combined with a firm administration of the existing law. England and Scotland are to have a large measure of local government next year; but Ireland is to wait till a more convenient season. A more complete reversal of the policy proclaimed last summer by the so-called Unionists cannot be imagined.

Still, however, the "Unionists" hope to be able some day to offer some form of self-government to Ireland. For party purposes they are wise in postponing that day to the latest possible period, for its advent will probably dissolve the union of the "Unionists." Lord Salisbury, Lord Hartington, Mr. Bright, and Mr. Chamberlain cannot agree upon any scheme which all can accept without a public recantation of previous professions. Mr. Bright is opposed to Home Rule "in any shape or form." Mr. Chamberlain, on the other hand, is in favour of a great National Council, on Mr. Butt's lines or on the lines of the Canadian plan; either of which would give the National Council control over education and the maintenance of law and order. Latterly, indeed, Mr. Chamberlain has advocated a separate treatment for Ulster. But the first act of an Ulster Provincial Assembly would probably be to declare the union of that Province with the rest of Ireland. Ulster, be it remembered, returns a majority of Nationalists to the Imperial Parliament. To exclude Ulster from any share in the settlement offered to the other three Provinces would therefore be impracticable; and Mr. Bright has lately expressed his opinion emphatically in that sense. In any case, Lord Hartington could be no party to any scheme so advanced as Mr. Chamberlain's. For although he declared, in his Belfast speech, that "complete self-government" was the goal of his policy for Ireland, he was careful to explain that "the extension of Irish management over Irish affairs must be a growth from small beginnings." But this "growth from small beginnings" would be, in Lord Salisbury's opinion, a very dangerous and mischievous policy. The establishment of self-government in Ireland, as distinct from what is commonly known as Home Rule, he pronounced in his Newport speech to be "a very difficult question;" and in the following passage he placed his finger upon the kernel of the difficulty:--"A local authority is more exposed to the temptation, and has more of the facility for enabling a majority to be unjust to the minority, than is the case when the authority derives its sanction and extends its jurisdiction over a wide area. That is one of the weaknesses of local authorities. In a large central authority the wisdom of several parts of the country will correct the folly or the mistakes of one. In a local authority that correction to a much greater extent is wanting; and it would be impossible to leave that out of sight in the extension of any such local authority to Ireland."

This seems to me a much wiser and more statesmanlike view than a system of elective boards scattered broadcast over Ireland. A multitude of local boards all over Ireland, without a recognized central authority to control them, would inevitably become facile instruments in the hands of the emissaries of disorder and sedition. And, even apart from any such sinister influences, they would be almost certain to yield to the temptation of being oppressive, extravagant, and corrupt, if there were no executive power to command their confidence and enforce obedience. Without the previous creation of some authority of that kind it would be sheer madness to offer Ireland the fatal boon of local self-government. It would enormously increase without conciliating the power of the Nationalists, and would make the administration of Ireland by constitutional means simply impossible. The policy of the Liberal Unionists is thus much too large or much too small. It is too small to conciliate, and therefore too large to be given with safety. All these proposed concessions are liable to one insuperable objection; they would each and all enable the Irish to extort Home Rule, but under circumstances which would rob it of its grace and repel gratitude. Mill has some admirable observations bearing on this subject, and I venture to quote the following passage: "The greatest imperfection of popular local institutions, and the chief cause of the failure which so often attends them, is the low calibre of the men by whom they are almost always carried on. That these should be of a very miscellaneous character is, indeed, part of the usefulness of the institution; it is that circumstance chiefly which renders it a school of political capacity and general intelligence. But a school supposes teachers as well as scholars; the utility of the instruction greatly depends on its bringing inferior minds into contact with superior, a contact which in the ordinary course of life is altogether exceptional, and the want of which contributes more than anything else to keep the generality of mankind on one level of contented ignorance.... It is quite hopeless to induce persons of a high class, either socially or intellectually, to take a share of local administration in a corner by piecemeal as members of a Paving Board or a Drainage Commission."[17]

Mr. Mill goes on to argue that it is essential to the safe working of any scheme of local self-government that it should be under the control of a central authority in harmony with public opinion.

When the "Unionists" begin, if they ever do begin, seriously to deliberate on the question of self-government for Ireland, they will find that they have only two practicable alternatives--the maintenance of the present system, or some scheme of Home Rule on the lines of Mr. Gladstone's much misunderstood Bill. And the ablest men among the "Unionists" are beginning to perceive this. The Spectator has in a recent article implored Mr. Chamberlain to desist from any further proposal in favour of self-government for Ireland, because the inevitable result would be to split up the Unionist party; and Mr. Chamberlain, as we have seen, has accepted the advice. Another very able and very logical opponent of Home Rule has candidly avowed that the only alternative to Home Rule is the perpetuation of "things as they are." Ireland, he thinks, "possesses none of the conditions necessary for local self-government." His own view, therefore, is "that in Ireland, as in France, an honest, centralized administration of impartial officials, and not local self-government, would best meet the real wants of the people."

"The name of 'Self-government' has a natural fascination for Englishmen; but a policy which cannot satisfy the wishes of Home Rulers, which may--it is likely enough--be of no benefit to the Irish people, which will certainly weaken the Government in its contest with lawlessness and oppression, is not a policy which obviously commends itself to English good sense."[18]

Well may this distinguished "Supporter of things as they are" declare: "The maintenance of the Union [on such terms] must necessarily turn out as severe a task as ever taxed a nation's energies; for to maintain the Union with any good effect, means that, while refusing to accede to the wishes of millions of Irishmen, we must sedulously do justice to every fair demand from Ireland; must strenuously, and without fear or favour, assert the equal rights of landlords and tenants, of Protestants and Catholics; and must, at the same time, put down every outrage and reform every abuse."

What hope is there of this? Our only guide to the probabilities of the future is our experience of the past And what has that been in Ireland? In every year since the Legislative Union there have been multitudes of men in England as upright, as enlightened, as well-intentioned towards Ireland, as Professor Dicey, and with better opportunities of translating their thoughts into acts. Yet what has been the result? Si monumentum requiris circumspice. Behold Ireland at this moment, and examine every year of its history since the Union. Do the annals of any constitutional Government in the world present so portentous a monument of Parliamentary failure, so vivid an example of a moral and material ruin "paved with good intentions"? Therein lies the pathos of it. Not from malice, not from cruelty, not from wanton injustice, not even from callous indifference to suffering and wrong, does our misgovernment of Ireland come. If the evil had its root in deliberate wrong-doing on the part of England it would probably have been cured long ago. But each generation, while freely confessing the sins of its fathers, has protested its own innocence and boasted of its own achievements, and then, with a pharisaic sense of rectitude, has complacently pointed to some inscrutable flaw in the Irish character as the key to the Irish problem. The generation which passed the Act of Union, oblivious of British pledges solemnly given and lightly broken, wondered what had become of the prosperity and contentment which the promoters of the Union had promised to Ireland. The next generation made vicarious penance, and preferred the enactment of Catholic emancipation to the alternative of civil war; and then wondered in its turn that Ireland still remained unpacified. Then came a terrible famine, followed by evictions on a scale so vast and cruel that the late Sir Robert Peel declared that no parallel could be found for such a tale of inhumanity in "the records of any country, civilized or barbarous." Another generation, pluming itself on its enlightened views and kind intentions, passed the Encumbered Estates Act, which delivered the Irish tenants over to the tender mercies of speculators and money-lenders; and then Parliament for a time closed its eyes and ears, and relied upon force alone to keep Ireland quiet. It rejected every suggestion of reform in the Land laws; and a great Minister, himself an Irish landlord, dismissed the whole subject in the flippant epigram that "tenant-right was landlord-wrong." Since then the Irish Church has been disestablished, and two Land Acts have been passed; yet we seem to be as far as ever from the pacification of Ireland. Surely it is time to inquire whether the evil is not inherent in our system of governing Ireland, and whether there is any other cure than that which De Beaumont suggested, namely, the destruction of the system. It is probable that there is not in all London a more humane or a more kind-hearted man than Lord Salisbury. Yet Lord Salisbury's Government will do some harsh and inequitable things in Ireland this winter, just as Liberal Governments have done during their term of office. The fault is not in the men, but in the system which they have to administer. I see no reason to doubt that Sir M. Hicks-Beach did the best he could under the circumstances; but, unfortunately, bad is the best. In a conversation which I had with Dr. Dilinger while he was in full communion with his Church, I ventured to ask him whether he thought that a new Pope, of Liberal ideas, force of character, and commanding ability, would make any great difference in the Papal system.

"No," he replied, "the Curial system is the growth of centuries, and there can be no change of any consequence while it lasts. Many a Pope has begun with brave projects of reform; but the struggle has been brief, and the end has been invariably the same: the Pope has been forced to succumb. His entourage has been too much for him. He has found himself enclosed in a system which was too strong for him, wheel within wheel; and while the system lasts the most enlightened ideas and the best intentions are in the long run unavailing." This criticism applies, mutatis mutandis, to what may be called the Curial system of Dublin Castle. It is a species of political Ultramontanism, exercising supreme power behind the screen of an official infallibility on which there is practically no check, since Parliament has never hitherto refused to grant it any power which it demanded for enforcing its decrees.

There is, moreover, another consideration which must convince any dispassionate mind which ponders it, that the British Parliament is incompetent to manage Irish affairs, and must become increasingly incompetent year by year. In ordinary circumstances Parliament sits about twenty-seven weeks out of the fifty-two. Five out of the twenty-seven may safely be subtracted for holidays, debates on the Address, and other debates apart from ordinary business. That leaves twenty-two weeks, and out of these two nights a week are at the disposal of the Government and three at the disposal of private members; leaving in all forty-four days for the Government and sixty-six for private members. Into those forty-four nights Government must compress all its yearly programme of legislation for the whole of the British Empire, from the settlement of some petty dispute about land in the Hebrides, to some question of high policy in Egypt, India, or other portions of the Queen's world-wide empire; and all this amidst endless distractions, enforced attendance through dreary debates and vapid talk, and a running fire of cross-examination from any volunteer questioner out of the six hundred odd members who sit outside the Government circle. The consequence is, that Parliament is getting less able every year to overtake the mass of business which comes before it. Each year contributes its quota of inevitable arrears to the accumulated mass of previous Sessions, and the process will go on multiplying in increasing ratio as the complex and multiform needs of modern life increase. The large addition recently made to the electorate of the United Kingdom is already forcing a crop of fresh subjects on the attention of Parliament, as well as presenting old ones from new points of view. Plans of devolution and Grand Committees will fail to cope with this evil. To overcome it we need some organic change in our present Parliamentary system, some form of decentralization, which shall leave the Imperial Parliament supreme over all subordinate bodies, yet relegate to the historic and geographical divisions of the United Kingdom the management severally of their own local affairs.

I should have better hope from governing Ireland (if it were possible) as we govern India, than from the present Unionist method of leaving "things as they are." A Viceroy surrounded by a Council of trained officials, and in semi-independence of Parliament, would have settled the Irish question, land and all, long ago. But imagine India governed on the model of Ireland: the Viceroy and the most important member of his Government changing with every change of Administration at Westminster;[19] his Council and the official class in general consisting almost exclusively of native Mussulmans, deeply prejudiced by religious and traditional enmity against the great mass of the population; himself generally subordinate to his Chief Secretary, and exposed to the daily criticism of an ignorant Parliament and to the determined hostility of eighty-six Hindoos, holding seats in Parliament as the representatives of the vast majority of the people of India, and resenting bitterly the domination of the hereditary oppressors of their race. How long could the Government of India be carried on under such conditions?

Viewing it all round, then, it must be admitted that the problem of governing Ireland while leaving things as they are is a sufficiently formidable one. Read the remarkable admissions which the facts have forced from intelligent opponents of Home Rule like Mr. Dicey, and add to them all the other evils which are rooted in our existing system of Irish government, and then consider what hope there is, under "things as they are," of "sedulously doing justice to every demand from Ireland," "strenuously, and without fear or favour, asserting the equal rights of landlords and tenants, Protestants and Catholics," "putting down every outrage, and reforming every abuse;" and all the "while refusing to accede to the wishes of millions of Irishmen" for a fundamental change in a political arrangement that has for centuries produced all the mischief which the so-called Unionist party are forced to admit, and much more besides, while it has at the same time frustrated every serious endeavour to bring about the better state of things which they expect from--what? From "things as they are!" As well expect grapes from thorns, or figs from thistles. While the tree remains the same, no amount of weeding, or pruning, or manuring, or change of culture, will make it bring forth different fruit. Mr. Dicey, among others, has demolished what Lord Beaconsfield used to call the "bit-by-bit" reformers of Irish Government--those who would administer homoeopathic doses of local self-government, but always under protest that the supply was to stop short of what would satisfy the hunger of the patient. But a continuance of "things as they are," gilded with a thin tissue of benevolent hopes and aspirations, is scarcely a more promising remedy for the ills of Ireland. Is it not time to try some new treatment--one which has been tried in similar cases, and always with success? One only policy has never been tried in Ireland--honest Home Rule.

Certainly, if Home Rule is to be refused till all the prophets of evil are refuted, Ireland must go without Home Rule for ever. "If the sky fall, we shall catch larks." But he would be a foolish bird-catcher who waited for that contingency. And not less foolish is the statesman who sits still till every conceivable objection to his policy has been mathematically refuted in advance, and every wild prediction falsified by the event; for that would ensure his never moving at all. Sedet 鐵 ernumque sedebit. A proper enough attitude, perhaps, on the part of an eristic philosopher speculating on politics in the silent shade of academic groves, but hardly suitable for a practical politician who has to take action on one of the most burning questions of our time. Human affairs are not governed by mathematical reasoning. You cannot demonstrate the precise results of any legislative measure beforehand as you can demonstrate the course of a planet in the solar system. "Probability," as Bishop Butler says, "is the guide of life;" and an older philosopher than Butler has warned us that to demand demonstrative proof in the sphere of contingent matter is the same kind of absurdity as to demand probable reasoning in mathematics. You cannot confute a prophet before the event; you can only disbelieve him. The advocates of Home Rule believe that their policy would in general have an exactly contrary effect to that predicted by their opponents. In truth, every act of legislation is, before experience, amenable to such destructive criticism as these critics urge against Home Rule. I have not a doubt that they could have made out an unanswerable "case" against the Great Charter at Runnymede; and they would find it easy to prove on ?priorigrounds that the British Constitution is one of the most absurd, mischievous, and unworkable instruments that ever issued from human brains or from the evolution of events. By their method of reasoning the Great Charter and other fundamental portions of the Constitution ought to have brought the Government of the

British Empire to a deadlock long ago. Every suspension of the Habeas Corpus Act, every Act of Attainder, every statute for summary trial and conviction before justices of the peace, is a violation of the fundamental article of the Constitution, which requires that no man shall be imprisoned or otherwise punished except after lawful trial by his peers.[20] Consider also the magazines of explosive materials which lie hidden in the constitutional prerogatives of the Crown, if they could only be ignited by the match of an ingenious theorist. The Crown, as Lord Sherbrooke once somewhat irreverently expressed it, "can turn every cobbler in the land into a peer," and could thus put an end, as the Duke of Wellington declared, to "the Constitution of this country."[21] "The Crown is not bound by Act of Parliament unless named therein by special and particular words."[22] The Crown can make peace or war without consulting Parliament, can by secret treaty saddle the nation with the most perilous obligations, and give away all such portions of the empire as do not rest on Statute. The prerogative of mercy, too, would enable an eccentric Sovereign, aided by an obsequious Minister, to open the jails and let all the convicted criminals in the land loose upon society.[22] But criticism which proves too much in effect proves nothing.

In short, every stage in the progress of constitutional reform has, in matter of fact, been marked by similar predictions falsified by results, and the prophets who condemn Home Rule have no better credentials; indeed, much worse, for they proclaim the miserable failure of "things as they are," whereas their predecessors were in their day satisfied with things as they were.[23]

It is, high time, therefore, to call upon the opponents of Home Rule to tell us plainly where they stand. They claim a mandate from the country for their policy. They neither asked nor received a mandate to support the system of Government which prevailed in Ireland at the last election, and still less the policy of coercion which they have substituted for that system. Do they mean to go back or forward? They cannot stand still. They have already discovered that one act of repression leads to another, and they will find ere long that they have no alternative except Home Rule or the suppression of Parliamentary Government in Ireland. Men may talk lightly of the ease with which eighty-six Irish members may be kept in order in Parliament. They forget that the Irish people are behind the Irish members. How is Ireland to be governed on Parliamentary principles if the voice of her representatives is to be forcibly silenced or disregarded? Could even Yorkshire or Lancashire be governed permanently in that way? Let it be observed that we have now reached this pass, namely, that the opponents of Home Rule are opposed to the Irish members, not on any particular form of self-government for Ireland, but on any form; in other words, they resist the all but unanimous demand of Ireland for what "Unionists" of all parties declared a year ago to be a reasonable demand. No candidate at the last election ventured to ask the suffrages of any constituency as "a supporter of things as they are." Yet that is practically the attitude now assumed by the Ministerial party, both Conservatives and Liberal Unionists. It is an attitude of which the country is getting weary, as the bye-elections have shown. But the "Unionists," it must be admitted, are in a sore dilemma. Their strength, such as it is, lies in doing nothing for the reform of Irish Government. Their bond of union consists of nothing else but opposition to Mr. Gladstone's policy. They dare not attempt to formulate any policy of their own, knowing well that they would go to pieces in the process. Their hope and speculation is that something may happen to remove Mr. Gladstone from the political arena before the next dissolution. But, after all, Mr. Gladstone did not create the Irish difficulty. It preceded him and will survive him, unless it is settled to the satisfaction of the Irish people before his departure. And the difficulty of the final settlement will increase with every year of delay. Nor will the difficulty be confined to Ireland. The Irish question is already reacting upon kindred, though not identical, problems in England and Scotland, and the longer it is kept open, so much the worse will it be for what are generally regarded as Conservative interests. It is not the Moderate Liberals or Conservatives who are gaining ground by the prolongation of the controversy, and the disappearance of Mr. Gladstone from the scene would have the effect of removing from the forces of extreme Radicalism a conservative influence, which his political opponents will discover when it is too late to restore it. Their regret will then be as unavailing as the lament of William of Deloraine over his fallen foe--

"I'd give the lands of Deloraine Dark Musgrave were alive again."

The Irish landlords have already begun to realize the mistake they made when they rejected Mr. Gladstone's policy of Home Rule and Land Purchase. It is the old story of the Sibyl's books. No British Government will ever again offer such terms to the Irish landlords as they refused to accept from Mr. Gladstone. On the other hand, Home Rule is inevitable. Can any reflective person really suppose that the democracy of Great Britain will consent to refuse to share with the Irish people the boon of self-government which will be offered to themselves next year? Any attempt to exclude the Irish from the benefits of such a scheme, after all the promises of the last general election, would almost certainly wreck the government; for constituencies have ways and means of impressing their wills on their representatives in Parliament even without a dissolution. If, on the other hand, Ireland should be included in a general scheme of local Government, the question of who shall control the police will arise. In Great Britain the police, of course, will be under local control. To refuse this to Ireland would be to offer a boon with a stigma attached to it. The Irish members agreed to let the control of the constabulary remain, under Mr. Gladstone's scheme, for some years in the hands of the British Government; but they would not agree to this while Dublin Castle ruled the country. Moreover, the formidable difficulty suggested by Lord Salisbury and Mr. John Stuart Mill (see pp. 115, 116) would appear the moment men began seriously to consider the question of local government for Ireland. The government of Dublin Castle would have to go, but something would have to be put in its place; and when that point has been reached it will probably be seen that nothing much better or safer can be found than some plan on the main lines of Mr. Gladstone's Bill.

FOOTNOTES:

[Footnote 15: Speech at Manchester, May 7, 1886, by Mr. Shaw-Lefevre, who was a member of the Cabinet to which Mr. Chamberlain's scheme was submitted.]

[Footnote 16: Hansard, vol. 220, pp. 708, 715.]

[Footnote 17: Considerations on Representative Government, p. 281.]

[Footnote 18: Dicey's England's Case against Home Rule, pp. 25-31, and Letter in Spectator of September 17th, 1887.]

[Footnote 19: From the beginning of 1880 till now there have been six Viceroys and ten Chief Secretaries in Dublin--namely, Duke of Marlborough, Earls Cowper and Spencer, Earls of Carnarvon and Aberdeen, and the Marquis of Londonderry; Mr. Lowther, Mr. Forster, Lord F. Cavendish, Mr. Trevelyan, Mr. Campbell Bannerman, Sir W. Hart Dyke, Mr. W.H. Smith, Mr. J. Morley,

Sir M. Hicks-Beach, and Mr. A. Balfour. A fine example, truly, of stable government and continuous policy!]

[Footnote 20: Creasy's Imperial and Colonial Constitutions of the Britannic Empire, p. 155.]

[Footnote 21: May's Const. Hist., i. 313.]

[Footnote 22: Blackstone's Commentaries, by Stephen, ii. 491, 492, 497, 507.]

[Footnote 23: We need not go far afield for illustrations. A few samples will suffice. "It was natural," says Mill (Rep. Gov., p. 311), "to feel strong doubts before trial had been made how such a provision [as the Supreme Court of the United States] would work; whether the tribunal would have the courage to exercise its constitutional power; if it did, whether it would exercise it wisely, and whether the Government would consent peaceably to its decision. The discussions on the American Constitution, before its final adoption, give evidence that these natural apprehensions were strongly felt; but they are now entirely quieted, since, during the two generations and more which have subsequently elapsed, nothing has occurred to verify them, though there have at times been disputes of considerable acrimony, and which became the badges of parties respecting the limits of the authority of the Federal and State Governments." The Austrian opponents of Home Rule in Hungary predicted that it would lead straight to separation. The opponents of the Canadian Constitution prophesied that Canada would in a few years be annexed to the United States; and Home Rule in Australia was believed by able statesmen to involve independence at an early date. Mr. Dicey himself tells us "that the wisest thinkers of the eighteenth century (including Burke) held that the independence of the American Colonies meant the irreparable ruin of Great Britain. There were apparently solid reasons for this belief: experience has proved it to be without foundation." The various changes in our own Constitution, and even in our Criminal Code, were believed by "men of light and leading" at the time to portend national ruin. All the judges in the land, all the bankers, and the professions generally, petitioned against alteration in the law which sent children of ten to the gallows for the theft of a pocket-handkerchief. The great Lord Ellenborough declared in the House of Lords that "the learned judges were unanimously agreed" that any mitigation in that law would imperil "the public security." "My Lords," he exclaimed, "if we suffer this Bill to pass we shall not know where we stand; we shall not know whether we are on our heads or on our feet." Mr. Perceval, when leader of the House of Commons in 1807, declared that "he could not conceive a time or change of circumstances which would render further concessions to the Catholics consistent with the safety of the State." (Croker Papers, i. 12.) Croker was a very astute man; but here is his forecast of the Reform Act of 1832: "No kings, no lords, no inequalities in the social system; all will be levelled to the plane of the petty shopkeepers and small farmers: this, perhaps, not without bloodshed, but certainly by confiscations and persecutions." "There can be no longer any doubt that the Reform Bill is a stepping-stone in England to a Republic, and in Ireland to separation." Croker met the Queen in 1832, considered her very good-looking, but thought it not unlikely that "she may live to be plain Miss Guelph." Even Sir Robert Peel wrote: "If I am to be believed, I foresee revolution as the consequence of this Bill;" and he "felt that it had ceased to be an object of ambition to any man of equable and consistent mind to enter into the service of the Crown." And as late as 1839, so robust a character as Sir James Graham thought the world was coming to an end because the young Queen gave her confidence to a Whig Minister. "I begin to share all your apprehensions and forebodings," he writes to Croker, "with regard to the probable issue of the present struggle. The Crown in alliance with Democracy baffles every calculation on the balance of power in our mixed form of Government. Aristocracy and Church cannot contend against Queen and people mixed; they must yield in the first instance, when the Crown, unprotected, will meet its fate, and the accustomed round of anarchy and despotism will run its course." And he prays that he may "lie cold before that dreadful day." (Ibid., ii. 113, 140, 176, 181, 356.) Free Trade created a similar panic. "Good God!" Croker exclaimed, "what a chaos of anarchy and misery do I foresee in every direction, from so comparatively small a beginning as changing an average duty of 8s. into a fixed duty of 8s., the fact being that the fixed duty means no duty at all; and no duty at all will be the overthrow of the existing social and political system of our country!" (Ibid., iii. 13.) And what have become of Mr. Lowe's gloomy vaticinations as to the terrible consequences of the very moderate Reform Bill of 1866, followed as it was by a much more democratic measure?]

A LAWYER'S OBJECTIONS TO HOME RULE.

BY E.L. GODKIN.

Mr. Dicey in his Case against Home Rule does me the honour to refer to an article which I wrote a year ago on "American Home Rule,"[24] expressing in one place "disagreement in the general conclusion to which the article is intended to lead," and in another "inability to follow the inference" which he supposes me to draw "against all attempts to enforce an unpopular law." Now the object of that article, I may be permitted to explain, was twofold. I desired, in the first place, to combat the notion which, it seemed to me, if I might judge from a great many of the speeches and articles on the Irish question, was widely diffused even among thoughtful Englishmen that the manner in which the Irish have expressed their discontent--that is, through outrage and disorder--was indicative of incapacity for self-government, and even imposed upon the Englishmen the duty, in the interest of morality (I think it was the Spectator who took this view), and as a disciplinary measure, of refusing to such a people the privilege of managing their own affairs. I tried to show by several noted examples occurring in this country that prolonged displays of lawlessness, and violence, and even cruelty, such as the anti-rent movement in the State of New York, the Ku-Klux outrages in the South, and the persecution of Miss Prudence Crandall in Connecticut, were not inconsistent with the possession of marked political capacity. I suggested that it was hardly adult politics to take such things into consideration in passing on the expediency of conceding local self-government to a subject community. There was to me something almost childish in the arguments drawn from Irish lawlessness in the discussion of Home Rule, and in the moral importance attached by some Englishmen to the refusal to such wicked men as the Irish of the things they most desire. It is only in kindergartens, I said, that rulers are able to do equal and exact justice, and see that the naughty are brought to grief and the good made comfortable. Statesmen occupy themselves with the more serious business of curing discontent. They concern themselves but little, if at all, with the question whether it might not be manifested by less objectionable methods.

The Irish methods of manifesting it, I endeavoured to show, were not exceptional, and did not prove either inability to make laws or unwillingness to obey them. I illustrated this by examples drawn from the United States. I might, had I had more time and space, have made these examples still more numerous and striking. I might have given very good reasons for believing that, were Ireland a state in the American Union, there probably would not have been any rent paid in the island within the last fifty years, and that the armed resistance of the tenants would have had the open or secret sympathy of the great bulk of the American people. In truth, the importance of Irish crime as a political symptom is grossly exaggerated by English writers. I venture to assert that more murders unconnected with robbery are committed in the State of Kentucky in one year than in Ireland in ten, and the condition of some other Southern and Western States is nearly as bad. All good Americans lament this and are ashamed of it, but it never enters into the heads of even the most lugubrious American moralists that Kentucky or any other State should be disfranchised and remanded to the condition of a Territory, because the offences against the person committed in it are so numerous, and the punishment of them, owing to popular sympathy or apathy, so difficult.

There are a great many Englishmen who think that when they show that Grattan's Parliament was a venal and somewhat disorderly body, which occasionally indulged in mixed metaphor, they have proved the impossibility of giving Ireland a Parliament now. But then, as they are obliged to admit, Walpole's Parliament was very corrupt, and no one would say that for that reason it would have been wise to suspend constitutional government in England in the eighteenth century. It is only through the pernicious habit of thinking of Irishmen as exceptions to all political rules that Grattan's Parliament is considered likely, had it lasted, to have come down to our time unreformed and unimproved.

Those have misunderstood me who suppose that I draw from the success of the anti-rent movement in this State between 1839 and 1846 an inference against "all attempts to enforce an unpopular law." Such was not by any means my object. What I sought to show by the history of this movement was that there was nothing peculiar or inexplicable in the hostility to rent-paying in Ireland. The rights of the New York landlords were as good in law and morals as the rights of the Irish landlords, and their mode of asserting them far superior. Moreover, those who resisted them were not men of a different race, religion, or nationality, and had, as Mr. Dicey says, "none of the excuses that can be urged in extenuation of half-starved tenants." Their mode of setting the law at defiance was exactly similar to that adopted by the Irish, and it was persisted in for a period of ten years, or until they had secured a substantial victory. The history of the anti-rent agitation in New York also illustrates strikingly, as it seems to me, the perspicacity of a remark made, in substance, long ago by Mr. Disraeli, which, in my eyes at least, threw a great deal of light on the Irish problem, namely, that Ireland was suffering from suppressed revolution. As Mr. Dicey says, "The crises called revolutions are the ultimate and desperate cures for the fundamental disorganization of society. The issue of a revolutionary struggle shows what is the true sovereign power in the revolutionized state. So strong is the interest of mankind, at least in any European country, in favour of some sort of settled rule, that civil disturbance will, if left to itself, in general end in the supremacy of some power which by securing the safety at last gains the attachment of the people. The Reign of Terror begets the Empire; even wars of religion at last produce peace, albeit peace may be nothing better than the iron uniformity of despotism. Could Ireland have been left for any lengthened period to herself, some form of rule adapted to the needs of the country would in all probability have been established. Whether Protestants or Catholics would have been the predominant element in the State; whether the landlords would have held their own, or whether the English system of tenure would long ago have made way for one more in conformity with native traditions; whether hostile classes and races would at last have established some modus vivendi favourable to individual freedom, or whether despotism under some of its various forms would have been sanctioned by the acquiescence of its subjects, are matters of uncertain speculation. A conclusion which, though speculative, is far less uncertain, is that Ireland, if left absolutely to herself, would have arrived, like every other country, at some lasting settlement of her difficulties" (p. 87). That is to say, that in Ireland as in New York the attempt to enforce unpopular land laws would have been abandoned, had local self-government existed. For "revolution" is, after all, only a fine name for the failure or refusal of the rulers of a country to persist in executing laws which the bulk of the population find obnoxious. When the popular hostility to the law is strong enough to make its execution impossible, as it was in New York in the rent affair, it is accepted as the respectable solution of a very troublesome problem. When, as in Ireland, it is strong enough to produce turbulence and disorder, but not strong enough to tire out and overcome the authorities, it simply ruins the political manners of the people. If the Irish landlords had had from the beginning to face the tenants single-handed and either hold them down by superior physical force, or come to terms with them as the New York landlords had to do, conditions of peace and good will would have assuredly been discovered long ago. The land question, in other words, would have been adjusted in accordance with "Irish ideas," that is, in some way satisfactory to the tenants. The very memory of the conflict would probably by this time have died out, and the two classes would be living in harmony on the common soil. If in New York, on the other hand, the Van Rensselaers and Livingstons had been able to secure the aid of martial law and of the Federal troops in asserting their claims, and in preventing local opinion having any influence whatever on the settlement of the dispute, there can be no doubt that a large portion of this State would to-day be as poor and as savage, and apparently as little fitted for the serious business of government, as the greater part of Ireland is.

There is, in truth, no reason to doubt that the idea of property in land, thoroughly accepted though it be in the United States, is nevertheless held under the same limitations as in the rest of the world. No matter what the law may say in any country, in no country is the right of the landed proprietor in his acres as absolute as his right in his movables. A man may own as much land as he can purchase, and may assert his ownership in its most absolute form against one, two, or three occupants, but the minute he began to assert it against a large number of occupants, that is, to act as if his rights were such that he had only to buy a whole state or a whole island in order to be able to evict the entire population, he would find in America, as he finds in Ireland, that he cannot have the same title to land as to personal property. He would, for instance, if he tried to oust the people of a whole district or of a village from their homes on any plea of possession, or of a contract, find that he was going too far, and that no matter what the judges might say, or the sheriff might try to do for him, his legal position was worth very little to him. Consequently a large landlord in America, if he were lucky enough to get tenants at all, would be very chary indeed about quarrelling with more than one of them at a time. The tenants would no more submit to wholesale ejectment than the farmers in Missouri would submit some years ago to a tax levy on their property to pay county bonds given in aid of a railroad. The goods of some of them were seized, but a large body of them attended the sale armed with rifles, having previously issued a notice that the place would be very "unhealthy" for outside bidders.

The bearing of this condition of American opinion on the Irish question will be plainer if I remind English readers that the Irish in the United States numbered in 1880 nearly 2,000,000, and that the number of persons of Irish parentage is probably between 4,000,000 and 5,000,000. In short there are, as well as one can judge, more Irish nationalists in the United States than in Ireland. The Irish-Americans are to-day the only large and prosperous Irish community in the world. The children of the Irish born in the United States or brought there in their infancy are just as Irish in their politics as those who have grown up at home. Patrick Ford, for instance, the editor of the Irish World, who is such a shape of dread to some Englishmen, came to America in childhood, and has no personal knowledge nor recollection of Irish wrongs. Of the part this large Irish community plays in stimulating agitation--both agrarian and political--at home I need not speak; Englishmen are very familiar with it, and are very indignant over it. The Irish-Americans not only send over a great deal of American money to their friends at home, but they send over American ideas, and foremost among them American hostility to large landowners, and American belief in Home Rule. Now, to me, one of the most curious things in the English state of mind about the Irish problem is the apparent expectation that this Irish-American interference is transient, and will probably soon die out. It is quite true, as Englishmen are constantly told, that "the best Americans," that is, the literary people and the commercial magnates, whom travelling Englishmen see on the Atlantic coast, dislike the Irish anti-English agitation. But it is also true that the disapproval of the "best Americans" is not of the smallest practical consequence, particularly as it is largely due to complete indifference to, and ignorance of, the whole subject. There are probably not a dozen of them who would venture to express their disapproval publicly. The mass of the population, particularly in the West, sympathize, though half laughingly, with the efforts of the transplanted Irish to "twist the British lion's tail," and all the politicians either sympathize with them, or pretend to do so. I am not now expressing any opinion as to whether this state of things is good or bad. What I wish to point out is that this Irish-American influence on Irish affairs is very powerful, and may, for all practical purposes, be considered permanent, and must be taken into account as a constant element in the Irish problem. I will indeed venture on the assertion that it is the appearance of the Irish-Americans on the scene which has given the Irish question its present seriousness. The attempts of the Irish at physical resistance to English authority have been steadily diminishing in gravity during the present century--witness the descent from the rebellion of 1798 to Smith O'Brien's rebellion and the Fenian rising of 1867. On the other hand the power of the Irish to act as a disturbing agency in English politics has greatly increased, and the reason is that the stream of Irish discontent is fed by thousands of rills from the United States. Every emigrant's letter, every Irish-American newspaper, every returned emigrant with money in his pocket and a good coat on his back, helps to swell it, and there is not the slightest sign, that

I can see, of its drying up.

Where Mr. Dicey is most formidable to the Home Rulers, as it seems to me, is in his chapter on "Home Rule as Federalism," which is the form in which the Irish ask for it. He attacks this in two ways. One is by maintaining that the necessary conditions for a federal union between Great Britain and Ireland do not exist. This disposes at one blow of all the experience derived from the working of the foreign federations, on which the advocates of Home Rule have relied a good deal. The other is what I may call predictions that the federation even if set up would not work. Either the state of facts on which all other federations have been built does not exist in Ireland, or if it now exists, will not, owing to the peculiarities of Irish character, continue to exist. In other words, the federation will either fail at the outset, or fail in the long run. No one can admire more than I do the force and ingenuity and wealth of illustration with which Mr. Dicey supports this thesis. But unfortunately the arguments by which he assails Irish federalism might be, or might have been, used against all federations whatever. They might have been used, as I shall try to show, against the most successful of them all, the Government of the United States. I was reminded, while reading Mr. Dicey's account of the impossibility of an Anglo-Irish federation, of Mr. Madison's rehearsal in the Federalist(No. 38) of the objections made to the Federal Constitution after the Convention had submitted it to the States. These objections covered every feature in it but one; and that, the mode of electing the President, curiously enough, is the only one which can be said to have utterly failed. A more impressive example of the danger of ?prioriattacks on any political arrangement, history does not contain. Mr. Madison says: "This one tells me that the proposed Constitution ought to be rejected, because it is not a confederation of the states, but a government over individuals. Another admits that it ought to be a government over individuals to a certain extent, but by no means to the extent proposed. A third does not object to the government over individuals, or to the extent proposed, but to the want of a bill of rights. A fourth concurs in the absolute necessity of a bill of rights, but contends that it ought to be declaratory not of the personal rights of individuals, but of the rights reserved to the states in their political capacity. A fifth is of opinion that a bill of rights of any sort would be superfluous and misplaced, and that the plan would be unexceptionable but for the fatal power of regulating the times and places of election. An objector in a large state exclaims loudly against the unreasonable equality of representation in the Senate. An objector in a small state is equally loud against the dangerous inequality in the House of Representatives. From one quarter we are alarmed with the amazing expense, from the number of persons who are to administer the new government. From another quarter, and sometimes from the same quarter, on another occasion the cry is that the Congress will be but the shadow of a representation, and that the government would be far less objectionable if the number and the expense were doubled. A patriot in a state that does not import or export discerns insuperable objections against the power of direct taxation. The patriotic adversary in a state of great exports and imports is not less dissatisfied that the whole burden of taxes may be thrown on consumption. This politician discovers in the constitution a direct and irresistible tendency to monarchy. That is equally sure it will end in aristocracy. Another is puzzled to say which of these shapes it will ultimately assume, but sees clearly it must be one or other of them. Whilst a fourth is not wanting, who with no less confidence affirms that the Constitution is so far from having a bias towards either of these dangers, that the weight on that side will not be sufficient to keep it upright and firm against the opposite propensities. With another class of adversaries to the Constitution, the language is, that the legislative, executive, and judiciary departments are intermixed in such a manner as to contradict all the ideas of regular government and all the requisite precautions in favour of liberty. Whilst this objection circulates in vague and general expressions, there are not a few who lend their sanction to it. Let each one come forward with his particular explanation, and scarcely any two are exactly agreed on the subject. In the eyes of one the junction of the Senate with the President in the responsible function of appointing to offices, instead of vesting this power in the executive alone, is the vicious part of the organization. To another the exclusion of the House of Representatives, whose numbers alone could be a due security against corruption and partiality in the exercise of such a power, is equally obnoxious. With a third the admission of the President into any share of a power which must ever be a dangerous engine in the hands of the executive magistrate is an unpardonable violation of the maxims of republican jealousy. No part of the arrangement, according to some, is more inadmissible than the trial of impeachments by the Senate, which is alternately a member both of the legislative and executive departments, when this power so evidently belonged to the judiciary department. We concur fully, reply others, in the objection to this part of the plan, but we can never agree that a reference of impeachments to the judiciary authority would be an amendment of the error; our principal dislike to the organization arises from the extensive powers already lodged in that department. Even among the zealous patrons of a council of state, the most irreconcilable variance is discovered concerning the mode in which it ought to be constituted."

Mr. Madison's challenge to the opponents of the American Constitution to agree on some plan of their own, and his humorous suggestion that if the American people had to wait for some such agreement to be reached they would go for a long time without a government, are curiously applicable to the opponents of Irish Home Rule. They are very fertile in reasons for thinking that neither the Gladstone plan nor any other plan can succeed, but no two of them, so far as I know, have yet hit upon any other mode of pacifying Ireland, except the use of force for a certain period to maintain order, and oddly enough, even when they agree on this remedy, they are apt to disagree about the length of time during which it should be tried.

Mr. Dicey, in conceding the success of the American Constitution, seems to me unmindful, if I may use the expression, of the judgments he would probably have passed on it had it been submitted to him at the outset were he in the frame of mind to which a prolonged study of the Irish problem has now brought him. The Supreme Court, for instance, which he now recognizes as an essential feature of the Federal Constitution, and the absence of which in the Gladstonian arrangement he treats as a fatal defect, would have undoubtedly appeared to him a preposterous contrivance. It would have seemed to him impossible that a legislature like Congress, with the traditions of parliamentary omnipotence still strong in the minds of the members, would ever submit to have its acts nullified by a board composed of half a dozen elderly lawyers. Nor would he have treated as any more reasonable the expectation that the State tribunals, which had existed in each colony from its foundation, and had earned the respect and confidence of the people, would quietly submit to have their jurisdiction curtailed, their decisions overruled, causes torn from their calendar, and prisoners taken out of their custody by new courts of semi-foreign origin, which the State neither paid nor controlled. He would, too, very probably have been most incredulous about the prospect of the growth of loyalty on the part of New-Yorkers and Massachusetts men to a new-fangled government, which was to make itself only slightly felt in their daily lives, and was to sit a fortnight away in an improvised village in the midst of a Virginian forest.

He would, too, have ridiculed the notion that State legislatures would refrain, in obedience to the Constitution, from passing any law which local sentiment strongly favoured or local convenience plainly demanded, such as a law impairing the obligation of obnoxious contracts, or levying duties on imports or exports. The possibility that the State militia could ever be got to obey federal officers, or form an efficient part of a federal army, he would have scouted. On the feebleness of the front which federation would present to a foreign enemy he would have dwelt with emphasis, and would have pointed with confidence to the probability that in the event of a war some of the states would make terms with him or secretly favour his designs. National allegiance and local allegiance would divide and perplex the feelings of loyal citizens. Unless the national sentiment predominated--and it could not predominate without having had time to grow--the federation would go to pieces at any of those crises when the interests or wishes of any of the states conflicted with the interests or wishes of the Union. That the national sentiment could grow at all rapidly, considering the maturity of the communities which composed the Union and the differences of origin, creed, and manners which separated them, no calm observer of human nature would believe for one moment.

The American Constitution is flecked throughout with those flaws which a lawyer delights to discover and point out, and which the framers of a federal contract can only excuse by maintaining that they are inevitable. It is true that Mr. Dicey does not even now acknowledge the success of the American Constitution to be complete. He points out that if the "example either of America or of Switzerland is to teach us anything worth knowing, the history of these countries must be read as a whole. It will then be seen that the two most successful confederacies in the world have been kept together only by the decisive triumph through force of arms of the central power over real or alleged State rights" (p. 192).

It is odd that such objectors do not see that the decisive triumph of the central power in the late civil war in America was, in reality, a striking proof of the success of the federation. The armies which General Grant commanded, and the enormous resources in money and devotion from which he was able to draw, were the product of the Federal Union and of nothing else. One of the greatest arguments its founders used in its favour was that if once established it would supply overwhelming force for the suppression of any attempt to break it up. They did not aim at setting up a government which neither foreign malice nor domestic treason, would ever assail, for they knew that this was something beyond the reach of human endeavour. They tried to set up one which, if attacked either from within or from without, would make a successful resistance, and we now know that they accomplished their object. Somewhat the same answer may be made to the objection, which is supposed to have fatal applicability to the case of Ireland, that among the "special faults of federalism" is that it does not provide "sufficient protection of the legal rights of unpopular minorities," and that "the moral of it all is that the [American] Federal Government is not able to protect the rights of individuals against strong local sentiment" (p. 194 of Mr. Dicey's book). He says, moreover, if I understand the argument rightly, that it was bound to protect free speech in the States because "there is not and never was a word in the Articles of the Constitution forbidding American citizens to criticize the institutions of the State." It would seem from this as if Mr. Dicey were under the impression that in America the citizen of a State has a right to do in his State whatever he is not forbidden to do by the Federal Constitution, and in doing it has a right to federal protection. But the Federal Government can only do what the Constitution expressly authorizes it to do, and the Constitution does not authorize it to protect a citizen in criticizing the institutions of his own State. This arrangement, too, is just as good federalism as the committal of free speech to federal guardianship would have been. The goodness or badness of the federal system is in no way involved in the matter.

The question to what extent a minority shall rely on the federation for protection, and to what extent on its own State, is a matter settled by the contract which has created the federation. The settlement of this is, in fact, the great object of a Constitution. Until it is settled somehow, either by writing or by understanding, there is, and can be, no federation. If I, as a citizen of the State of New York, could call on the United States Government to protect me under all circumstances and against all wrongs, it would show that I was not living under a federation at all, but under a centralized republic. The reason why I have to rely on the United States for protection against some things and not against others is that it was so stipulated when the State of New York entered the Union. There is nothing in the nature of the federal system to prevent the United States Government from protecting my freedom of speech. Nor is there anything in the federal system which forbids its protecting me against the establishment of a State Church, which, as a matter of fact, it does not do. Nor is there anything in the federal system compelling the Government to protect me against the establishment of an order of nobility, which, as a matter of fact, it does do. The reason why it does not do one of these things and does the other is simply and solely that it was so stipulated, after much discussion, in the contract. Most thinking men are to-day of opinion that the United States ought to have exclusive jurisdiction of marriage, so that the law of marriage might be uniform in all parts of the Union. The reason why they do not possess such jurisdiction is not that Congress is not fully competent to pass such a law or the federal courts to execute it, but that no such jurisdiction is conferred by the Constitution. In fact it seems to me just as reasonable to cite the ease of divorce in various States of the Union as a defect in the federal system, as to cite the oppression of local minorities in matters not placed under federal authority by the organic law.

If one may judge from a great deal of writing on American matters which one sees in English journals and the demands for federal interference in America in State affairs which they constantly make, the greatest difficulty Irish Home Rule has to contend with is the difficulty which men bred in a united monarchy and under an omnipotent Parliament experience in grasping what I may call the federal idea. The influence of association on their minds is so strong that they can hardly conceive of a central power, worthy of the name of a government, standing by and witnessing disorders or failures of justice in any place within its borders, without stepping in to set matters right, no matter what the Constitution may say. They remind me often of an old verger in Westminster Abbey during the American civil war who told me that "he always knew a government without a head couldn't last." Permanence and peace were in his mind inseparably linked with kingship. That even Mr. Dicey has not been able to escape this influence appears frequently in his discussions of federalism. He, of course, thoroughly understands the federal system as a jurist, but when he comes to discuss it as a politician he has evidently some difficulty in seeing how a government with a power to enforce any commands can be restrained by contract from enforcing all commands which may seem to be expedient or salutary. Consequently the cool way in which the Federal Government here looks on at local disorders seems to him a sign, not of the fidelity of the President and Congress to the federal pact, but of some inherent weakness in the federal system.

The true way to judge the federal system, however, either in the United States or elsewhere, is by observing the manner in which it has performed the duties assigned to it by the Constitution. If the Government at Washington performs these faithfully, its failure to prevent lawlessness in New York or the oppression of minorities in Connecticut is of no more consequence than its failure to put down brigandage in Macedonia. Possibly it would have been better to saddle it with greater responsibility for local peace; but the fact is that the framers of the Constitution decided not to do so. They did not mean to set up a government which would see that every man living under it got his due. They could not have got the States to accept such a government. They meant to set up a government which should represent the nation worthily in all its relations with foreigners, which should carry on war effectively, protect life and property on the high seas, furnish a proper currency, put down all resistance to its lawful authority, and secure each State against domestic violence on the demand of its Legislature.

There is no common form for federal contracts, and no rules describing what such a contract must contain in order that the Government may be federal and not unitarian. There is no hard and fast line which must, under the federal system, divide the jurisdiction of the central Government from the jurisdiction of each State Government. The way in which the power is divided between the two must necessarily depend on the traditions, manners, aims, and needs of the people of the various localities. The federal system is not a system manufactured on a regulation model, which can be sent over the world like iron huts or steam launches, in detached pieces, to be put together when the scene of operation is reached. Therefore I am unable to see the force of the argument that, as the conditions under which all existing federations were established differ in some respects from those under which the proposed federal union between England and Ireland would have to be established, therefore the success of these confederations, such as it is, gives them no value as precedents. A system which might have worked very well for the New England States would not have worked well for a combination which included also the middle and southern States. And the framers of the American Constitution were not so simple-minded as to inquire, either before beginning their labours or before ending them--as Mr. Dicey would apparently have the English and Irish do--whether this or that style of constitution was "the correct thing" in federalism. Assuming that the people desired to form a nation as regarded the world outside, they addressed themselves to the task of discovering how much power the various States were willing to surrender for this purpose. That was ascertained, as far as it could be ascertained, by assembling their delegates in convention, and discussing the wishes and fears and suggestions of the different localities in a friendly and conciliatory spirit. They had no precedents to guide them. There had not existed a federal government, either in ancient or modern times, whose working afforded an example by which the imagination or the understanding of the American people was likely to be affected in the smallest degree. They, therefore, had to strike out an entirely new path for themselves, and they ended by producing an absolutely new kind of federation, which was half Unitarian, that is, in some respects a union of states, and in others a centralized government; and it was provided for a Territory one end of which was more than a month's distance from the other.

It is not in its details, therefore, but in the manner of its construction, that the American Constitution furnishes anything in the way of guidance or suggestion to those who are now engaged in trying to find a modus vivendi between England and Ireland. The same thing may be said of the Swiss Constitution and of the Austro-Hungarian Constitution. Both of them contain many anomalies--that is, things that are not set down in the books as among the essentials of federalism. But both are adapted to the special wants of the people who live under them, and were framed in reference to those wants.

The Austro-Hungarian Delegations are another exception to the rule. These Delegations undoubtedly control the ministry of the Empire, or at all events do in practice displace it by their votes. It is made formally responsible to them by the Constitution. All that Mr. Dicey can say to this is that "the real responsibility of the Ministry to the Delegations admits of a good deal of doubt," and that, at all events, it is not like the responsibility of Mr. Gladstone or Lord Salisbury to the British Parliament. This may be true, but the more mysterious or peculiar it is the better it illustrates the danger of speaking of any particular piece of machinery or of any particular division of power as an essential feature of a federal constitution.

We are told by the critics of the Gladstonian scheme that federalism is not "a plan for disuniting the parts of a united state." But whether it is or not once more depends on circumstances. Federalism, like the British or French Constitution, is an arrangement intended to satisfy the people who set it up by gratifying some desire or removing some cause of discontent. If that discontent be due to unity, federalism disunites; if it be due to disunion, federalism unites.

In the case of the Austro-Hungarian Empire, for instance, it clearly is a "plan for disuniting the parts of a united state." Austria and Hungary were united in the sense in which the opponents of Home Rule use the word for many years before 1867, but the union did not work, that is, did not produce moral as well as legal unity. A constitution was therefore invented which disunites the two countries for the purposes of domestic legislation, but leaves them united for the purposes of foreign relations. This may be a queer arrangement. Although it has worked well enough thus far, it may not continue to work well, but it does work well now. It has succeeded in converting Hungary from a discontented and rebellious province and a source of great weakness to Austria into a loyal and satisfied portion of the Empire. In other words, it has accomplished its purpose. It was not intended to furnish a symmetrical piece of federalism. It was intended to conciliate the Hungarian people. When therefore the professional federal architects make their tour of inspection and point out to the Home Ruler what flagrant departures from the correct federal model the Austro-Hungarian Constitution contains, how improbable it is that so enormous a structure can endure, and how, after all, the Hungarians have not got rid of the Emperor, who commands the army and represents the brute force of the old r 間 ime, I do not think he need feel greatly concerned. This may be all true, and yet the Austro-Hungarian federalism is a valuable thing. It has proved that the federal remedy is good for more than one disease, that it can cure both too much unity and too little. The truth is that there are only two essentials of a federal government. One is an agreement between the various communities who are to live under it as to the manner in which the power is to be divided between the general and local governments; the other is an honest desire on the part of all concerned to make it succeed. As a general rule, whatever the parties agree on and desire to make work is likely to work, just as a Unitarian government is sure to succeed if the people who live under it determine that it shall succeed. If a federal plan be settled in the only right way, by amicable and mutually respectful discussion between representative men, all the more serious obstacles are certain to be revealed and removed. Those which are not brought to light by such discussions are pretty sure to be comparatively trifling, and to disappear before the general success of arrangement. But by a "mutually respectful discussion" I mean discussion in which good faith and intelligence of all concerned are acknowledged on both sides.

In what I have said by way of criticism of a book which may be taken as a particularly full exposition of the legal criticism that may be levelled at Mr. Gladstone's scheme, I have not touched on the arguments against Home Rule which Mr. Dicey draws from the amount of disturbance it would cause in English political habits and arrangements. I freely admit the weight of these arguments. The task of any English statesman who gives Home Rule to Ireland in the only way in which it can be given--with the assent of the British people--will be a very arduous one. But this portion of Mr. Dicey's book, producing, as it does, the distinctively English objections to Home rule, is to me much the most instructive, because it shows the difficulty there would be in creating the state of mind in England about any federal relation to Ireland which would be necessary to make it succeed. I do not think it an exaggeration to say that two-thirds of the English objections to Home Rule as federalism are unconscious expressions of distrust of Irish sincerity or intelligence thrown into the form of prophecy, and prophets, as we all know, cannot be refuted. For instance, "the changes necessitated by federalism would all tend to weaken the power of Great Britain" (Dicey, p. 173). The question of the command of the army could not be arranged; the Irish army could not be depended on by the Crown (p. 174); the central Government would be feeble against foreign aggression, and the Irish Parliament would give aid to a foreign enemy (pp. 176-7). Federalism would aggravate or increase instead of diminishing the actual Irish disloyalty to the Crown (pp. 179-80); the Irish expectations of material prosperity from Home Rule are baseless or grossly exaggerated (p. 182); the probability is, it would produce increased poverty and hardship; there would be frequent quarrels between the two countries over questions of nullification, secession, and federal taxation (p. 184); neither side would acquiesce in the decision either of the Privy Council or of any other tribunal on these questions; Home Rulers would be the first to resist these decisions (p. 185). Irish federation "would soon generate a demand that the whole British Empire should be turned into a Confederacy" (p. 188). Finally, as "the one prediction which may be made with absolute confidence," "federalism would not generate the goodwill between England and Ireland which, could it be produced, would be an adequate compensation even for the evils and inconveniences of a federal system" (p. 191).

Now I do not myself believe these things, but what else can any advocate of Home Rule say in answer to them? They are in their very nature the utterances of a prophet--an able, acute, and fair-minded prophet, I grant, but still a prophet--and before a prophet the wisest man has to be silent, or content himself by answering in prophecy also. What makes the sceptical frame of mind in which Mr. Dicey approaches the Home Rule question so important is not simply that it probably represents that of a very large body of educated Englishmen, but that it is one in which a federal system cannot be produced. Faith, hope, and charity are political as well as social virtues. The minute you leave the region of pure despotism and try any form of government in which the citizen has in the smallest degree to co-operate in the execution of the laws, you have need of these virtues at every step. As soon as you give up the attempt to rule men by drumhead justice, you have to begin to trust in some degree to their intelligence, to their love of order, to their self-respect, and to their desire for material prosperity, and the nearer you get to what is called free government the larger this trust has to be. It has to be very large indeed in order to carry on such a government as that of Great Britain or of the United States; it has to be larger still in order to set up and administer a federal government. In such a government the worst that can happen is very patent. The opportunities which the best-drawn federal constitution offers for outbreaks of what Americans call "pure cussedness"--that is, for the indulgence of anarchical tendencies and impulses--is greater than in any other. Therefore, to set it up, or even to discuss it with any profit, your faith in the particular variety of human nature, which is to live under it, has to be great. No communities can live under it together and make it work which do not respect each other. I say respect, I do not say love, each other. The machine can be made to go a good while without love, and if it goes well it will bring love before long; but mutual respect is necessary from the first day. This is why Mr. Dicey's book is discouraging. The arguments which he addressed to Englishmen would not, I think, be formidable but for the mood in which he finds Englishmen, and that this mood makes against Home Rule there can be little doubt.

I am often asked by Americans why the English do not call an Anglo-Irish convention in the American fashion, and discuss the Irish question with the Irish, find out exactly what they will take to be quiet, and settle with them in a rational way. I generally answer that, in the first place, a convention is a constitution-making agency with which the English public is totally unfamiliar, and that, in the second place, Englishmen's temper is too imperial, or rather imperious, to make the idea of discussion on equal terms with the Irish at all acceptable. They are, in fact, so far from any such arrangement that-- preposterous and even funny as it seems to the American mind--to say that an

English statesman is carrying on any sort of communication with the representatives of the Irish people is to bring against him, in English eyes, a very damaging accusation. When a man like Mr. Matthew Arnold writes to the Times to contend that Englishmen should find out what the Irish want solely for the purpose of not letting them have it, and a journal like the Spectator maintains that the sole excuse for extending the suffrage in Ireland, as it has lately been extended in England, was that the Irish as a minority would not be able to make any effective use of it; and when another political philosopher writes a long and very solemn letter in which, while conceding that in governing Ireland a sympathetic regard for Irish feelings and interests should be displayed, he mentions, as one of the leading facts of the situation, that in "the Irish character there is a grievous lack of independence, of self-respect, of courage, and above all of truthfulness"--when men of this kind talk in this way, it is easy to see that the mental and moral conditions necessary to the successful formation of a federal union are still far off. No federal government, and no government requiring loyalty and fidelity for its successful working, was ever set up by, or even discussed between, two parties, one of which thought the other so unreasonable that it should be carefully denied everything it asked for and as unfit for any sort of political co-operation as mendacity, cowardice, and slavishness could make it.

Finally let me say that there is nothing in Mr. Dicey's book which has surprised me more, considering with what singular intellectual integrity he attacks every point, than his failure to make any mention or to take any account of the large part which time and experience must necessarily play in bringing to perfection any political arrangement which is made to order, if I may use the expression, no matter how carefully it may be drafted. Hume says on this point with great wisdom, "To balance the large state or society, whether monarchical or republican, on general laws, is a work of so great difficulty, that no human genius, however comprehensive, is able by the mere dint of reason or reflection to effect it. The judgments of many must unite in the work, experience must guide their labour, time must bring it to perfection, and the feeling of inconveniences must correct the mistakes which they inevitably fall into in their first trial and experiments."[25]

This has proved true of the American and Swiss federations; it will probably prove true of the Austro-Hungarian federation and of any that may be set up by Great Britian [Transcriber: sic.] and her colonies. It will prove still more true of any attempt that may be made at federation between Great Britain and Ireland. No corrections which could be made in the Gladstonian or any other constitution would make it work exactly on the lines laid down by its framers. Even if it were revised in accordance with Mr. Dicey's criticism, it would probably be found, as in the case of the American Constitution, that few of the dangers which were most feared for it had beset it, and that some of the inconveniences which were most distinctly foreseen as likely to arise from it were among the things which had materially contributed to its success. History is full of the gentle ridicule which the course of events throws on statesmen and philosophers.

FOOTNOTES:

[Footnote 24: Printed in the earlier part of this volume.]

[Footnote 25: Essay on the Rise and Progress of the Arts and Sciences.]

THE "UNIONIST" CASE FOR HOME RULE.

BY R. BARRY O'BRIEN.

I am often asked, What are the best books to read on the Irish question? and I never fail to mention Mr. Lecky's Leaders of Public Opinion in Ireland and the History of England in the Eighteenth Century; Mr. Goldwin Smith's Irish History and Irish Character, Three English Statesmen, The Irish Question, and Professor Dicey's admirable work, England's Case against Home Rule.

Indeed, the case for Home Rule, as stated in these books, is unanswerable; and it redounds to the credit of Mr. Lecky, Mr. Goldwin Smith, and Mr. Dicey that their narrative of facts should in no wise be prejudiced by their political opinions.

That their facts are upon one side and their opinions on the other is a minor matter. Their facts, I venture to assert, have made more Home Rulers than their opinions can unmake.

To put this assertion to the test I propose to quote some extracts from the works above mentioned. These extracts shall be full and fair. Nothing shall be left out that can in the slightest degree qualify any statement of fact in the context. Arguments will be omitted, for I wish to place facts mainly before my readers. From these facts they can draw their own conclusions. Neither shall I take up space with comments of my own. I shall call my witnesses and let them speak for themselves.

I.--MR. LECKY.

In the introduction to the new edition of the Leaders of Public Opinion in Ireland, published in 1871--seventy-one years after Mr. Pitt's Union, which was to make England and Ireland one nation--we find the following "contrast" between "national life" in the two countries:--

"There is, perhaps, no Government in the world which succeeds more admirably in the functions of eliciting, sustaining, and directing public opinion than that of England. It does not, it is true, escape its full share of hostile criticism, and, indeed, rather signally illustrates the saying of Bacon, that 'the best Governments are always subject to be like the finest crystals, in which every icicle and grain is seen which in a fouler stone is never perceived;' but whatever charges may be brought against the balance of its powers, or against its legislative efficiency, few men will question its eminent success as an organ of public opinion. In England an even disproportionate amount of the national talent takes the direction of politics. The pulse of an energetic national life is felt in every quarter of the land. The debates of Parliament are followed with a warm, constant, and intelligent interest by all sections of the community. It draws all classes within the circle of political interests, and is the centre of a strong and steady patriotism, equally removed from the apathy of many Continental nations in time of calm, and from their feverish and spasmodic energy in time of excitement. Its decisions, if not instantly accepted, never fail to have a profound and calming influence on the public mind. It is the safety-valve of the nation. The discontents, the suspicions, the peccant humours that agitate the people, find there their vent, their resolution, and their end.

"It is impossible, I think, not to be struck by the contrast which, in this respect, Ireland presents to England. If the one country furnishes us with an admirable example of the action of a healthy public opinion, the other supplies us with the most unequivocal signs of its disease. The Imperial Parliament exercises for Ireland legislative functions, but it is almost powerless upon opinion--it allays no discontent, and attracts no affection. Political talent, which for many years was at least as abundant among Irishmen as in any equally numerous section of the people, has been steadily declining, and marked decadence in this respect among the representatives of the nation reflects but too truly the absence of public spirit in their constituents.

"The upper classes have lost their sympathy with and their moral ascendency over their tenants, and are thrown for the most part into a policy of mere obstruction. The genuine national enthusiasm never flows in the channel of imperial politics. With great multitudes sectarian considerations have entirely superseded national ones, and their representatives are accustomed systematically to subordinate all party and all political questions to ecclesiastical interests; and while calling themselves Liberals, they make it the main object of their home politics to separate the different classes of their fellow-countrymen during the period of their education, and the main object of their foreign policy to support the temporal power of the Pope. With another and a still larger class the prevailing feeling seems to be an indifference to all Parliamentary proceedings; an utter scepticism about constitutional means of realizing their ends; a blind, persistent hatred of England. Every cause is taken up with an enthusiasm exactly proportioned to the degree in which it is supposed to be injurious to English interests. An amount of energy and enthusiasm which if rightly directed would suffice for the political regeneration of Ireland is wasted in the most insane projects of disloyalty; while the diversion of so much public feeling from Parliamentary politics leaves the Parliamentary arena more and more open to corruption, to place-hunting, and to imposture.

"This picture is in itself a very melancholy one, but there are other circumstances which greatly heighten the effect. In a very ignorant or a very wretched population it is natural that there should be much vague, unreasoning discontent, but the Irish people are at present neither wretched nor ignorant. Their economical condition before the famine was, indeed, such that it might well have made reasonable men despair. With the land divided into almost microscopic farms, with a population multiplying rapidly to the extreme limits of subsistence, accustomed to the very lowest standard of comfort, and marrying earlier than in any other northern country in Europe, it was idle to look for habits of independence or self-reliance, or for the culture which follows in the train of leisure and comfort. But all this has been changed. A fearful famine and the long-continued strain of emigration have reduced the nation from eight millions to less than five, and have effected, at the price of almost intolerable suffering, a complete economical revolution. The population is now in no degree in excess of the means of subsistence. The rise of wages and prices has diffused comfort through all classes. ... Probably no country in Europe has advanced so rapidly as Ireland within the last ten years, and the tone of cheerfulness, the improvement of the houses, the dress, and the general condition of the people must have struck every observer.[26] ... If industrial improvement, if the rapid increase of material comforts among the poor, could allay political discontent, Ireland should never have been so loyal as at present.

"Nor can it be said that ignorance is at the root of the discontent. The Irish people have always, even in the darkest period of the penal laws, been greedy for knowledge, and few races show more quickness in acquiring it. The admirable system of national education established in the present century is beginning to bear abundant fruit, and, among the younger generation at least, the level of knowledge is quite as high as in England. Indeed, one of the most alarming features of Irish disloyalty is its close and evident connection with education. It is sustained by a cheap literature, written often with no mean literary skill, which penetrates into every village, gives the people their first political impressions, forms and directs their enthusiasm, and seems likely in the long leisure of the pastoral life to exercise an increasing power. Close observers of the Irish character will hardly have failed to notice the great change which since the famine has passed over the amusements of the people. The old love of boisterous out-of-door sports has almost disappeared, and those who would have once sought their pleasures in the market or the fair now gather in groups in the public-house, where one of their number reads out a Fenian newspaper. Whatever else this change may portend, it is certainly of no good omen for the future loyalty of the people.

"It was long customary in England to underrate this disaffection by ascribing it to very transitory causes. The quarter of a century that followed the Union was marked by almost perpetual disturbance; but this it was said was merely the natural ground swell of agitation which followed a great reform. It was then the popular theory that it was the work of O'Connell, who was described during many years as the one obstacle to the peace of Ireland, and whose death was made the subject of no little congratulation, as though Irish discontent had perished with its organ. It was as if, the Aeolian harp being shattered, men wrote an epitaph upon the wind. Experience has abundantly proved the folly of such theories. Measured by mere chronology, a little more than seventy years have passed since the Union, but famine and emigration have compressed into these years the work of centuries. The character, feelings, and conditions of the people have been profoundly altered. A long course of remedial legislation has been carried, and during many years the national party has been without a leader and without a stimulus. Yet, so far from subsiding, disloyalty in Ireland is probably as extensive, and is certainly as malignant, as at the death of O'Connell, only in many respects the public opinion of the country has palpably deteriorated. O'Connell taught an attachment to the connection, a loyalty to the crown, a respect for the rights of property, a consistency of Liberalism, which we look for in vain among his successors; and that faith in moral force and constitutional agitation which he made it one of his greatest objects to instil into the people has almost vanished with the failure of his agitation."[27]

Few Irish Nationalists have drawn a weightier indictment against the Union than this. After a trial of seventy years, Mr. Lecky sums up the case against the Union in these pregnant sentences:--

"The Imperial Parliament allays no discontent, and attracts no affection;" "The genuine national enthusiasm never flows in the channel of imperial politics;" the people have "an utter scepticism about constitutional means of realizing their ends," and are imbued with "a blind, persistent hatred of England." Worse still, neither the material progress of the country, nor the education of the people, has reconciled them to the Imperial Parliament. Indeed, their disloyalty has increased with their prosperity and enlightenment. This is the story which Mr. Lecky has to tell. But why are the Irish disloyal? Mr. Lecky shall answer the question.

"The causes of this deep-seated disaffection I have endeavoured in some degree to investigate in the following essays. To the merely dramatic historian the history of Ireland will probably appear less attractive than that of most other countries, for it is somewhat deficient in great characters and in splendid episodes; but to a philosophic student of history it presents an interest of the very highest order. In no other history can we trace more clearly the chain of causes and effects, the influence of past legislation, not only upon the material condition, but also upon the character of a nation. In no other history especially can we investigate more fully the evil consequences which must ensue from disregarding that sentiment of nationality which, whether it be wise or foolish, whether it be desirable or the reverse, is at least one of the strongest and most enduring of human passions. This, as I conceive, lies at the root of Irish discontent. It is a question of nationality as truly as in Hungary or in Poland. Special grievances or anomalies may aggravate, but do not cause it, and they become formidable only in as far as they are connected with it. What discontent was felt against the Protestant Established Church was felt chiefly because it was regarded as an English garrison sustaining an anti-national system; and the agrarian difficulty never assumed its full intensity till by the repeal agitation the landlords had been politically alienated from the people."[28]

Let those who imagine that the Irish question can be completely settled by the redress of material grievances take those words to heart.

But, it is said, Scotch national sentiment is as strong as Irish, why should not a legislative union be as acceptable to Ireland as to Scotland? Mr. Lecky shall answer this question too.

"It is hardly possible to advert to the Scotch Union, without pausing for a moment to examine why its influence on the loyalty of the people should have ultimately been so much happier than that of the legislative union which, nearly a century later, was enacted between England and Ireland. A very slight attention to the circumstances of the case will explain the mystery, and will at the same time show the extreme shallowness of those theorists who can only account for it by reference to original peculiarities of national character. The sacrifice of a nationality is a measure which naturally produces such intense and such enduring discontent that it never should be exacted unless it can be accompanied by some political or material advantages to the lesser country that are so great and at the same time so evident as to prove a corrective. Such a corrective in the case of Scotland, was furnished by the commercial clauses. The Scotch Parliament was very arbitrary and corrupt, and by no means a faithful representation of the people. The majority of the nation were certainly opposed to the Union, and, directly or indirectly, it is probable that much corruption was employed to effect it; but still the fact remains that by it one of the most ardent wishes of all Scottish patriots was attained, that there had been for many years a powerful and intelligent minority who were prepared to purchase commercial freedom even at the expense of the fusion of legislatures, and that in consequence of the establishment of free trade the next generation of Scotchmen witnessed an increase of material well-being that was utterly unprecedented in the history of their country. Nothing equivalent took place in Ireland. The gradual abolition of duties between England and Ireland was, no doubt, an advantage to the lesser country, but the whole trade to America and the other English colonies had been thrown open to Irishmen between 1775 and 1779. Irish commerce had taken this direction; the years between 1779 and the rebellion of 1798 were probably the most prosperous in Irish history, and the generation that followed the Union was one of the most miserable. The sacrifice of nationality was extorted by the most enormous corruption in the history of representative institutions. It was demanded by no considerable section of the Irish people. It was accompanied by no signal political or material benefit that could mitigate or counteract its unpopularity, and it was effected without a dissolution, in opposition to the votes of the immense majority of the representatives of the counties and considerable towns, and to innumerable addresses from every part of the country. Can any impartial man be surprised that such a measure, carried in such a manner, should have proved unsuccessful?"[29]

In the Leaders of Public Opinion in Ireland Mr. Lecky traces the current of events which have led to the present situation. He shows how the Treaty of Limerick was shamelessly violated, and how the native population was oppressed and degraded.

"The position of Ireland was at this time [1727] one of the most deplorable that can be conceived.... The Roman Catholics had been completely prostrated by the battle of the Boyne and by the surrender of Limerick. They had stipulated indeed for religious liberty, but the Treaty of Limerick was soon shamelessly violated, and it found no avengers. Sarsfield and his brave companions had abandoned a country where defeat left no opening for their talents, and had joined the Irish Brigade which had been formed in the service of France.... But while the Irish Roman Catholics abroad found free scope for their ambition in the service of France, those who remained at home had sunk into a condition of utter degradation. All Catholic energy and talent had emigrated to foreign lands, and penal laws of atrocious severity crushed the Catholics who remained."[30]

Mr. Lecky's account of these "penal laws" is upon the whole, I think, the best that has been written.

"The last great Protestant ruler of England was William III., who is identified in Ireland with the humiliation of the Boyne, with the destruction of Irish trade, and with the broken Treaty of Limerick. The ceaseless exertions of the extreme Protestant party have made him more odious in the eyes of the people than he deserves to be; for he was personally far more tolerant than the great majority of his contemporaries, and the penal code was chiefly enacted under his successors. It required, indeed, four or five reigns to elaborate a system so ingeniously contrived to demoralize, to degrade, and to impoverish the people of Ireland. By this code the Roman Catholics were absolutely excluded from the Parliament, from the magistracy, from the corporations, from the bench, and from the bar. They could not vote at Parliamentary elections or at vestries; they could not act as constables, or sheriffs, or jurymen, or serve in the army or navy, or become solicitors, or even hold the positions of gamekeeper or watchman. Schools were established to bring up their children as Protestants; and if they refused to avail themselves of these, they were deliberately assigned to hopeless ignorance, being excluded from the university, and debarred, under crushing penalties, from acting as schoolmasters, as ushers, or as private tutors, or from sending their children abroad to obtain the instruction they were refused at home. They could not marry Protestants, and if such a marriage were celebrated it was annulled by law, and the priest who officiated might be hung. They could not buy land, or inherit or receive it as a gift from Protestants, or hold life-annuities, or leases for more than thirty-one years, or any lease on such terms that the profits of the land exceeded one-third of the rent. If any Catholic leaseholder by his industry so increased his profits that they exceeded this proportion, and did not immediately make a corresponding increase in his payments, any Protestant who gave the information could enter into possession of his farm. If any Catholic had secretly purchased either his old forfeited estate, or any other land, any Protestant who informed against him might become the proprietor. The few Catholic landowners who remained were deprived of the right which all other classes possessed of bequeathing their lands as they pleased. If their sons continued Catholics, it was divided equally between them. If, however, the eldest son consented to apostatize, the estate was settled upon him, the father from that hour became only a life-tenant, and lost all power of selling, mortgaging, or otherwise disposing of it.

If the wife of a Catholic abandoned the religion of her husband, she was immediately free from his control, and the Chancellor was empowered to assign to her a certain proportion of her husband's property. If any child, however young, professed itself a Protestant, it was at once taken from the father's care, and the Chancellor could oblige the father to declare upon oath the value of his property, both real and personal, and could assign for the present maintenance and future portion of the converted child such proportion of that property as the court might decree. No Catholic could be guardian either to his own children or to those of another person; and therefore a Catholic who died while his children were minors had the bitterness of reflecting upon his death-bed that they must pass into the care of Protestants. An annuity of from twenty to forty pounds was provided as a bribe for every priest who would become a Protestant. To convert a Protestant to Catholicism was a capital offence. In every walk of life the Catholic was pursued by persecution or restriction. Except in the linen trade, he could not have more than two apprentices. He could not possess a horse of the value of more than five pounds, and any Protestant, on giving him five pounds, could take his horse. He was compelled to pay double to the militia. He was forbidden, except under particular conditions, to live in Galway or Limerick. In case of war with a Catholic power, the Catholics were obliged to reimburse the damage done by the enemy's privateers. The Legislature, it is true, did not venture absolutely to suppress their worship, but it existed only by a doubtful connivance--stigmatized as if it were a species of licensed prostitution, and subject to conditions which, if they had been enforced, would have rendered its continuance impossible. An old law which prohibited it, and another which enjoined attendance at the Anglican worship, remained unrepealed, and might at any time be revived; and the former was, in fact, enforced during the Scotch rebellion of 1715. The parish priests, who alone were allowed to officiate, were compelled to be registered, and were forbidden to keep curates or to officiate anywhere except in their own parishes. The chapels might not have bells or steeples. No crosses might be publicly erected. Pilgrimages to the holy wells were forbidden. Not only all monks and friars, but also all Catholic archbishops, bishops, deacons, and other dignitaries, were ordered by a certain day to leave the country; and if after that date they were found in Ireland they were liable to be first imprisoned and then banished; and if after that banishment they returned to discharge their duty in their dioceses, they were liable to the punishment of death. To facilitate the discovery of offences against the code, two justices of the peace might at any time compel any

Catholic of eighteen years of age to declare when and where he last heard Mass, what persons were present, and who officiated; and if he refused to give evidence they might imprison him for twelve months, or until he paid a fine of twenty pounds. Any one who harboured ecclesiastics from beyond the seas was subject to fines which for the third offence amounted to confiscation of all his goods. A graduated scale of rewards was offered for the discovery of Catholic bishops, priests, and schoolmasters; and a resolution of the House of Commons pronounced 'the prosecuting and informing against Papists' 'an honourable service to the Government.'

"Such were the principal articles of this famous code--a code which Burke truly described as 'well digested and well disposed in all its parts; a machine of wise and elaborate contrivance, and as well fitted for the oppression, impoverishment, and degradation of a people, and the debasement in them of human nature itself, as ever proceeded from the perverted ingenuity of man.'"[31]

The effects of these laws Mr. Lecky has described thus:

"The economical and moral effects of the penal laws were, however, profoundly disastrous. The productive energies of the nation were fatally diminished. Almost all Catholics of energy and talent who refused to abandon their faith emigrated to foreign lands. The relation of classes was permanently vitiated; for almost all the proprietary of the country belonged to one religion, while the great majority of their tenants were of another. The Catholics, excluded from almost every possibility of eminence, deprived of their natural leaders, and consigned by the Legislature to utter ignorance, soon sank into the condition of broken and dispirited helots. A total absence of industrial virtues, a cowering and abject deference to authority, a recklessness about the future, a love of secret illegal combinations, became general among them. Above all, they learned to regard law as merely the expression of force, and its moral weight was utterly destroyed. For the greater part of a century, the main object of the Legislature was to extirpate a religion by the encouragement of the worst, and the punishment of some of the best qualities of our nature. Its rewards were reserved for the informer, for the hypocrite, for the undutiful son, or for the faithless wife. Its penalties were directed against religious constancy and the honest discharge of ecclesiastical duty.

"It would, indeed, be scarcely possible to conceive a more infamous system of legal tyranny than that which in the middle of the eighteenth century crushed every class and almost every interest in Ireland."[32]

But laws were not only passed against the native race and the national religion. Measures were taken to destroy the industries of the country, and to involve natives and colonists, Protestants and Catholics, in common ruin. Mr. Lecky shall tell the story.

"The commercial and industrial condition of the country was, if possible, more deplorable than its political condition, and was the result of a series of English measures which for deliberate and selfish tyranny could hardly be surpassed. Until the reign of Charles II. the Irish shared the commercial privileges of the English; but as the island had not been really conquered till the reign of Elizabeth, and as its people were till then scarcely removed from barbarism, the progress was necessarily slow. In the early Stuart reigns, however, comparative repose and good government were followed by a sudden rush of prosperity. The land was chiefly pasture, for which it was admirably adapted; the export of live cattle to England was carried on upon a large scale, and it became a chief source of Irish wealth. The English landowners, however, took the alarm. They complained that Irish rivalry in the cattle market was reducing English rents; and accordingly, by an Act which was first passed in 1663, and was made perpetual in 1666, the importation of cattle into England was forbidden.

"The effect of a measure of this kind, levelled at the principal article of the commerce of the nation, was necessarily most disastrous. The profound modification which it introduced into the course of Irish industry was sufficiently shown by the estimate of Sir W. Petty, who declares that before the statute three-fourths of the trade of Ireland was with England, but not one-fourth of it since that time. In the very year when this Bill was passed another measure was taken not less fatal to the interest of the country. In the first Navigation Act, Ireland was placed on the same terms as England; but in the Act as amended in 1663 she was omitted, and was thus deprived of the whole Colonial trade. With the exception of a very few specified articles no European merchandise could be imported into the British Colonies except directly from England, in ships built in England, and manned chiefly by English sailors. No articles, with a few exceptions, could be brought from the

Colonies to Europe without being first unladen in England. In 1670 this exclusion of Ireland was confirmed, and in 1696 it was rendered more stringent, for it was enacted that no goods of any sort could be imported directly from the Colonies to Ireland. It will be remembered that at this time the chief British Colonies were those of America, and that Ireland, by her geographical position, was naturally of all countries most fitted for the American trade.

"As far, then, as the Colonial trade was concerned, Ireland at this time gained nothing whatever by her connection with England. To other countries, however, her ports were still open, and in time of peace a foreign commerce was unrestricted. When forbidden to export their cattle to England, the Irish turned their land chiefly into sheep-walks, and proceeded energetically to manufacture the wool. Some faint traces of this manufacture may be detected from an early period, and Lord Strafford, when governing Ireland, had mentioned it with a characteristic comment. Speaking of the Irish he says, 'There was little or no manufactures amongst them, but some small beginnings towards a cloth trade, which I had and so should still discourage all I could, unless otherwise directed by His Majesty and their Lordships. It might be feared that they would beat us out of the trade itself by underselling us, which they were able to do.' With the exception, however, of an abortive effort by this governor, the Irish wool manufacture was in no degree impeded, and was indeed mentioned with special favour in many Acts of Parliament; and it was in a great degree on the faith of this long-continued legislative sanction that it was so greatly expanded. The poverty of Ireland, the low state of civilization of a large proportion of its inhabitants, the effects of the civil wars which had so recently convulsed it, and the exclusion of its products from the English Colonies, were doubtless great obstacles to manufacturing enterprise; but, on the other hand, Irish wool was very good, living was cheaper, taxes were lighter than in England, a spirit of real industrial energy began to pervade the country, and a considerable number of English manufacturers came over to colonize it. There appeared for a time every probability that the Irish would become an industrial nation, and, had manufactures arisen, their whole social, political, and economical condition would have been changed. But English jealousy again interposed. By an Act of crushing and unprecedented severity, which was introduced in 1698 and carried in 1699, the export of the Irish woollen manufactures, not only to England, but also to all other countries, was absolutely forbidden.

"The effects of this measure were terrible almost beyond conception. The main industry of the country was at a blow completely and irretrievably annihilated. A vast population was thrown into a condition of utter destitution. Several thousands of manufacturers left the country, and carried their skill and enterprise to Germany, France, and Spain. The western and southern districts of Ireland are said to have been nearly depopulated. Emigration to America began on a large scale, and the blow was so severe that long after, a kind of chronic famine prevailed."[33]

Mr. Lecky relates with pride how the penal code was relaxed, and the commercial restrictions were removed, while the Irish Parliament, essentially a Protestant and landlord body, still existed, and shows how the cause of Catholic Emancipation was retarded by the Union.

"The Relief Bill of '93 naturally suggests a consideration of the question so often agitated in Ireland, whether the Union was really a benefit to the Roman Catholic cause. It has been argued that Catholic Emancipation was an impossibility as long as the Irish Parliament lasted; for in a country where the great majority were Roman Catholics, it would be folly to expect the members of the dominant creed to surrender a monopoly on which their ascendency depended. The arguments against this view are, I believe, overwhelming. The injustice of the disqualification was far more striking before the Union than after it. In the one case, the Roman Catholics were excluded from the Parliament of a nation of which they were the great majority; in the other, they were excluded from the Parliament of an empire in which they were a small minority. Grattan, Plunket, Curran, Burrowes, and Ponsonby were the great supporters of Catholic Emancipation, and the great opponents of the Union. Clare and Duigenan were the two great opponents of emancipation, and the great supporters of the Union. At a time when scarcely any public opinion existed in Ireland, when the Roman Catholics were nearly quiescent, and when the leaning of Government was generally liberal, the Irish Protestants admitted their fellow-subjects to the magistracy, to the jury-box, and to the franchise. By this last measure they gave them an amount of political power which necessarily implied complete emancipation. Even if no leader of genius had arisen in the Roman Catholic ranks, and if no spirit of enthusiasm had animated their councils, the influence possessed by a body who formed three fourths of the population, who were rapidly rising in wealth, and who could send their representatives to Parliament, would have been sufficient to ensure their triumph. If the Irish Legislature had continued, it would have been found impossible to resist the demand for reform; and every reform, by diminishing the overgrown power of a few Protestant landholders, would have increased that of the Roman Catholics. The concession accorded in 1793 was, in fact, far greater and more important than that accorded in 1829, and it placed the Roman Catholics, in a great measure, above the mercy of Protestants. But this was not all. The sympathies of the Protestants were being rapidly enlisted in their behalf. The generation to which Charlemont and Flood belonged had passed away, and all the leading intellects of the country, almost all the Opposition, and several conspicuous members of the Government, were warmly in favour of emancipation. The rancour which at present exists between the members of the two creeds appears then to have been almost unknown, and the real obstacle to emancipation was not the feelings of the people, but the policy of the Government. The Bar may be considered on most subjects a very fair exponent of the educated opinion of the nation; and Wolf Tone observed, in 1792, that it was almost unanimous in favour of the Catholics; and it is not without importance, as showing the tendencies of the rising generation, that a large body of the students of Dublin University in 1795 presented an address to Grattan, thanking him for his labours in the cause. The Roman Catholics were rapidly gaining the public opinion of Ireland, when the Union arrayed against them another public opinion which was deeply prejudiced against their faith, and almost entirely removed from their influence. Compare the twenty years before the Union with the twenty years that followed it, and the change is sufficiently manifest. There can scarcely be a question that if Lord Fitzwilliam had remained in office the Irish Parliament would readily have given emancipation. In the United Parliament for many years it was obstinately rejected, and if O'Connell had never arisen it would probably never have been granted unqualified by the veto. In 1828 when the question was brought forward in Parliament, sixty-one out of ninety-three Irish members, forty-five out of sixty-one Irish county members, voted in its favour. Year after year Grattan and Plunket brought forward the case of their fellow-countrymen with an eloquence and a perseverance worthy of their great cause; but year after year they were defeated. It was not till the great tribune had arisen, till he had moulded his co-religionists into one compact and threatening mass, and had brought the country to the verge of revolution, that the tardy boon was conceded. Eloquence and argument proved alike unavailing when unaccompanied by menace, and Catholic Emancipation was confessedly granted because to withhold it would be to produce a rebellion."[34]

Many people will think that this is a sufficiently weighty condemnation of the Union, but what follows is a still graver reflection on that untoward measure.

"In truth the harmonious co-operation of Ireland with England depends much less upon the framework of the institutions of the former country than upon the dispositions of its people and upon the classes who guide its political life. With a warm and loyal attachment to the connection pervading the nation, the largest amount of self-government might be safely conceded, and the most defective political arrangement might prove innocuous. This is the true cement of nations, and no change, however plausible in theory, can be really advantageous which contributes to diminish it. Theorists may argue that it would be better for Ireland to become in every respect a province of England; they may contend that a union of Legislatures, accompanied by a corresponding fusion of characters and identification of hopes, interests, and desires, would strengthen the empire; but as a matter of fact this was not what was effected in 1800. The measure of Pitt centralized, but it did not unite, or rather, by uniting the Legislatures it divided the nations. In a country where the sentiment of nationality was as intense as in any part of Europe, it destroyed the national Legislature contrary to the manifest wish of the people, and by means so corrupt, treacherous, and shameful that they are never likely to be forgotten. In a country where, owing to the religious difference, it was peculiarly necessary that a vigorous lay public opinion should be fostered to dilute or restrain the sectarian spirit, it suppressed the centre and organ of political life, directed the energies of the community into the channels of sectarianism, drove its humours inwards, and thus began a perversion of public opinion which has almost destroyed the elements of political progress. In a country where the people have always been singularly destitute of self-reliance, and at the same time eminently faithful to their leaders, it withdrew the guidance of affairs from the hands of the resident gentry, and, by breaking their power, prepared the ascendency of the demagogue or the rebel. In two plain ways it was dangerous to the connection: it incalculably increased the aggregate disloyalty of the people, and it destroyed the political supremacy of the class that is most attached to the connection. The Irish Parliament, with all its faults, was an eminently loyal body. The Irish people through the eighteenth century, in spite of great provocations, were on the whole a loyal people till the recall of Lord Fitzwilliam, and even then a few very moderate measures of reform might have reclaimed them. Burke, in his Letters on a Regicide Peace, when reviewing the elements of strength on which England could confide in her struggle with revolutionary France, placed in the very first rank the co-operation of Ireland. At the present day, it is to be feared that most impartial men would regard Ireland, in the event of a great European war, rather as a source of weakness than of strength. More than seventy years have passed since the boasted measure of Pitt, and it is unfortunately incontestable that the lower orders in Ireland are as hostile to the system of government under which they live as the Hungarian people have ever been to Austrian, or the Roman to Papal rule; that Irish disloyalty is multiplying enemies of England wherever the English tongue is spoken; and that the national sentiment runs so strongly that multitudes of Irish Catholics look back with deep affection to the Irish Parliament, although no Catholic could sit within its walls, and although it was only during the last seven years of its independent existence that Catholics could vote for its members. Among the opponents of the Union were many of the most loyal, as well as nearly all the ablest men in Ireland; and Lord Charlemont, who died shortly before the measure was consummated, summed up the feelings of many in the emphatic sentence with which he protested against it. 'It would more than any other measure,' he said, 'contribute to the separation of two countries the perpetual connection of which is one of the warmest wishes of my heart.'

"In fact, the Union of 1800 was not only a great crime, but was also, like most crimes, a great blunder. The manner in which it was carried was not only morally scandalous; it also entirely vitiated it as a work of statesmanship. No great political measure can be rationally judged upon its abstract merits, and without considering the character and the wishes of the people for whom it is intended. It is now idle to discuss what might have been the effect of a Union if it had been carried before 1782, when the Parliament was still unemancipated; if it had been the result of a spontaneous movement of public opinion; if it had been accompanied by the emancipation of the Catholics. Carried as it was prematurely, in defiance of the national sentiment of the people and of the protests of the unbribed talent of the country, it has deranged the whole course of political development, driven a large proportion of the people into sullen disloyalty, and almost destroyed healthy public opinion. In comparing the abundance of political talent in Ireland during the last century with the striking absence of it at present, something no doubt may be attributed to the absence of protection for literary property in Ireland in the former period, which may have directed an unusual portion of the national talent to politics, and something to the Colonial and Indian careers which have of late years been thrown open to competition; but when all due allowances have been made for these, the contrast is sufficiently impressive. Few impartial men can doubt that the tone of political life and the standard of political talent have been lowered, while sectarian animosity has been greatly increased, and the extent to which Fenian principles have permeated the people is a melancholy comment upon the prophesies that the Union would put an end to disloyalty in Ireland."[35]

Mr. Lecky's views as to what ought to have been done in 1800 deserve to be set forth.

"While, however, the Irish policy of Pitt appears to be both morally and politically deserving of almost unmitigated condemnation, I cannot agree with those who believe that the arrangement of 1782 could have been permanent. The Irish Parliament would doubtless have been in time reformed, but it would have soon found its situation intolerable. Imperial policy must necessarily have been settled by the Imperial Parliament, in which Ireland had no voice; and, unlike Canada or Australia, Ireland is profoundly affected by every change of Imperial policy. Connection with England was of overwhelming importance to the lesser country, while the tie uniting them would have been found degrading by one nation and inconvenient to the other. Under such circumstances a Union of some kind was inevitable. It was simply a question of time, and must have been demanded by Irish opinion. At the same time, it would not, I think, have been such a Union as that of 1800. The conditions of Irish and English politics are so extremely different, and the reasons for preserving in Ireland a local centre of political life are so powerful, that it is probable a Federal Union would have been preferred. Under such a system the Irish Parliament would have continued to exist, but would have been restricted to purely local subjects, while an Imperial Parliament, in which Irish representatives sat, would have directed the policy of the empire."[36]

MR. GOLDWIN SMITH.

None of the recent opponents of Home Rule have written against that policy with more brilliance and epigrammatic keenness than Mr. Goldwin Smith. But no one has stated with more force the facts and considerations which, operating on men's mind for years past, have made the Liberal party Home Rulers now. His coup d'oeil remains the most pointed indictment ever drawn from the historical annals of Ireland against the English methods of governing that country. Twenty years ago he anticipated the advice recently given by Mr. Gladstone. In 1867 he wrote:--

"I have myself sought and found in the study of Irish history the explanation of the paradox, that a people with so many gifts, so amiable, naturally so submissive to rulers, and everywhere but in their own country industrious, are in their own country bywords of idleness, lawlessness, disaffection, and agrarian crime."[37] He explains the paradox thus: "But it is difficult to distinguish the faults of the Irish from their misfortunes. It has been well said of their past industrial character and history,--'We were reckless, ignorant, improvident, drunken, and idle. We were idle, for we had nothing to do; we were reckless, for we had no hope; we were ignorant, for learning was denied us; we were improvident, for we had no future; we were drunken, for we sought to forget our misery. That time has passed away for ever.' No part of this defence is probably more true than that which connects the drunkenness of the Irish people with their misery. Drunkenness is, generally speaking, the vice of despair; and it springs from the despair of the Irish peasant as rankly as from that of his English fellow. The sums of money which have lately been transmitted by Irish emigrants to their friends in Ireland seem a conclusive answer to much loose denunciation of the national character, both in a moral and an industrial point of view.... There seems no good reason for believing that the Irish Kelts are averse to labour, provided they be placed, as people of all races require to be placed, for two or three generations in circumstances favourable to industry."[38] He shows that the Irish have not been so placed. "Still more does justice require that allowance should be made on historical grounds for the failings of the Irish people. If they are wanting in industry, in regard for the rights of property, in reverence for the law, history furnishes a full explanation of their defects, without supposing in them any inherent depravity, or even any inherent weakness. They have never had the advantage of the training through which other nations have passed in their gradual rise from barbarism to civilization. The progress of the Irish people was arrested at almost a primitive stage, and a series of calamities, following close upon each other, have prevented it from ever fairly resuming its course. The pressure of overwhelming misery has now been reduced; government has become mild and just; the civilizing agency of education has been introduced; the upper classes are rapidly returning to their duty, and the natural effect is at once seen in the improved character of the people. Statesmen are bound to be well acquainted with the historical sources of the evil with which they have to deal, especially when those evils are of such a nature as, at first aspect, to imply depravity in a nation. There are still speakers and writers who seem to think that the Irish are incurably vicious, because the accumulated effects of so many centuries cannot be removed at once by a wave of the legislator's wand. Some still believe, or affect to believe, that the very air of the island is destructive of the characters and understandings of all who breathe it."[39]

Elsewhere he adds, referring to the land system:

"How many centuries of a widely different training have the English people gone through in order to acquire their boasted love of law."[40]

Of the "training" through which the Irish went, he says--

"The existing settlement of land in Ireland, whether dating from the confiscations of the Stuarts, or from those of Cromwell, rests on a proscription three or four times as long as that on which the settlement of land rests over a considerable part of France. It may, therefore, be considered as placed upon discussion in the estimation of all sane men; and, this being the case, it is safe to observe that no inherent want of respect for property is shown by the Irish people if a proprietorship which had its origin within historical memory in flagrant wrong is less sacred in their eyes than it would be if it had its origin in immemorial right."[41]

The character which he gives of Irish landlordism deserves to be quoted:

"The Cromwellian landowners soon lost their religious character, while they retained all the hardness of the fanatic and the feelings of Puritan conquerors towards a conquered Catholic people. 'I have eaten with them,' said one, 'drunk with them, fought with them; but I never prayed with them.' Their descendants became, probably, the very worst upper class with which a country was ever afflicted. The habits of the Irish gentry grew beyond measure brutal and reckless, and the coarseness of their debaucheries would have disgusted the crew of Comus. Their drunkenness, their blasphemy, their ferocious duelling, left the squires of England far behind. If there was a grotesque side to their vices which mingles laughter with our reprobation, this did not render their influence less pestilent to the community of which the motive of destiny had made them social chiefs. Fortunately, their recklessness was sure, in the end, to work, to a certain extent, its own cure; and in the background of their swinish and uproarious drinking-bouts, the Encumbered Estates Act rises to our view."[42]

Mr. Goldwin Smith deals with agrarian crime thus:

"The atrocities perpetrated by the Whiteboys, especially in the earlier period of agrarianism (for they afterwards grew somewhat less inhuman), are such as to make the flesh creep. No language can be too strong in speaking of the horrors of such a state of society. But it would be unjust to confound these agrarian conspiracies with ordinary crime, or to suppose that they imply a propensity to ordinary crime either on the part of those who commit them, or on the part of the people who connive at and favour their commission. In the districts where agrarian conspiracy and outrage were most rife, the number of ordinary crimes was very small. In Munster, in 1833, out of 973 crimes, 627 were Whiteboy, or agrarian, and even of the remainder, many, being crimes of violence, were probably committed from the same motive.

"In plain truth, the secret tribunals which administered the Whiteboy code were to the people the organs of a wild law of social morality by which, on the whole, the interest of the peasant was protected. They were not regular tribunals; neither were the secret tribunals of Germany in the Middle Ages, the existence of which, and the submission of the people to their jurisdiction, implied the presence of much violence, but not of much depravity, considering the wildness of the times. The Whiteboys 'found in their favour already existing a general and settled hatred of the law among the great body of the peasantry.'[43] We have seen how much the law, and the ministers of the law, had done to deserve the peasant's love. We have seen, too, in what successive guises property had presented itself to his mind: first as open rapine; then as robbery carried on through the roguish technicalities of an alien code; finally as legalized and systematic oppression. Was it possible that he should have formed so affectionate a reverence either for law or property as would be proof against the pressure of starvation?"[44] "A people cannot be expected to love and reverence oppression because it is consigned to the statute-book, and called law."[45]

These extracts are taken from Irish History and Irish Character, which was published in 1861. But in 1867 Mr. Goldwin Smith wrote a series of letters to the Daily News, which were republished in 1868 under the title of The Irish Question; and these letters form, perhaps, the most statesmanlike and far-seeing pronouncement that has ever been made on the Irish difficulty.

In the preface Mr. Goldwin Smith begins:

"The Irish legislation of the last forty years, notwithstanding the adoption of some remedial measures, has failed through the indifference of Parliament to the sentiments of Irishmen; and the harshness of English public opinion has embittered the effects on Irish feeling of the indifference of Parliament. Occasionally a serious effort has been made by an English statesman to induce Parliament to approach Irish questions in that spirit of sympathy, and with that anxious desire to be just, without which a Parliament in London cannot legislate wisely for Ireland. Such efforts have hitherto met with no response; is it too much to hope that it will be otherwise in the year now opening?"[46]

The only comment I shall make on these words is: they were penned more than half a century after Mr. Pitt's Union, which was to shower down blessings on the Irish people.

Mr. Goldwin Smith's first letter was written on the 23rd of November, 1867, the day of the execution of the Fenians Allen, Larkin, and O'Brien. He says--

"There can be no doubt, I apprehend, that the Irish difficulty has entered on a new phase, and that Irish disaffection has, to repeat an expression which I heard used in Ireland, come fairly into a line with the other discontented nationalities of Europe. Active Fenianism probably pervades only the lowest class; passive sympathy, which the success of the movement would at once convert into active co-operation, extends, it is to be feared, a good deal higher.

"England has ruin before her, unless she can hit on a remedy, and overcome any obstacles of class interest or of national pride which would prevent its application, the part of Russia in Poland, or of Austria in Italy--a part cruel, hateful, demoralizing, contrary to all our high principles and professions, and fraught with dangers to our own freedom. Our position will be worse than that of Russia in this respect, that, while her Poland is only a province, our Fenianism is an element pervading every city of the United Kingdom in which Irish abound, and allying itself with kindred misery, discontent, and disorder. Wretchedness, the result of misgovernment, has caused the Irish people to multiply with the recklessness of despair, and now here are their avenging hosts in the midst of us, here is the poison of their disaffection running through every member of our social frame. Not only so, but the same wretchedness has sent millions of emigrants to form an Irish nation in the United States, where the Irish are a great political power, swaying by their votes the councils of the American Republic, and in immediate contact with those Transatlantic possessions of England, the retention of which it is now patriotic to applaud, and will one day be patriotic to have dissuaded.

" ... That Ireland is not at this moment, materially speaking, in a particularly suffering state, but, on the contrary, the farmers are rather prosperous, and wages, even when allowance is made for the rise in the price of provisions, considerably higher than they were, only adds to the significance of this widespread disaffection.

"The Fenian movement is not religious, nor radically economical (though no doubt it has in it a socialistic element), but national, and the remedy for it must be one which cures national discontent. This is the great truth which the English people have to lay to heart."[47]

Mr. Goldwin Smith then dispels the notion that the Irish question is a religious one.

"When Fenianism first appeared, the Orangemen, in accordance with their fixed idea, ascribed it to the priests. They were undeceived, I was told, by seeing a priest run away from the Fenians in fear of his life."[48]

Neither was it a question of the land.

"The land question, no doubt, lies nearer to the heart of the matter, and it is the great key to Irish history in the past; but I do not believe that even this is fundamental."

He then states what is "fundamental."[49]

"The real root of the disaffection which exhibits itself at present in the guise of Fenianism, and which has been suddenly kindled into flame by the arming of the Irish in the American civil war, but which existed before in a nameless and smouldering state, is, as I believe, the want of national institutions, of a national capital, of any objects of national reverence and attachment, and consequently of anything deserving to be called national life. The English Crown and Parliament the Irish have never learnt, nor have they had any chance of learning, to love, or to regard as national, notwithstanding the share which was given them, too late, in the representation. The greatness of England is nothing to them. Her history is nothing, or worse. The success of Irishmen in London consoles the Irish in Ireland no more than the success of Italian adventurers in foreign countries (which was very remarkable) consoled the Italian people. The drawing off of Irish talent, in fact, turns to an additional grievance in their minds. Dublin is a modern Tara, a metropolis from which the glory has departed; and the viceroyalty, though it pleases some of the tradesmen, fails altogether to satisfy the people. 'In Ireland we can make no appeal to patriotism, we can have no patriotic sentiments in our schoolbooks, no patriotic emblems in our schools, because in Ireland everything patriotic is rebellious.' These were the words uttered in my hearing, not by a complaining demagogue, but by a desponding statesman. They seemed to me pregnant with fatal truths.

"If the craving for national institutions, and the disaffection bred in this void of the Irish people's heart, seem to us irrational and even insane, in the absence of any more substantial grievance, we ought to ask ourselves what would become of our own patriotism if we had no national institutions, no objects of national loyalty and reverence, even though we might be pretty well governed, at least in intention, by a neighbouring people whom we regarded as aliens, and who, in fact, regarded us pretty much in the same light. Let us first judge ourselves fairly, and then judge the Irish, remembering always that they are more imaginative and sentimental, and need some centre of national feeling and affection more than ourselves."[50]

And all this was written sixty-seven years after the Union of 1800.

Mr. Goldwin Smith then deals with the subject of the Irish and Scotch unions much in the same way as Mr. Lecky.

"The incorporation of the Scotch nation with the English, being conducted on the right principles by the great Whig statesman of Anne, has been perfectly successful. The attempt to incorporate the Irish nation with the English and Scotch, the success of which would have been, if possible, a still greater blessing, being conducted by very different people and on very different principles, has unhappily failed. What might have been the result if even the Hanoverian sovereigns had done the personal duty to their Irish kingdom which they have unfortunately neglected, it is now too late to inquire. The Irish Union has missed its port, and, in order to reach it, will have to tack again. We may hold down a dependency, of course, by force, in Russian and Austrian fashion; but force will never make the hearts of two nations one, especially when they are divided by the sea. Once get rid of this deadly international hatred, and there will be hope of real union in the future."[51]

Mr. Goldwin Smith finally proposes a "plan" by which the "deadly international hatred" might be got rid of, and a "real union" brought about. Here it is.

"1. The residence of the Court at Dublin, not merely to gratify the popular love of royalty and its pageantries, which no man of sense desires to stimulate, but to assure the Irish people, in the only way possible as regards the mass of them, that the sovereign of the United Kingdom is really their sovereign, and that they are equally cared for and honoured with the other subjects of the realm. This would also tend to make Dublin a real capital, and to gather and retain there a portion of the Irish talent which now seeks its fortune elsewhere.

"2. An occasional session (say once in every three years) of the Imperial Parliament in Dublin, partly for the same purposes as the last proposal, but also because the circumstances of Ireland are likely to be, for some time at least, really peculiar, and the personal acquaintance of our legislators with them is the only sufficient security for good Irish legislation. There could be no serious difficulty in holding a short session in the Irish capital, where there is plenty of accommodation for both Houses.

"3. A liberal measure of local self-government for Ireland. I would not vest the power in any single assembly for all Ireland, because Ulster is really a different country from the other provinces. I would give each province a council of its own, and empower that council to legislate (subject, of course, to the supremacy of the Imperial Parliament) on all matters not essential to the political and legal unity of the empire, in which I would include local education. The provincial councils should of course be elective, and the register of electors might be the same as that of electors to the Imperial Parliament. In England itself the extension of local institutions, as political training schools for the masses, as checks upon the sweeping action of the great central assembly, and as the best organs of legislation in all matters requiring (as popular education, among others, does) adaptation to the circumstances of particular districts, would, I think, have formed a part of any statesmanlike revision of our political system. Here, also, much good might be done, and much evil averted, by committing the present business of quarter sessions, other than the judicial business, together with such other matters as the central legislative might think fit to vest in local hands, to an assembly elected by the county."[52]

Thus it will be seen that twenty years ago Mr. Goldwin Smith anticipated Mr. Chamberlain's scheme of provincial councils, and got a good way on the road to an Irish Parliament.

* * * * *

MR. DICEY.

A fairer controversalist, or an abler supporter of the "paper Union," than Mr. Dicey there is not; nevertheless no man has fired more effective shots into Mr. Pitt's unfortunate arrangement of 1800.

How well has the "failure" of that arrangement been described in these pithy sentences--"Eighty-six years have elapsed since the conclusion of the Treaty of Union between England and Ireland. The two countries do not yet form an united nation. The Irish people are, if not more wretched (for the whole European world has made progress, and Ireland with it), yet more conscious of wretchedness, and Irish disaffection to England is, if not deeper, more widespread than in 1800. An Act meant by its authors to be a source of the prosperity and concord which, though slowly, followed upon the Union with Scotland, has not made Ireland rich, has not put an end to Irish lawlessness, has not terminated the feud between Protestants and Catholics, has not raised the position of Irish tenants, has not taken away the causes of Irish discontent, and has, therefore, not removed Irish disloyalty. This is the indictment which can fairly be brought against the Act of Union."[53]

What follows reflects honour on Mr. Dicey as an honest opponent who does not shrink from facts; but what a wholesale condemnation of the policy of the Imperial Parliament!

"On one point alone (it may be urged) all men, of whatever party or of whatever nation, who have seriously studied the annals of Ireland are agreed-- the history is a record of incessant failure on the part of the Government, and of incessant misery on the part of the people. On this matter, if on no other, De Beaumont, Froude, and Lecky are at one. As to the guilt of the failure or the cause of the misery, men may and do differ; that England, whether from her own fault or the fault of the Irish people, or from perversity of circumstances, has failed in Ireland of achieving the elementary results of good government is as certain as any fact of history or of experience. Every scheme has been tried in turn, and no scheme has succeeded or has even, it may be suggested, produced its natural effects. Oppression of the Catholics has increased the adherents and strengthened the hold of Catholicism. Protestant supremacy, while it lasted, did not lead even to Protestant contentment, and the one successful act of resistance to the English dominion was effected by a Protestant Parliament supported by an army of volunteers, led by a body of Protestant officers. The independence gained by a Protestant Parliament led, after eighteen years, to a rebellion so reckless and savage that it caused, if it did not justify, the destruction of the Parliament and the carrying of the Union. The Act of Union did not lead to national unity, and a measure which appeared on the face of it (though the appearance, it must be admitted, was delusive) to be a copy of the law which bound England and Scotland into a common country inspired by common patriotism, produced conspiracy and agitation, and at last placed England and Ireland further apart, morally, than they stood at the beginning of the century. The Treaty of Union, it was supposed, missed its mark because it was not combined with Catholic Emancipation. The Catholics were emancipated, but emancipation, instead of producing loyalty, brought forth the cry for repeal. The Repeal movement ended in failure, but its death gave birth to the attempted rebellion in 1848. Suppressed rebellion begot Fenianism, to be followed in its turn by the agitation for Home Rule. The movement relies, it is said, and there is truth in the assertion, on constitutional methods for obtaining redress. But constitutional measures are supplemented by boycotting, by obstruction, by the use of dynamite. A century of reform has given us Mr. Parnell instead of Grattan, and it is more than possible that Mr. Parnell may be succeeded by leaders in whose eyes Mr. Davitt's policy may appear to be tainted with moderation. No doubt, in each case the failure of good measures admits, like every calamity in public or private life, of explanation, and after the event it is easy to see why, for example, the Poor Law, when extended to Ireland, did not produce even the good effects such as they are which in England are to be set against its numerous evils; or why an emigration of unparalleled proportions has diminished population without much diminishing poverty; why the disestablishment of the Anglican Church has increased rather than diminished the hostility to England of the Catholic priesthood; or why two Land Acts have not contented Irish farmers. It is easy enough, in short, and this without having any recourse to theory of race, and without attributing to Ireland either more or less of original sin than falls to the lot of humanity, to see how it is that imperfect statesmanship--and all statesmanship, it should be remembered, is imperfect--has failed in obtaining good results at all commensurate with its generally good intentions. Failure, however, is none the less failure because its causes admit of analysis. It is no defence to bankruptcy that an insolvent can, when brought before the Court, lucidly explain the errors which resulted in disastrous speculations. The failure of English statesmanship, explain it as you will, has produced the one last and greatest evil which misgovernment can cause. It has created hostility to the law in the minds of the people. The law cannot work in Ireland because the classes whose opinion in other countries supports the actions of the courts, are in Ireland, even when not law-breakers, in full sympathy with law-breakers."[54]

No Home Ruler has described the evils of English misrule in Ireland with such vigour as this.

"Bad administration, religious persecution, above all, a thoroughly vicious land tenure, accompanied by such sweeping confiscations as to make it, at any rate, a plausible assertion that all land in Ireland has during the course of Irish history been confiscated at least thrice over, are admittedly some of the causes, if they do not constitute the whole cause, of the one immediate difficulty which perplexes the policy of England. This is nothing else than the admitted disaffection to the law of the land prevailing among large numbers of Irish people. The existence of this disaffection, whatever be the inference to be drawn from it, is undeniable. A series of so-called Coercion Acts, passed both before and since the Act of Union, give undeniable evidence, if evidence were wanted, of the ceaseless and, as it would appear, almost irrepressible resistance in Ireland offered by the people to the enforcement of the law. I have not the remotest inclination to underrate the lasting and formidable character of this opposition between opinion and law, nor can any jurist who wishes to deal seriously with a serious and infinitely painful topic, question for a moment that the ultimate strength of law lies in the sympathy, or at the lowest the acquiescence, of the mass of the population. Judges, constables, and troops become almost powerless when the conscience of the people permanently opposes the execution of the law. Severity produces either no effect or bad effects; executed criminals are regarded as heroes or martyrs; and jurymen and witnesses meet with the execration and often with the fate of criminals. On such a point it is best to take the opinion of a foreigner unaffected by prejudices or passions from which no Englishman or Irishman has a right to suppose himself free.

The next passage is a trenchant condemnation of the "Union."

"There exists in Europe no country so completely at unity with itself as Great Britain. Fifty years of reform have done their work, and have removed the discontents, the divisions, the disaffection, and the conspiracies which marked the first quarter, or the first half of this century. Great Britain, if left to herself, could act with all the force, consistency, and energy given by unity of sentiment and community of interests. The distraction and the uncertainty of our political aims, the feebleness and inconsistency with which they are pursued, arise, in part at least, from the connection with Ireland. Neither Englishmen nor Irishmen are to blame for the fact that it is difficult for communities differing in historical associations and in political conceptions to keep step together in the path of progress. For other evils arising from the connection the blame must rest on English Statesmen. All the inherent vices of party government, all the weaknesses of the parliamentary system, all the evils arising from the perverse notion that reform ought always to be preceded by a period of lengthy and more than half factitious agitation met by equally factitious resistance, have been fostered and increased by the interaction of Irish and English politics. No one can believe that the inveterate habit of ruling one part of the United Kingdom on principles which no one would venture to apply to the government of any other part of it, can have produced anything but the most injurious effect on the stability of our Government and the character of our public men. The advocates of Home Rule find by far their strongest arguments for influencing English opinion, in the proofs which they produce that England, no less than Ireland, has suffered from a political arrangement under which legal union has failed to secure moral union. These arguments, whatever their strength, are, however, it must be noted, more available to a Nationalist than to an advocate of federalism."[56]

The words which I have italicised are an expression of opinion; but nothing can alter the damning statement of fact--"legal union has failed to secure moral union." Nevertheless, Mr. Dicey advocates the maintenance of this legal union as it stands.

"On the whole, then, it appears that, whatever changes or calamities the future may have in store, the maintenance of the Union is at this day the one sound policy for England to pursue. It is sound because it is expedient; it is sound because it is just."[57]

I shall not discuss the question of Home Rule with the eminent writers whose works I have cited. It is enough that they demonstrate the failure of the Union. So convinced was Mr. Lecky, in 1871, of its failure, that he suggested a readjustment of the relations of the two countries on a federal basis;[58] and Mr. Goldwin Smith, in 1868, contended that the Irish difficulty could only be settled by the establishment of Provincial Councils, and an occasional session of the Imperial Parliament in Dublin. Mr. Dicey clings to the existing Union while demonstrating its failure, because he has persuaded himself that the only alternative is separation.

Irishmen may be pardoned for acting on Mr. Dicey's facts, and disregarding his prophecies. The mass of Irishmen believe, with Grattan, that the ocean protests against separation as the sea protests against such a union as was attempted in 1800.[59]

FOOTNOTES:

[Footnote 26: Omissions here and elsewhere are merely for purposes of space. In some places the omitted parts would strengthen the Irish case; in no place would they weaken it.]

[Footnote 27: Lecky, Leaders of Public Opinion in Ireland, new edit. (1871), Introduction, pp. viii., xiv.]

[Footnote 28: Lecky, Leaders of Public Opinion in Ireland, new edit. (1871), Introduction, pp. xiv., xv.]

[Footnote 29: Lecky, History of England in the Eighteenth Century, vol. ii. pp. 59, 60.]

[Footnote 30: Leaders of Public Opinion, pp. 33, 34.]

[Footnote 31: Leaders of Public Opinion, pp. 120-123.]

[Footnote 32: Leaders of Public Opinion, pp. 125, 126.]

[Footnote 33: Leaders of Public Opinion, pp. 34-37.]

[Footnote 34: Leaders of Public Opinion, pp. 134-137.]

[Footnote 35: Leaders of Public Opinion, pp. 192-195.]

[Footnote 36: Leaders of Public Opinion, pp. 195, 196.]

[Footnote 37: Goldwin Smith, Three English Statesmen, p. 274.]

[Footnote 38: Irish History and Irish Character, pp. 13, 14.]

[Footnote 39: Ibid., p. 194.]

[Footnote 40: Ibid., p. 142.]

[Footnote 41: Irish History and Irish Character, p. 101.]

[Footnote 42: Irish History and Irish Character, pp. 139, 140.]

[Footnote 43: Sir George Cornewall Lewis, Irish Disturbances, p. 97.]

[Footnote 44: Irish History and Irish Character, pp. 153-157.]

[Footnote 45: Ibid., pp. 70, 71]

[Footnote 46: The Irish Question, Preface, pp. iii., iv.]

[Footnote 47: The Irish Question, pp. 3-5.]

[Footnote 48: Ibid., p. 6.]

[Footnote 49: Ibid., p. 7.]

[Footnote 50: The Irish Question, pp. 7-9.]

[Footnote 51: Irish Question, p. 10.]

[Footnote 52: The Irish Question, pp. 16-18.]

[Footnote 53: Dicey, England's Case against Home Rule, p. 128.]

[Footnote 54: Dicey, England's Case against Home Rule, pp. 72-74.]

[Footnote 55: Dicey, England's Case against Home Rule, pp. 92-94.--The foreigner is De Beaumont.]

[Footnote 56: Dicey, England's Case against Home Rule, pp. 151, 152.]

[Footnote 57: Ibid., p. 288.]

[Footnote 58: I hope I am not doing Mr. Lecky an injustice in this statement. I rely on the extract quoted from the Leaders of Public Opinion in Ireland, at p. 176 of this volume; but see Introduction, p. xix.]

[Footnote 59: Irish House of Commons, January 15th, 1800.]

IRELAND'S ALTERNATIVES.

Ireland is a component member of the most complex political body the world has yet known; any inquiry, then, into the fitness of any particular form of government for that country involves an investigation of the structures of various composite nations, or nations made up of numerous political communities more or less differing from each other. From the examination of the nature of the common tie, and the circumstances which caused it to be adopted or imposed on the component peoples, we cannot but derive instruction, and be furnished with materials which will enable us to take a wide view of the question of Home Rule, and assist us in judging between the various remedies proposed for the cure of Irish disorders.

The nature of the ties which bind, or have bound, the principal composite nations of the world together may be classified as--

1. Confederate unions. 2. Federal unions. 3. Imperial unions.

A confederate union may be defined to mean an alliance between the governments of independent States, which agree to appoint a common superior authority having power to make peace and war and to demand contributions of men and money from the confederate States. Such superior authority has no power of enforcing its decrees except through the medium of the governments of the constituent States; or, in other words, in case of disobedience, by armed force.

A federal union differs from a confederate union in the material fact that the common superior authority, instead of acting on the individual subjects of the constituent States through the medium of their respective governments, has a power, in respect of all matters within its jurisdiction, of enacting laws and issuing orders which are binding directly on the individual citizens.

The distinguishing characteristics of an imperial union are, that it consists of an aggregate of communities, one of which is dominant, and that the component communities have been brought into association, not by arrangement between themselves, but by colonization, cession, and by other means emanating from the resources or power of the dominant community.

The above-mentioned distinction between a Government having communities only for its subjects, and incapable of enforcing its orders by any other means than war, and a Government acting directly on individuals, must be constantly borne in mind, for in this lies the whole difference between a confederate and federal union; that is to say, between a confederacy which, in the case of the United States, lasted a few short years, and a federal union which, with the same people as subjects, has lasted nearly a century, and has stood the strain of the most terrible war of modern times.

The material features of the Constitution of the United States have been explained in a previous article.[61] All that is necessary to call to mind here is, that the Government of the United States exercises a power of taxation throughout the whole Union by means of its own officers, and enforces its decrees through the medium of its own Courts. A Supreme Court has also been established, which has power to adjudicate on the constitutionality of all laws passed by the Legislature of the United States, or of any State, and to decide on all international questions.

Switzerland was till 1848 an example of a confederate union or league of semi-independent States, which, unlike other confederacies, had existed with partial interruptions for centuries. This unusual vitality is attributed by Mill[62] to the circumstance that the confederate government felt its weakness so strongly that it hardly ever attempted to exercise any real authority. Its present government, finally settled in 1874, but based on fundamental laws passed in 1848, is a federal union formed on the pattern of the American Constitution. It consists of a federal assembly comprising two Chambers--the Upper Chamber composed of forty-four members chosen by the twenty-two cantons, two for each canton; the Lower consisting of 145 members chosen by direct election at the rate of one deputy for every 20,000 persons. The chief executive authority is deputed to a federal council consisting of seven members elected for three years by the federal assembly, and having at their head a president and vice-president, who are the first magistrates of the republic. There is also a federal tribunal, having similar functions to those of the supreme court of the United States of America, consisting of nine members elected for six years by the federal assembly.

The Empire of Germany is a federal union, differing from the United States and Switzerland in having an hereditary emperor as its head. It comprises twenty-six States, who have "formed an eternal union for the protection of the realm, and the care of the welfare of the German people."[63] The King of Prussia, under the title of German Emperor, represents the empire in all its relations to foreign nations, and has the power of making peace and war, but if the war be more than a defensive war he must have the assent of the Upper House. The legislative body of the empire consists of two Houses--the Upper, called the Bundesrath, representing the several component States in different proportions according to their relative importance; the lower, the Reichstag, elected by the voters in 397 electoral districts, which are distributed amongst the constituent States in unequal numbers, regard being had to the population and circumstances of each State.

The Austro-Hungarian Empire is a federal union, differing alike in its origin and construction from the federal unions above mentioned. In the beginning Austria and Hungary were independent countries--Austria a despotism, Hungary a constitutional monarchy, with ancient laws and customs dating back to the foundation of the kingdom in 895. In the sixteenth century the supreme power in both countries--that is to say, the despotic monarchy in Austria and the constitutional monarchy in Hungary--became vested in the same person; as might have been anticipated, the union was not a happy one. If we dip into Heeren's Political System of Europe at intervals selected almost at random, the following notices will be found in relation to Austria and Hungary:--Between 1671 and 1700 "political unity in the Austrian monarchy was to have been enforced especially in the principal country (Hungary), for this was regarded as the sole method of establishing power; the consequence was an almost perpetual revolutionary state of affairs."[64] Again, in the next chapter, commenting on the period between 1740 and 1786: "Hungary, in fact the chief, was treated like a conquered province; subjected to the most oppressive commercial restraints, it was regarded as a colony from which Austria exacted what she could for her own advantage. The injurious consequences of this internal discord are evident." Coming to modern times we find that oppression followed oppression with sickening monotony, and that at last the determination of Austria to stamp out the Constitution in Hungary gave rise to the insurrection of 1849, which Austria suppressed with the assistance of Russia, and as a penalty declared the Hungarian Constitution to be forfeited, and thereupon Hungary was incorporated with Austria, as Ireland was incorporated with Great Britain in 1800. Both events were the consequences of unsuccessful rebellions; but the junction which, in the case of Hungary, was enforced by the sword, was in Ireland more smoothly carried into effect by corruption. Hungary, sullen and discontented, waited for Austria's calamity as her opportunity, and it came after the battle of Sadowa. Austria had just emerged from a fearful conflict, and Count Beust[65] felt that unless some resolute effort was made to meet the views of the constitutional party in Hungary, the dismemberment of the empire must be the result. Now, what was the course he took? Was it a tightening of the bonds between Austria and Hungary? On the contrary, to maintain the unity of the empire he dissolved its union and restored to Hungary its ancient constitutional privileges. Austria and Hungary each had its own Parliament for local purposes. To manage the imperial concerns of peace and war, and the foreign relations, a controlling body, called the Delegations, was established, consisting of 120 members, of whom half represent and are chosen by the Legislature of Austria, and the other half by that of Hungary; the Upper House of each country returning twenty members, and the Lower House forty.[66] Ordinarily the delegates sit and vote in two Chambers, but if they disagree the two branches must meet together and give their final vote without debate, which is binding on the whole empire.[67]

The question arises, What is the magnetic influence which induces communities of men to combine together in federal unions? Undoubtedly it is the feeling of nationality; and what is nationality? Mr. Mill says,[68] "a portion of mankind may be said to constitute a nationality if they are united among themselves by common sympathies which do not exist between them and any others; which make them co-operate with each other more willingly than other people; desire to be under the same government, and desire that it should be a government by themselves or a portion of themselves exclusively." He then proceeds to state that the feeling of nationality may have been generated by various causes. Sometimes it is the identity of race and descent; community of language and community of religion greatly contribute to it; geographical limits are one of its causes; but the strongest of all is identity of political antecedents: the possession of a national history and consequent community of recollections--collective pride and humiliation, pleasure and regret--connected with the same incidents in the past.

The only point to be noted further in reference to the foregoing federal unions, is that the same feeling of nationality which, in the United States, Switzerland, and the German Empire, produced a closer legal bond of union, in the case of

Austria-Hungary operated to dissolve the amalgamation formed in 1849 of the two States, and to produce a federal union of States in place of a single State.

One conclusion seems to follow irresistibly from any review of the construction of the various States above described: that the stability of a nation bears no relation whatever to the legal compactness or homogeneity of its component parts. Russia and France, the most compact political societies in Europe, do not, to say the least, rest on a firmer basis than Germany and Switzerland, the inhabitants of which are subjected to the obligations of a double nationality. Above all, no European nation, except Great Britain, can for a moment bear comparison with the United States in respect of the devotion of its people to their Constitution.

An imperial union, though resembling somewhat in outward form a federal union, differs altogether from it both in principle and origin. Its essential characteristic is that one community is absolutely dominant while all the others are subordinate. In the case of a federal union independent States have agreed to resign a portion of their powers to a central Government for the sake of securing the common safety. In an imperial union the dominant or imperial State delegates to each constituent member of the union such a portion of local government as the dominant State considers the subordinate member entitled to, consistently with the integrity of the empire. The British Empire furnishes the best example of an imperial union now existing in the world. Her Majesty, as common head, is the one link which binds the empire together and connects with each other every constituent member. The Indian Empire and certain military dependencies require no further notice in these pages; but a summary of our various forms of colonial government is required to complete our knowledge of the forms of Home Rule possibly applicable to Ireland.

The colonies, in relation to their forms of government, may be classified as follows:--

I. Crown colonies, in which laws may be made by the Governor alone, or with the concurrence of a Council nominated by the Crown.

2. Colonies possessing representative institutions, but not responsible government, in which the Crown has only a veto on legislation, but the Home Government retains the control of the executive.

3. Colonies possessing representative institutions and responsible government, in which the Crown has only a veto on legislation, and the Home Government has no control over any public officer except the Governor.

The British Colonial Governments thus present an absolute gradation of rule; beginning with absolute despotism and ending with almost absolute legal independence, except in so far as a veto on legislation and the presence of a Governor named by the Crown mark the dependence of the colony on the mother country.

It is to be remembered, moreover, that the colonies which have received this complete local freedom are the great colonies of the earth--nations themselves possessing territories as large or larger than any European State--namely, Canada, the Cape, New South Wales, Victoria, Queensland, South Australia, New Zealand, Tasmania. And this change from dependence to freedom has been effected with the good-will both of the mother country and the colony, and without it being imputed to the colonists, when desiring a larger measure of self-government, that they were separatists, anarchists, or revolutionists.

Such are the general principles of colonial government, but one colony requires special mention, from the circumstance of its Constitution having been put forward as a model for Ireland; this is the Dominion of Canada. The Government of Canada is, in effect, a subordinate federal union; that is to say, it possesses a central Legislature, having the largest possible powers of local self-government consistent with the supremacy of the empire, with seven inferior provincial Governments, exercising powers greater than those of an English county, but not so great as those of an American State. The advantage of such a form of government is that, without weakening the supremacy of the empire or of the central local power, it admits of considerable diversities being made in the details of provincial government, where local peculiarities and antecedents render it undesirable to make a more complete assimilation of the Governments of the various provinces.

Materials have now been collected which will enable the reader to judge of the expediency or inexpediency of the course taken by Mr. Gladstone's Government in dealing with Ireland. Three alternatives were open to them--

1. To let matters alone. 2. To pass a Coercion Bill. 3. To change the government of Ireland, and at the same time to pass a Land Bill.

The two last measures are combined under the head of one alternative, as it will be shown in the sequel that no effective Land Bill can be passed without granting Home Rule in Ireland.

Now, the short answer to the first alternative is, that no party in the State-- Conservative, Whig, Radical, Unionist, Home Ruler, Parnellite--thought it possible to leave things alone. That something must be done was universally admitted.

The second alternative has found favour with the present Government, and certainly is a better example of the triumph of hope over experience, than even the proverbial second marriage.

Eighty-six years have elapsed since the Union. During the first thirty-two years only eleven years, and during the last fifty-four years only two years have been free from special repressive legislation; yet the agitation for repeal of the Union, and general discontent, are more violent in 1887 than in any one of the eighty-six previous years. In the name of common-sense, is there any reason for supposing that the Coercion Bill of 1887 will have a better or more enduring effect than its numerous predecessors? The prim?facie case is at all events in favour of the contention that, when so many trials of a certain remedy have failed, it would be better not to try the same remedy again, but to have recourse to some other medicine. What, then, was the position of Mr. Gladstone's Government at the close of the election of 1885? What were the considerations presented to them as supreme supervisors and guardians of the British Empire? They found that vast colonial empire tranquil and loyal beyond previous expectation--the greater colonies satisfied with their existing position; the lesser expecting that as they grew up to manhood they would be treated as men, and emancipated from childish restraints. The Channel Islands and the Isle of Man were contented with their sturdy dependent independence, loyal to the backbone. One member only stood aloof, sulky and dissatisfied, and though in law integrally united with the dominant community, practically was dissociated from it by forming within Parliament (the controlling body of the whole) a separate section, of which the whole aim was to fetter the action of the entire supreme body in order to bring to an external severance the practical disunion which existed between that member and Great Britain. This member--Ireland--as compared with other parts of the empire, was small and insignificant; measured against Great Britain, its population was five millions to thirty-one millions, and its estimated capital was only one twenty-fourth part of the capital of the United Kingdom. Measured against Australia, its trade with Great Britain was almost insignificant. Its importance arose from the force of public opinion in Great Britain, which deemed England pledged to protect the party in Ireland which desired the Union to be maintained, and from the power of obstructing English legislation through the medium of the Irish contingent, willing and ready on every occasion to intervene in English debates. The first step to be taken obviously was to find out what the great majority of Irish members wanted. The answer was, that they would be contented to quit the British Parliament on having a Parliament established on College Green, with full powers of local government, and that they would accept on behalf of their country a certain fixed annual sum to be paid to the Imperial Exchequer, on condition that such sum should not be increased without the consent of the Irish representatives. Here there were two great points gained without any sacrifice of principle. Ireland could not be said to be taxed without representation when her representatives agreed to a certain fixed sum to be paid till altered with their consent; while at the same time all risk of obstruction to English legislation by Irish means was removed by the proposal that the Irish representatives should exercise local powers in Dublin instead of imperial powers at Westminster.

On the basis of the above arrangement the Bill of Mr. Gladstone was founded. Absolute local autonomy was conferred on Ireland; the assent of the Irish members to quit the Imperial Parliament was accepted; and the Bill provided that after a certain day the representative Irish peers should cease to sit in the House of Lords, and the Irish members vacate their places in the House of Commons. Provisions were then made for the absorption in the Irish Legislative Body of both the Irish representative peers and Irish members.

The legislative supremacy of the British Parliament was maintained by an express provision excepting from any interference on the part of Irish Legislature all imperial powers, and declaring any enactment void which infringed that provision; further, an enactment was inserted for the purpose of securing to the English Legislature in the last resource the absolute power to make any law for the government of Ireland, and therefore to repeal, or suspend, the Irish Constitution.

Technically these reservations of supremacy to the English Legislature were unnecessary, as it is an axiom of constitutional law that a sovereign Legislature, such as the Queen and two Houses of Parliament in England, cannot bind their successors, and consequently can repeal or alter any law, however fundamental, and annul any restrictions on alteration, however strongly expressed. Practically they were never likely to be called into operation, as it is the custom of Parliament to adhere, under all but the most extraordinary and unforeseen circumstances, to any compact made by Act of Parliament between itself and any subordinate legislative body. The Irish Legislature was subjected to the same controlling power which has for centuries been applied to prevent any excess of jurisdiction in our Colonial Legislatures, by a direction that an appeal as to the constitutionality of any laws which they might pass should lie to the Judicial Committee of the Privy Council. This supremacy of the imperial judicial power over the action of the Colonial Legislatures was a system which the founders of the American Constitution copied in the establishment of their supreme Court, and thereby secured for that legislative system a stability which has defied the assaults of faction and the strain of civil war.

The Executive Government of Ireland was continued in her Majesty, and was to be carried on by the Lord Lieutenant on her behalf, by the aid of such officers and such Council as her Majesty might from time to time see fit. The initiative power of recommending taxation was also vested in the Queen, and delegated to the Lord Lieutenant. These clauses are co-ordinate and correlative with the clause conferring complete local powers on the Irish Legislature, while it preserves all imperial powers to the Imperial Legislature. The Governor is an imperial officer, and will be bound to watch over imperial interests with a jealous scrutiny, and to veto any Bill which may be injurious to those interests. On the other hand, as respects all local matters, he will act on and be guided by the advice of the Irish Executive Council. The system is self-acting. The Governor, for local purposes, must have a Council which is in harmony with the Legislative Body. If the Governor and a Council, supported by the Legislative Body, do not agree, the Governor must give way, unless he can, by dismissing his Council, and dissolving the Legislative Body, obtain both a Council and a Legislative Body which will support his views. As respects imperial questions, the case is different; here the last word rests with the mother country, and in the last resort a determination of the Executive Council, backed by the Legislative Body, to resist imperial rights, must be deemed an act of rebellion on the part of the Irish people, and be dealt with accordingly.

In acceding to the claims of the National Party for Home Rule in Ireland another question had to be considered: the demands of the English garrison, as it is called--or, in plain words, of the class of Irish landlords--for protection. They urged that to grant Home Rule in Ireland would be to hand them over to their enemies, their tenants, and to lead to an immediate, or to all events a proximate, confiscation of their properties. Without admitting the truth of these apprehensions to the full extent, or indeed to any great extent, it was undoubtedly felt by the framers of the Home Rule Bill that a moral obligation rested on the Imperial Government to remove, if possible, "the fearful exasperations attending the agrarian relations in Ireland," rather than leave a question so fraught with danger, so involved in difficulty, to be determined by the Irish Government on its first entry on official existence. Hence the Land Bill, the scheme of which was to frame a system under which the tenants, by being made owners of the soil, should become interested as a class in the maintenance of social order, while the landlords should be enabled to rid themselves on fair terms of their estates, in cases where, from apprehension of impending changes, or for pecuniary reasons, they were desirous of relieving themselves from the responsibilities of ownership. Of the land scheme brought into Parliament in 1886, it need only here be said that it proposed to lend the Irish Government 3 per cent. stock at 3-1/8 per cent. interest, the Irish Government undertaking to purchase, from any Irish landlord desirous of selling, his estate at (as a general rule) twenty years' purchase on the net rental. The money thus disbursed by the Irish Government was repaid to them by an annuity, payable by the tenant for forty-nine years, of 4 per cent. on a capital sum equal to twenty times the gross rental; the result being that, were the Bill passed into law, the tenant would become immediate owner of the land, subject to the payment of an annuity considerably less than the previous rent-- that the Irish Government would make a considerable profit on the transaction, inasmuch as it would receive from the tenant interest calculated on the basis of the gross rental, whilst it would pay to the English Government interest calculated on the basis of the net rental--and that the English Government would sustain no loss if the interest were duly received by them.

The effect of such a plan appears almost magical: Ireland is transformed at one stroke from a nation of landlords into a nation of peasant proprietors-- apparently without loss to any one, and with gain to everybody concerned, except the British Government, who neither gain nor lose in the matter. The practicability, however, of such a scheme depends altogether on the security against loss afforded to the British tax-payer, for he is industrious and heavily burdened, and cannot be expected to assent to any plan which will land him in any appreciable loss. Here it is that the plan of Mr. Gladstone's Land Bill differs from all other previous plans. Act after Act has been passed enabling the tenant to borrow money from the British Government on the security of the holding, for the purpose of enabling him to purchase the fee-simple. In such transactions the British Government becomes the mortgagee, and can only recover its money, if default is made in payment, by ejecting the tenant and becoming the landlord. In proportion, then, as any existing purchase Act succeeds, in the same proportion the risk of the British taxpayer increases. He is ever placed in the most invidious of all lights; instead of posing as the generous benefactor who holds forth his hand to rescue the landlord and tenant from an intolerable position, he stands forward either as the grasping mortgagee or as the still more hated landlord, who, having deprived the tenant of his holding, is seeking to introduce another man into property which really belongs to the ejected tenant. Such a position may be endurable when the number of purchasing tenants is small, but at once breaks down if agrarian reform in Ireland is to be extended so far as to make any appreciable difference in the relations of landlord and tenant; still more, if it become general. Now, what is the remedy of such a state of things? Surely to interpose the Irish Government between the Irish debtor and his English creditor, and to provide that the Irish revenues in bulk, not the individual holdings of each tenant, shall be the security for the English creditor. This was the scheme embodied in the Land Act of 1886. The punctual payment of all money due from the Government of Ireland to the Government of Great Britain was to have been secured by the continuance in the hands of the British Government of the Excise and Customs duties, and by the appointment of an Imperial Receiver-General, assisted by subordinate officers, and protected by an Imperial Court. This officer would have received not only all the imperial taxes, but also the local taxes; and it would have been his duty to satisfy the claims of the British Government before he allowed any sum to pass into the Irish Exchequer. In effect, the British Government, in relation to the levying of imperial taxes, would have stood in the same relation to Ireland as Congress does to the United States in respect to the levying of federal taxes. The fiscal unity of Great Britain and Ireland would have been in this way secured, and the British Government protected against any loss of interest for the large sums to be expended in carrying into effect in Ireland any agrarian reform worthy of the name.

The Irish Bills of 1886, as above represented, had at least three recommendations:

1. They created a state of things in Ireland under which it was possible to make a complete agrarian reform without exposing the English Exchequer to any appreciable risk.

2. They enabled the Irish to govern themselves as respects local matters, while preserving intact the supremacy of the British Parliament and the integrity of the Empire.

3. They enabled the British Parliament to govern the British Empire without any obstructive Irish interference.

To the first of these propositions no attempt at an answer has been made. The Land Bill was never considered on its merits; indeed, was never practically discussed, but was at once swept into oblivion by the wave which overwhelmed the Home Rule Bill.

The contention against the second proposition was concerned in proving that the supremacy of the British Parliament was not maintained: the practical answer to this objection has been given above. Pushed to its utmost, it could only amount to proof that an amendment ought to have been introduced in Committee, declaring, in words better selected than those introduced for that purpose in the Bill, that nothing in the Act should affect the supremacy of the British Parliament. In short, the whole discussion here necessarily resolved itself into a mere verbal squabble as to the construction of a clause in a Bill not yet in Committee, and had no bottom or substance.

It was also urged that the concession of self-government to Ireland was but another mode of handing over the Loyalist party--or, as it is sometimes called, the English garrison--to the tender mercies of the Parnellites. The reply to this would seem to be, that as respects property the Land Bill effectually prevented any interference of the Irish Parliament with the land; nay, more, enabled any Irishman desirous of turning his land into money to do so on the most advantageous terms that ever had been--and with a falling market it may be confidently prophesied ever can be--offered to the Irish landlord; while as respect life and liberty, were it possible that they should be endangered, it was the duty of the imperial officer, the Lord Lieutenant, to take means for the preservation of peace and good order; and behind him, to enforce his behests, stand the strong battalions who, to our sorrow be it spoken, have so often been called upon to put down disturbance and anarchy in Ireland.

Competing plans have been put forward, with more or less detail, for governing Ireland. The suggestion that Ireland should be governed as a Crown colony need only be mentioned to be rejected. It means in effect, that Ireland should sink from the rank of an equal or independent member of the British Empire to the grade of the most dependent of her colonies, and should be governed despotically by English officials, without representation in the English Parliament or any machinery of local self-government. Another proposal has been to give four provincial Governments to Ireland, limiting their powers to local rating, education, and legislation in respect of matters which form the subjects of private Bill legislation at present; in fact, to place them somewhat on the footing of the provinces of Canada, while reserving to the English Parliament the powers vested in the Dominion of Canada. Such a scheme would seem adapted to whet the appetite of the Irish for nationality, without supplying them with any portion of the real article. It would supply no basis on which a system of agrarian reform could be founded, as it would be impossible to leave the determination of a local question, which is a unit in its dangers and its difficulties, to four different Legislatures; above all, the hinge on which the question turns--the sufficiency of the security for the British taxpayer--could not be afforded by provincial resources. Indeed, no alternative for the Land Bill of 1886 has been suggested which does not err in one of the following points: either it pledges English credit on insufficient security, or it requires the landowners to accept Irish debentures or some form of Irish paper money at par; in other words, it makes English taxes a fund for relieving Irish landlords, or else it compels the Irish landowner, if he sells at all, to sell at an inadequate price. Before parting with Canada, it may be worth while noticing that another, and more feasible, alternative is to imitate more closely the Canadian Constitution, and to vest the central or Dominion powers in a central

Legislature in Dublin, parcelling out the provincial powers, as they have been called, amongst several provincial Legislatures. This scheme might be made available as a means of protecting Ulster from the supposed danger of undue interference from the Central Government, and for making, possibly, other diversities in the local administration of various parts of Ireland in order to meet special local exigencies.

A leading writer among the dissentient Liberals has intimated that one of two forms of representative colonial government might be imposed on Ireland--either the form in which the executive is conducted by colonial officials, or the form of the great irresponsible colonies. The first of these forms is open to the objection, that it perpetuates those struggles between English executive measures and Irish opinion which has made Ireland for centuries ungovernable, and led to the establishment of the union and destruction of Irish independence in 1800; the second proposal would destroy the fiscal unity of the empire--leave the agrarian feud unextinguished, and aggravate the objections which have been urged against the Home Rule Bill of 1886. A question still remains, in relation to the form of the Home Rule Bill of 1886, which would not have deserved attention but for the prominence given to it in some of the discussions upon the subject. The Bill of 1886 provides "that the Legislature may make laws for the peace, order, and good government of Ireland," but subjects their power to numerous exceptions and restrictions. The Act establishing the Dominion of Canada enumerates various matters in respect of which the Legislature of Canada is to have exclusive power, but prefaces the enumeration with a clause "that the Dominion Legislature may make laws for the peace, order, and good government of Canada in relation to all matters not within the jurisdiction of the provincial Legislatures, although such matters may not be specially mentioned." In effect, therefore, the difference between the Irish Bill and the Canadian Act is one of expression and not of substance, and, although the Bill is more accurate in its form, it would scarcely be worth while to insist on legislating by exception instead of by enumeration if, by the substitution of the latter form for the former, any material opposition would be conciliated.

What, then, are the conclusions intended to be drawn from the foregoing premises?

1. That coercion is played out, and can no longer be regarded as a remedy for

the evils of Irish misrule.

2. That some alternative must be found, and that the only alternative within the range of practical politics is some form of Home Rule.

3. That there is no reason for thinking that the grant of Home Rule to Ireland--a member only, and not one of the most important members, of the British Empire--will in any way dismember, or even in the slightest degree risk the dismemberment of the Empire.

4. That Home Rule presupposes and admits the supremacy of the British Parliament.

5. That theory is in favour of Home Rule, as the nationality of Ireland is distinct, and justifies a desire for local independence; while the establishment of Home Rule is a necessary condition to the effectual removal of agrarian disturbances in Ireland.

6. That precedent is in favour of granting Home Rule to Ireland--e.g.the success of the new Constitution in Austria-Hungary, and the happy effects resulting from the establishment of the Dominion of Canada.

7. That the particular form of Home Rule granted is comparatively immaterial.

8. That the Home Rule Bill of 1886 may readily be amended in such a manner as to satisfy all real and unpartisan objectors.

9. That the Land Bill of 1886 is the best that has ever been devised, having regard to the advantages offered to the new Irish Government, the landlord, and the tenant.

FOOTNOTES:

[Footnote 60: Reprinted by permission, with certain omissions, from the Contemporary Review, August, 1887.]

[Footnote 61: "Home Rule and Imperial Unity:" Contemporary Review,

March, 1887.]

[Footnote 62: Mill on Representative Government, p. 310.]

[Footnote 63: See Statesman's Year-Book: Switzerland and Germany.]

[Footnote 64: Heeren's Political System of Europe, p. 152.]

[Footnote 65: Memoirs of Count Beust, vol. i., Introduction, p. xliii.]

[Footnote 66: Statesman's Year-Book.]

[Footnote 67: The Emperor of Austria is the head of the empire, with the title of King in Hungary. Austria-Hungary is treated as a federal, not as an imperial union, on the ground that Austria was never rightfully a dominant community over Hungary.]

[Footnote 68: Representative Government, p. 295.]

THE PAST AND FUTURE OF THE IRISH QUESTION[69]

BY JAMES BRYCE, M.P.

For half a century or more no question of English domestic politics has excited so much interest outside England as that question of resettling her relations with Ireland, which was fought over in the last Parliament, and still confronts the Parliament that has lately been elected. Apart from its dramatic interest, apart from its influence on the fortune of parties, and its effect on the imperial position of Great Britain, it involves so many large principles of statesmanship, and raises so many delicate points of constitutional law, as to deserve the study of philosophical thinkers no less than of practical politicians in every free country.

The circumstances which led to the introduction of the Government of Ireland Bill, in April, 1886, are familiar to Americans as well as Englishmen. Ever since the crowns and parliaments of Great Britain and Ireland were united, in A.D. 1800, there has been in Ireland a party which protested against that union as fraudulently obtained and inexpedient in itself. For many years this party, led by Daniel O'Connell, maintained an agitation for Repeal. After his death a more extreme section, which sought the complete independence of Ireland, raised the insurrection of 1848, and subsequently, under the guidance of other hands, formed the Fenian conspiracy, whose projected insurrection was nipped in the bud in 1867, though the conspiracy continued to menace the Government and the tranquillity of the island. In 1872 the Home Rule party was formed, demanding, not the Repeal of the Union, but the creation of an Irish Legislature, and the agitation, conducted in Parliament in a more systematic and persistent way than heretofore, took also a legitimate constitutional form. To this demand English and Scotch opinion was at first almost unanimously opposed. At the General Election of 1880, which, however, turned mainly on the foreign policy of Lord Beaconsfield's Government, not more than three or four members were returned by constituencies in Great Britain who professed to consider Home Rule as even an open question. All through the Parliament, which sat from 1880 till 1885, the Nationalist party, led by Mr. Parnell, and including at first less than half, ultimately about half, of the Irish members, was in constant and generally bitter opposition to the Government of Mr. Gladstone. But during these five years a steady, although silent and often unconscious, process of change was passing in the minds of English and Scotch members, especially Liberal members, due to their growing sense of the mistakes which Parliament committed in handling Irish questions, and of the hopelessness of the efforts which the Executive was making to pacify the country on the old methods. The adoption of a Home Rule policy by one of the great English parties was, therefore, not so sudden a change as it seemed. The process had been going on for years, though in its earlier stages it was so gradual and so unwelcome as to be faintly felt and reluctantly admitted by the minds that were undergoing it. In the spring of 1886 the question could be no longer evaded or postponed. It was necessary to choose between one of two courses; the refusal of the demand for self-government, coupled with the introduction of a severe Coercion Bill, or the concession of it by the introduction of a Home Rule Bill. There were some few who suggested, as a third course, the granting of a limited measure of local institutions, such as county boards; but most people felt, as did Mr. Gladstone's Ministry, that this plan would have had most of the dangers and few of the advantages of either of the two others.

How the Government of Ireland Bill was brought into the House of Commons on April 8th, amid circumstances of curiosity and excitement unparalleled since 1832; how, after debates of almost unprecedented length, it was defeated in June, by a majority of thirty; how the policy it embodied was brought before the country at the General Election, and failed to win approval--all this is too well known to need recapitulation here. But the causes of the disaster have not been well understood, for it is only now--now, when the smoke of the battle has cleared away from the field--that these causes have begun to stand revealed in their true proportions.

Besides some circumstances attending the production of the Bill, to which I shall refer presently, and which told heavily against it, there were three feelings which worked upon men's minds, disposing them to reject it.

The first of these was dislike and fear of the Irish Nationalist members. In the previous House of Commons this party had been uniformly and bitterly hostile to the Liberal Government. Measures intended for the good of Ireland, like the Land Act of 1881, had been ungraciously received, treated as concessions extorted, for which no thanks were due--inadequate concessions, which must be made the starting-point for fresh demands. Obstruction had been freely practised to defeat not only bills restraining the liberty of the subject in Ireland, but many other measures. Some few members of the Irish party had systematically sought to delay all English and Scotch legislation, and, in fact, to bring the work of Parliament to a dead stop. Much violent language had been used, even where the provocation was slight. The outbreaks of crime which had repeatedly occurred in Ireland had been, not, indeed, defended, but so often passed over in silence by Nationalist speakers, that English opinion was inclined to hold them practically responsible for disorders which, so it was thought, they had neither wished nor tried to prevent. (I am, of course, expressing no opinion as to the justice of this view, nor as to the excuses to be made for the Parliamentary tactics of the Irish party, but merely stating how their conduct struck many Englishmen.) There could be no doubt as to the hostility which they, still less as to that which their fellow-countrymen in the United States, had expressed toward England, for they had openly wished success to Russia while war seemed impending with her, and the so-called Mahdi of the Soudan was vociferously cheered at many a Nationalist meeting. At the Election of 1885 they had done their utmost to defeat Liberal candidates in every English and Scotch constituency where there existed a body of Irish voters, and had thrown some twenty seats or more into the hands of the Tories. Now, to many Englishmen, the proposal to create an Irish Parliament seemed nothing more or less than a proposal to hand over to these Irish members the government of Ireland, with all the opportunities thence arising to oppress the opposite party in Ireland and to worry England herself. It was all very well to urge that the tactics which the Nationalists had pursued when their object was to extort Home Rule would be dropped, because superfluous, when Home Rule had been granted; or to point out that an Irish Parliament would contain different men from those who had been sent to Westminster as Mr. Parnell's nominees. Neither of these arguments could overcome the suspicious antipathy which many Englishmen felt, nor dissolve the association in their minds between the Nationalist leaders and the forces of disorder. The Parnellites (thus they reasoned) are bad men; what they seek is therefore likely to be bad, and whether bad in itself or not, they will make a bad use of it. In such reasonings there was more of sentiment and prejudice than of reason, but sentiment and prejudice are proverbially harder than arguments to expel from minds where they have made a lodgment.

The internal condition of Ireland supplied more substantial grounds for alarm. As everybody knows, she is not, either in religion or in blood, or in feelings and ideas, a homogeneous country. Three-fourths of the people are Roman Catholics, one-fourth Protestants, and this Protestant fourth subdivided into bodies not fond of one another, who have little community of sentiment. Besides the Scottish colony in Ulster, many English families have settled here and there through the country. They have been regarded as intruders by the aboriginal Celtic population, and many of them, although hundreds of years may have passed since they came, still look on themselves as rather English than Irish. The last fifty years, whose wonderful changes have in most parts of the world tended to unite and weld into one compact body the inhabitants of each part of the earth's surface, connecting them by the ties of commerce, and of a far easier and swifter intercourse than was formerly possible, have in Ireland worked in the opposite direction. It has become more and more the habit of the richer class in Ireland to go to England for its enjoyment, and to feel itself socially rather English than Irish. Thus the chasm between the immigrants and the aborigines has grown deeper. The upper class has not that Irish patriotism which it showed in the days of the National Irish Parliament (1782-1800), and while there is thus less of a common national feeling to draw rich and poor together, the strife of landlords and tenants has continued, irritating the minds of both parties, and gathering them into two hostile camps. As everybody knows, the Nationalist agitation has been intimately associated with the Land agitation--has, in fact, found a strong motive-force in the desire of the tenants to have their rents reduced, and themselves secured against eviction. Now, many people in England assumed that an Irish Parliament would be under the control of the tenants and the humbler class generally, and would therefore be hostile to the landlords. They went farther, and made the much bolder assumption that as such a Parliament would be chosen by electors, most of whom were Roman Catholics, it would be under the control of the Catholic priesthood, and hostile to Protestants. Thus they supposed that the grant of self-government to Ireland would mean the abandonment of the upper and wealthier class, the landlords and the Protestants, to the tender mercies of their enemies. Such abandonment, it was proclaimed on a thousand platforms, would be disgraceful in itself, dishonouring to England, a betrayal of the very men who had stood by her in the past, and were prepared to stand by her in the future, if only she would stand by them. It was, of course, replied by the defenders of the Home Rule Bill, that what the so-called English party in Ireland really stood by was their own ascendency over the Irish masses--an oppressive ascendency, which had caused most of the disorders of the country. As to religion, there were many Protestants besides Mr. Parnell himself among the Nationalist leaders. There was no ill-feeling (except in Ulster) between Protestants and Roman Catholics in Ireland. There was no reason to expect that either the Catholic hierarchy or the priesthood generally would be supreme in an Irish Parliament, and much reason to expect the contrary. As regards Ulster, where, no doubt, there were special difficulties, due to the bitter antagonism of the Orangemen (not of the Protestants generally) and Catholics, Mr. Gladstone had undertaken to consider any special provisions which could be suggested as proper to meet those difficulties. These replies, however, made little impression. They were pronounced, and pronounced all the more confidently the more ignorant of Ireland the speaker was, to be too hypothetical. To many Englishmen the case seemed to be one of two hostile factions contending in Ireland for the last sixty years, and that the gift of self-government might enable one of them to tyrannize over the other. True, that party was the majority, and, according to the principles of democratic government, therefore entitled to prevail. But it is one thing to admit a principle and another to consent to its application. The minority had the sympathy of the upper classes in England, because the minority contained the landlords. It had the sympathy of a part of the middle class, because it contained the Protestants. And of those Englishmen who were impartial as between the Irish factions, there were some who held that England must in any case remain responsible for the internal peace and the just government of Ireland, and could not grant powers whose possession might tempt the one party to injustice, and the other to resist injustice by violence.

There was another anticipation, another forecast of evils to follow, which told most of all upon English opinion. This was the notion that Home Rule was only a stage in the road to the complete separation of the two islands. The argument was conceived as follows: "The motive passions of the Irish agitation have all along been hatred toward England and a desire to make Ireland a nation, holding her independent place among the nations of the world. This design was proclaimed by the Young Irelanders of 1848 and by the Fenian rebels of 1866; it has been avowed, in intervals of candour, by the present Nationalists themselves. The grant of an Irish Parliament will stimulate rather than appease this thirst for separate national existence. The nearer complete independence seems, the more will it be desired. Hatred to England will still be an active force, because the amount of control which England retains will irritate Irish pride, as well as limit Irish action; while all the misfortunes which may befall the new Irish Government will be blamed, not on its own imprudence, but on the English connection. And as the motives for seeking separation will remain, so the prospect of obtaining it will seem better. Agitation will have a better vantage-ground in an Irish Parliament than it formerly had among the Irish members of a British Legislature; and if actual resistance to the Queen's authority should be attempted, it will be attempted under conditions more favourable than the present, because the rebels will have in their hands the machinery of Irish Government, large financial resources, and a prima facietitle to represent the will of the Irish people. As against a rebellious party in Ireland, England has now two advantages--an advantage of theory, an advantage of fact. The advantage of theory is that she does not admit Ireland to be a distinct nation, but maintains that in the United Kingdom there is but one nation, whereof some inhabit Great Britain and some Ireland. The advantage of fact is that, through her control of the constabulary, the magistrates, the courts of justice, and, in fine, the whole administrative system of Ireland, she can easily quell insurrectionary movements. By creating an Irish Parliament and Government she would strip herself of both these advantages."

I need hardly say that I do not admit the fairness of this statement of the case, because some of the premises are untrue, and because it misrepresents the nature of the Irish Government which Mr. Gladstone's Bill would have created. But I am trying to state the case as it was sedulously and skilfully presented to Englishmen. And it told all the more upon English waverers, because the considerations above mentioned seemed, if well founded, to destroy and cut away the chief ground on which Home Rule had been advocated, viz. that it would relieve England from the constant pressure of Irish discontent and agitation, and bring about a time of tranquillity, permitting good feeling to grow up between the peoples. If Home Rule was, after all, to be nothing more than a half-way house to independence, an Irish Parliament only a means of extorting a more complete emancipation from imperial control, was it not much better to keep things as they were, and go on enduring evils, the worst of which were known already? Hence the advocates of the Bill denied not the weight of the argument, but its applicability. Separation, they urged, is impossible, for it is contrary to the nature of things, which indicates that the two islands must go together. It is not desired by the Irish people, for it would injure them far more than it could possibly injure England, since Ireland finds in England the only market for her produce, the only source whence capital flows to her. A small revolutionary party has, no doubt, conspired to obtain it. But the only sympathy they received was due to the fact that the legitimate demand of Ireland for a recognition of her national feeling and for the management of her own local affairs was contemptuously ignored by England. The concession of that demand will banish the notion even from those minds which now entertain it, whereas its continued refusal may perpetuate that alienation of feeling which is at the bottom of all the mischief, the one force that makes for separation.

It is no part of my present purpose to examine these arguments and counter arguments, but only to show what were the grounds on which a majority of the English voters refused to pronounce in favour of the Home Rule Bill. The reader will have observed that the issues raised were not only numerous, but full of difficulty. They were issues of fact, involving a knowledge both of the past history of Ireland and of her present state. They were also issues of inference, for even supposing the broad facts to be ascertained, these facts were susceptible of different interpretations, and men might, and did, honestly draw opposite conclusions from them. A more obscure and complicated problem, or rather group of problems, has seldom been presented to a nation for its decision. But the nation did not possess the requisite knowledge. Closely connected as Ireland seems to be with England, long as the Irish question has been a main trouble in English politics, the English and Scottish people know amazingly little about Ireland. Even in the upper class, you meet with comparatively few persons who have set foot on Irish soil, and, of course, far fewer who have ever examined the condition of the island and the sources of her discontent. Irish history, which is, no doubt, dismal reading, is a blank page to the English. In January, 1886, one found scarce any politicians who had ever heard of the Irish Parliament of 1782. And in that year, 1886, an Englishman anxious to discover the real state of the country did not know where to go for information. What appeared in the English newspapers, or, rather, in the one English newspaper which keeps a standing "own correspondent" in Dublin, was (as it still is) a grossly and almost avowedly partisan report, in which opinions are skilfully mixed with so-called facts, selected, consciously or unconsciously, to support the writer's view. The Nationalist press is, of course, not less strongly partisan on its own side, so that not merely an average Englishman, but even the editor of an English newspaper, who desires to ascertain the true state of matters and place it before his English readers, has had, until within the last few months, when events in Ireland began to be fully reported in Great Britain, no better means at his disposal for understanding Ireland than for understanding Bulgaria. I do not dwell upon this ignorance as an argument for Home Rule, though, of course, it is often so used. I merely wish to explain the bewilderment in which Englishmen found themselves when required to settle by their votes a question of immense difficulty. Many, on both sides, simply followed their party banners. Tories voted for Lord Salisbury; thorough-going admirers of Mr. Gladstone voted for Mr. Gladstone. But there was on the Liberal side a great mass who were utterly perplexed by the position. Contradictory statements of fact, as well as contradictory arguments, were flung at their heads in distracting profusion. They felt themselves unable to determine what was true and who was right. But one thing seemed clear to them. The policy of Home Rule was a new policy. They had been accustomed to censure and oppose it. Only nine months before, the Irish Nationalists had emphasized their hostility to the Liberal party by doing their utmost to defeat Liberal candidates in English constituencies. Hence, when it was proclaimed that Home Rule was the true remedy which the Liberal party must accept, they were startled and discomposed.

Now, the English are not a nimble-minded people. They cannot, to use a familiar metaphor, turn round in their own length. Their momentum is such as to carry them on for some distance in the direction wherein they have been moving, even after the order to stop has been given. They need time to appreciate, digest, and comprehend a new proposition. Timid they are not, nor, perhaps, exceptionally cautious, but they do not like to be hurried, and insist on looking at a proposition for a good while before they come to a decision regarding it. It is one of the qualities which make them a great people. As has been observed, this proposition was novel, was most serious, and raised questions which they felt that their knowledge was insufficient to determine. Accordingly, a certain section of the Liberal party refused to accept it. A great number, probably the majority, of these doubtful men abstained from voting. Others voted against the Home Rule Liberal candidates, not necessarily because they condemned the policy, but because, as they were not satisfied that it was right, they deemed delay a less evil than the committal of the nation to a new departure, which might prove irrevocable.

It must not, however, be supposed that it was only hesitation which drove many Liberals into the host arrayed against the Irish Government Bill. I have already said that among the leaders there were some, and those men of great influence, who condemned its principles. This was true also of a considerable, though a relatively smaller, section of the rank and file. And it was only what might have been expected. The proposal to undo much of the work done in 1800, to alter fundamentally the system which had for eighty-six years regulated the relations of the two islands, by setting up a Parliament in Ireland, was a proposal which not only had not formed a part of the accepted creed of the Liberal party, but fell outside party lines altogether. It might, no doubt, be argued, as was actually done, and as those who understand the history of the Liberal party have more and more come to see, that Liberal principles recommended it, since they involve faith in the people, and faith in the curative tendency of local self-government. But this was by no means axiomatic. Taking the whole complicated facts of the case, and taking Liberalism as it had been practically understood in England, a man might in July, 1886, deem himself a good Liberal and yet think that the true interests of both peoples would be best served by maintaining the existing Parliamentary system. Similarly, there was nothing in Toryism or Tory principles to prevent a fair-minded and patriotic Tory from approving the Home Rule scheme. It was a return to the older institutions of the monarchy, and not inconsistent with any of the doctrines which the Tory party had been accustomed to uphold. The question, in short, was one of those which cut across ordinary party lines, creating new divisions among politicians; and there might have been and ought to have been Liberal Home Rulers and Tory Home Rulers, Liberal opponents of Home Rule and Tory opponents of Home Rule.

But here comes in a feature, a natural but none the less a regrettable feature, of the English party system. As the object of the party in opposition is to turn out the party in power and seat itself in their place, every Opposition regards with the strongest prejudice the measures proposed by a ruling Ministry. Cases sometimes occur where these measures are so obviously necessary, or so evidently approved by the nation, that the Opposition accepts them. But in general it scans them with a hostile eye. Human nature is human nature; and when the defeat of Government can be secured by defeating a Government Bill, the temptation to the Opposition to secure it is irresistible. Now, the Tory party is far more cohesive than the Liberal party, far more obedient to its leaders, far less disposed to break into sections, each of which thinks and acts for itself. Accordingly, that division of opinion in the Tory party which might have been expected, and which would have occurred if those who composed the Tory party had been merely so many reflecting men, and not members of a closely compacted political organization, did not occur. Liberals were divided, as such a question would naturally divide them. Tories were not divided; they threw their whole strength against the Bill. I am far from suggesting that they did so against their consciences. Whatever may be said as to two or three of the leaders, whose previous language and conduct seemed to indicate that they would themselves, had the election of 1885 gone differently, have been inclined to a Home Rule policy, many of the Tory chiefs, as well as the great mass of the party, honestly disapproved Mr. Gladstone's measure. But their party motives and party affiliations gave it no chance of an impartial verdict at their hands. They went into the jury-box with an invincible prepossession against the scheme of their opponents. When all these difficulties are duly considered, and especially when regard is had to those which I have last enumerated, the suddenness with which the new policy was launched, and the fact that as coming from one party it was sure beforehand of the hostility of the other, no surprise can be felt at its fate. Those who, in England, now look back over the spring and summer of 1886 are rather surprised that it should come so near succeeding. To have been rejected by a majority of only thirty in Parliament, and of little over ten per cent. of the total number of electors who voted at the general election, is a defeat far less severe than any one who knew England would have predicted.

That the decision of the country is regarded by nobody as a final decision goes without saying. It was not regarded as final, even in the first weeks after it was given. This was not because the majority was comparatively small, for a smaller majority the other way would have been conclusive. It is because the country had not time enough for full consideration and deliberate judgment. The Bill was brought in on April 14th, the elections began on July 1st; no one can say what might have been the result of a long discussion, during which the first feelings of alarm (for alarm there was) might have worn off. And the decision is without finality, also, because the decision of the country was merely against the particular plan proposed by Mr. Gladstone, and not in favour of any alternative plan for dealing with Ireland, most certainly not for the coercive method which has since been adopted. One particular solution of the Irish problem was refused. The problem still stands confronting us, and when other modes of solving it have been in turn rejected, the country may come back to this mode.

We may now turn from the past to the future. Yet the account which has been given of the feelings and ideas arrayed against the Bill does not wholly belong to the past. They are the feelings to which the opponents of any plan of self-government for Ireland still appeal, and which will have to be removed or softened down before it can be accepted by the English. In particular, the probability of separation, and the supposed dangers to the Protestants and the landlords from an Irish Parliament, will continue to form the themes of controversy so long as the question remains unsettled.

What are the prospects of its settlement? What is the position which it now occupies? How has it affected the current politics of England?

It broke up the Liberal party in Parliament. The vast numerical majority of that party in the country supported, and still supports, Mr. Gladstone and the policy of Irish self-government. But the dissentient minority includes many men of influence, and constitutes in the House of Commons a body of about seventy members, who hold the balance between parties. For the present they are leagued with the Tory Ministry to resist Home Rule, and their support insures a parliamentary majority to that Ministry. But it is, of course, necessary for them to rally to Lord Salisbury, not only on Irish questions, but on all questions; for, under our English system, a Ministry defeated on any serious issue is bound to resign, or dissolve Parliament. Now, to maintain an alliance for a special purpose, between members of opposite parties, is a hard matter. Agreement about Ireland does not, of itself, help men to agree about foreign policy, or bimetallism, or free trade, or changes in land laws, or ecclesiastical affairs. When these and other grave questions come up in Parliament, the Tory Ministry and their Liberal allies must, on every occasion, negotiate a species of concordat, whereby the liberty of both is fettered. One party may wish to resist innovation, the other to yield to it, or even to anticipate it. Each is obliged to forego something in order to humour the other; neither has the pleasure or the credit of taking a bold line on its own responsibility. There is, no doubt, less difference between the respective tenets of the great English parties than there was twenty years ago, when Mr. Disraeli had not yet completed the education of one party, and economic laws were still revered by the other. But, besides its tenets, each party has its tendencies, its sympathies, its moral atmosphere; and these differ so widely as to make the co-operation of Tories and Liberals constrained and cumbrous. Moreover, there are the men to be considered, the leaders on each side, whose jealousies, rivalries, suspicions, personal incompatibilities, neither old habits of joint action nor corporate party feeling exist to soften. On the whole, therefore, it is unlikely that the league of these two parties, united for one question only, and that a question which will pass into new phases, can be durable. Either the league will dissolve, or the smaller party will be absorbed into the larger. In England, as in America, third parties rarely last. The attraction of the larger mass is irresistible, and when the crisis which created a split or generated a new group has passed, or the opinion the new group advocates has been either generally discredited or generally adopted, the small party melts away, its older members disappearing from public life, its younger ones finding their career in the ranks of one of the two great standing armies of politics. If the dissentient, or anti-Home Rule, Liberal party lives till the next general election, it cannot live longer, for at that election it will be ground to powder between the upper and nether millstones of the regular Liberals and the regular Tories.

The Irish struggle of 1886 has had another momentous consequence. It has brought the Nationalist or Parnellite party into friendly relations with the mass of English Liberals. When the Home Rule party was founded by Mr. Butt, some fifteen years ago, it had more in common with the Liberal than with the Tory party. But as it demanded what both English parties were then resolved to refuse, it was forced into antagonism to both; and from 1877 onward (Mr.

Butt being then dead) the antagonism became bitter, and, of course, specially bitter as toward the statesmen in power, because it was they who continued to refuse what the Nationalists sought. Mr. Parnell has always stated, with perfect candour, that he and his friends must fight for their own hand unhampered by English alliances, and getting the most they could for Ireland from the weakness of either English party. This position they still retain. If the Tory party will give them Home Rule, they will help the Tory party. However, as the Tory party has gained office by opposing Home Rule, this contingency may seem not to lie within the immediate future. On the other hand, the Gladstonian Liberals have lost office for their advocacy of Home Rule, and now stand pledged to maintain the policy they have proclaimed. The Nationalists have, therefore, for the first time since the days immediately following the Union of A.D. 1800 (a measure which the Whigs of those days resisted), a great English party admitting the justice of their claim, and inviting them to agitate for it by purely constitutional methods. For such an alliance the English Liberals are hotly reproached, both by the Tories and by the dissentients who follow Lord Harrington and Mr. Chamberlain. They are accused of disloyalty to England. The past acts and words of the Nationalists are thrown in their teeth, and they are told that in supporting the Irish claim they condone such acts, they adopt such words. They reply by denying the adoption, and by pointing out that the Tories themselves were from 1881 till 1886 in a practical, and often very close, though unavowed, Parliamentary alliance with the Nationalists in the House of Commons. The student of history will, however, conceive that the Liberals have a stronger and higher defence than any tu quoque. Issues that involve the welfare of peoples are far too serious for us to apply to them the same sentiments of personal taste and predilection which we follow in inviting a dinner party, or selecting companions for a vacation tour. If a man has abused your brother, or got drunk in the street, you do not ask him to go with you to the Yellowstone Park. But his social offences do not prevent you from siding with him in a political convention. So, in politics itself, one must distinguish between characters and opinions. If a man has shown himself unscrupulous or headstrong, you may properly refuse to vote him into office, or to sit in the same Cabinet with him, because you think these faults of his dangerous to the country. But if the cause he pleads be a just one, you have no more right to be prejudiced against it by his conduct than a judge has to be swayed by dislike to the counsel who argues a case. There were moderate men in America, who, in the days of the anti-slavery movement, cited against it the intemperate language of many abolitionists. There were aristocrats in England, who, during the struggle for the freedom and unity of Italy, sought to discredit the patriotic party by accusing them of tyrannicide. But the sound sense of both nations refused to be led away by such arguments, because it held those two causes to be in their essence righteous. In all revolutionary movements there are elements of excess and violence, which sober men may regret, but which must not disturb our judgment as to the substantial merits of an issue. The revolutionist of one generation is, like Garibaldi or Mazzini, the hero of the next; and the verdict of posterity applauds those who, even in his own day, were able to discern the justice of the cause under the errors or faults of its champion. Doubly is it the duty of a great and far-sighted statesman not to be repelled by such errors, when he can, by espousing a revolutionary movement, purify it of its revolutionary character, and turn it into a legitimate constitutional struggle. This is what Mr. Gladstone has done. If his policy be in itself dangerous and disloyal to the true interests of the people of our islands, let it be condemned. But if it be the policy which has the best promise for the peace, the prosperity, and the mutual good will of those peoples, he and those who follow him would be culpable indeed were they to be deterred by the condemnation which they have so often expressed, and which they still express, for some of the past acts of a particular party, from declaring that the aims of that party were substantially right aims, and from now pressing upon the country what their conscience approves.

However, as the Home Rule Liberals and Nationalists, taken together, are in a minority (although a minority which obtains recruits at many bye-elections) in the present Parliament, it is not from them that fresh proposals are expected. They will, of course, continue to speak, write, and agitate on behalf of the views they hold. But practical attempt to deal with Irish troubles must for the present come from the Tory Ministry; for in the English system of government those who command a Parliamentary majority are responsible for legislation as well as administration, and are censured not merely if their legislation is bad, but if it is not forthcoming when events call for it.

Why, it may be asked, should Lord Salisbury's Government burn its fingers over Ireland, as so many governments have burnt their fingers before? Why not let Ireland alone, giving to foreign affairs and to English and Scottish reforms all the attention which these too much neglected matters need?

Well would it be for England, as well as for English Ministries, if Ireland could be simply let alone, her maladies left to be healed by the soft, slow hand of nature. But Irish troubles call aloud to be dealt with, and that promptly. They stand in the way of all other reforms, indeed of all other business. Letting alone has been tried, and it has succeeded no better, even in times less urgent than the present, than the usual policy of coercion followed by concession, or concession followed by coercion.

There are three aspects of the Irish question, three channels by which the troubles of the "distressful island" stream down upon us, forcing whoever now rules or may come to rule in England to attempt some plan for dealing with them. I will take them in succession.

The first is the Parliamentary difficulty. In the British House of Commons, with its six hundred and seventy members, there are nearly ninety Irish Nationalists. They are a well-disciplined body, voting as one man, though capable of speaking enough for a thousand. They have no interest in English or Scotch or colonial or Indian affairs, but only in Irish, and look upon the vote which they have the right of giving upon the former solely as a means of furthering their own Irish aims. They are, therefore, in the British Parliament not merely a foreign body, indifferent to the great British and imperial issues confided to it, but a hostile body, opposed to its present constitution, seeking to discredit it in its authority over Ireland, and to make more and more palpable and incurable the incompetence for Irish business whereof they accuse it. Several modes of doing this are open to them. They may, as some of the more actively bitter among them did in the Parliaments of 1874 and 1880, obstruct business by long and frequent speeches, dilatory motions, and all those devices which in America are called filibustering. The House of Commons may, no doubt, try to check these tactics by more stringent rules of procedure, but the attempts already made in this direction have had but slight success, and every restriction of debate, since it trenches on the freedom of English and Scotch no less than of Irish members, injures Parliament as a whole. They may disgust the British people with the House of Commons by keeping it (as they have done in former years) so constantly occupied with Irish business as to leave it little time for English and Scotch measures. They may throw the weight of their collective vote into the scale of one or other British party, according to the amount of concession it will make to them, or, by always voting against the Ministry of the day, they may cause frequent and sudden changes of Government. This plan also they have followed in time past; for the moment it is not so applicable, because the Tories and dissentient Liberals, taken together, possess a majority in the House of Commons. But at any moment the alliance of those two sections may vanish, or another General Election may leave Tories and Liberals so nearly balanced that the Irish vote could turn the scale. Whoever reflects on the nature of Parliamentary Government will perceive that it is based on the assumption that the members of the ruling assembly, however much they may differ on other subjects, agree in desiring the strength, dignity, and welfare of the assembly itself, and in caring for the main national interests which it controls. He will therefore be prepared to expect countless and multiform difficulties in working such a Government, where a large section of the assembly seeks not to use, but to make useless, its forms and rules--not to preserve, but to lower and destroy, its honour, its credit, its efficiency. In vain are Irish members blamed for these tactics, for they answer that the interests of their own country require them to seek first her welfare, which can in their view be secured only by removing her from the direct control of what they deem a foreign assembly. Now that the demand for Irish self-government has obtained the sympathy of the bulk of English Liberals, they are unlikely forthwith to resume the systematic obstruction of past years. But they will be able, without alienating their English friends, to render the conduct of Parliamentary business so difficult that every English Ministry will be forced either to crush them, if it can, or to appease them by a series of concessions.

The second difficulty is that of maintaining social order in Ireland. What that difficulty is, and whence it arises, every one knows. It is chronic, but every second or third winter, when there has been a wet season, or the price of live stock declines, it becomes specially acute. The tenants refuse to pay rents which they declare to be impossible. The landlords, or the harsher among them, try to enforce rents by evictions; evictions are resisted by outrages and boycotting. Popular sentiment supports those who commit outrages, because it considers the tenantry to be engaged in a species of war, a righteous war, against the landlord. Evidence can seldom be obtained, and juries acquit in the teeth of evidence. Thus the enforcement of the law strains all the resources of authority, while a habit of lawlessness and discontent is transmitted from generation to generation. Of the remedies proposed for this chronic evil the most obvious is the strengthening of the criminal law. We have been trying this for more than one hundred years, since Whiteboyism appeared, and trying it in vain. Since the Union, Coercion Acts, of more or less severity, have been almost always in force in Ireland, passed for two or three years, then dropped for a year or two, then renewed in a form slightly varying, but always with the same result of driving the disease in for a time, but not curing it. Mr. Gladstone proposed to buy out the landlords and then leave an Irish Parliament to restore social order, with that authority which it would derive from having the will of the people behind it; because he held that when the people felt the law to be of their own making, and not imposed from without, their sentiment would be enlisted on its side, and the necessity for a firm Government recognized. This plan, has, however, been rejected, so the choice was left of a fresh Coercion Act, or of some scheme, necessarily a costly scheme, for getting rid of the source of trouble by transferring the land of Ireland to the peasantry. The present Government, while guided by Sir M. Hicks-Beach, who had some knowledge of Ireland, did its best to persuade the landlords to accept reduced rents, while the Nationalist leaders, on their side, sought to restrain the people from outrages. But the armistice did not last. The Ministry yielded to the foolish counsels of its more violent supporters, and entrusted Irish affairs to the hands of a Chief Secretary without previous knowledge of the island. An unusually severe Coercion Act has been brought in and passed by the aid of the dissentient Liberals. And we now see this Act administered with a mixture of virulence and incompetence to which even the dreary annals of Irish misgovernment present few parallels. The feeling of the English people is rising against the policy carried out in their name. So far from being solved, the problem of social order becomes every day more acute.

There remains the question of a reform of local government. For many years past, every English Ministry has undertaken to frame a measure creating a new system of popular rural self-government in England. It is the first large task of domestic legislation which we ask from Parliament. When such a scheme is proposed, can Ireland be left out of it? Should she be left out, the argument that she is being treated unequally and unfairly, as compared with England, would gain immense force; because the present local government of Ireland is admittedly less popular, less efficient, altogether less defensible, than even that of England which we are going to reform. If, therefore, the theory that the Imperial Parliament is both anxious and able to do its duty by Ireland is to be maintained, Ireland, too, must have her scheme of local government. And a scheme of local government is a large project, the discussion of which must pass into a discussion of the government of the island as a whole.

Since, then, we may conclude that whatever Ministry is in power will be bound to take up the state of Ireland--since Parliament and the nation will be occupied with the subject during the coming sessions fully as much as they have been during those that have recently passed--the next inquiry is, What will the tendency of opinion and legislation be? Will the reasons and forces described above bring us to Home Rule? and if so, when, how, and why?

There are grounds for answering these questions in the negative. A majority of the House of Commons, including the present Ministry and such influential Liberals as Mr. Bright, Lord Hartington, Mr. Chamberlain, stand pledged to resist it, and seem--such is the passion which controversy engenders--more disposed to resist it than they were in 1885. But this ground is less strong than it may appear. We have had too many changes of opinion--ay, and of action too--upon Irish affairs not to be prepared for further changes. A Ministry in power learns much which an Opposition fails to learn. Home Rule is an elastic expression, and some of those who were loudest in denouncing Mr. Gladstone's Bill will find it easy to explain, should they bring in a Bill of their own for giving self-government to Ireland, that their measure is a different thing, and free from the objections brought against his. Nor, if such a conversion should come, need it be deemed a dishonest one, for events are potent teachers, and governments now seek rather to follow than to form opinion. Although a decent interval must be allowed, no one will be astonished if the Tory leaders should move ere long in the direction indicated. Toryism itself, as has been remarked already, contains nothing opposed to the idea.

Far greater obstacles exist in the aversion which (as already observed) so many Englishmen of both parties have entertained for any scheme which should seem to leave the Protestant minority at the mercy of the peasant and Roman Catholic majority, and to carry us some way toward the ultimate separation of the islands. These alarms are genuine and deep seated. One who (like the present writer) thinks them, if not baseless, yet immensely overstrained, is, of course, convinced that they may be allayed. But time must first pass, and the plan that is to allay them may have to be framed on somewhat different lines from those of Mr. Gladstone's measure. It is even possible that a conflict more sharp and painful than any of recent years may intervene before a settlement is reached.

Nevertheless, great as are the obstacles in the way, bitter as are the reproaches with which Mr. Gladstone is pursued by the richer classes in England, there is good reason to believe that the current is setting toward his policy. In proceeding to state the grounds for this view, I must frankly own that I am no longer (as in most of the preceding pages) merely setting forth facts on which impartial men in England would agree. The forecast which I seek to give may be tinged by my own belief that the grant of self-government is the best, if not the only method, now open to us of establishing peace between the islands, relieving the English Parliament of work it is ill fitted to discharge, allowing Ireland opportunities to learn those lessons in politics which her people so much need. The future, even the near future, is more than usually dim. Yet, if we examine those three branches of the Irish question which have been enumerated above, we shall see how naturally, in each of them, the concession of self-government seems to open, I will not say the most direct, but the least dangerous way, out of our troubles.

The Parliamentary difficulty arises from the fact that the representatives of Ireland have the feelings of foreigners sitting in a foreign assembly, whose honour and usefulness they do not desire. While these are their feelings they cannot work properly in it, and it cannot work properly with them. The inconvenience may be endured, but the English will grow tired of it, and be disposed to rid themselves of it, if they see their way to do so without greater mischief. There are but two ways out of the difficulty. One is to get rid of the Irish members altogether; the other is to make them, by the concession of their just demands, contented and loyal members of a truly united Parliament. The experience of the Parliament of 1880, which was mainly occupied with Irish business, and began, being a strongly Liberal Parliament, with a bias toward the Irish popular party, showed how difficult it is for a House of Commons which is ignorant of Ireland to legislate wisely for it. In the House of Lords there is not a single Nationalist; indeed, up till 1886, that exalted chamber contained only one peer, Lord Dalhousie (formerly member for Liverpool), who had ever said a word in favour of Home Rule. The more that England becomes sensible, as she must become sensible, of the deficiencies of the present machinery for appreciating the needs and giving effect to the wishes of Irishmen, the more disposed will she be to grant them some machinery of their own.

As regards social order, I have shown that the choice which lies before the opponents of Home Rule is either to continue the policy of coercing the peasantry by severe special legislation, or to remove the source of friction by buying out the landlords for the benefit of the tenants. The present Ministry have chosen the former alternative, but they dangle before the eyes of their supporters some prospect that they may ultimately revert to the latter. Now, the only way that has yet been pointed out of buying out the landlords, without imposing tremendous liabilities of loss upon the British Treasury, is the creation of a strong Home Rule Government in Dublin. Supposing, however, that some other plan could be discovered, which would avoid the fatal objections to which an extension of the plan of the (Salisbury) Land Purchase Act of 1885 is open, such a plan would remove one of the chief objections to an Irish Parliament, by leaving no estates for such a Parliament to confiscate. As for coercion every day, I might say, every bye-election shows us how it becomes more and more odious to the British democracy. They dislike severity; they dislike the inequality involved in passing harsher laws for Ireland than those that apply to England and Scotland. They find themselves forced to sympathize with acts of violence in Ireland which they would condemn in Great Britain, because these acts seem the only way of resisting harsh and unjust laws. When the recoil comes, it will be more violent than in former days. The wish to discover some other course will be very strong, and the obvious other course will be to leave it to an Irish authority to enforce social order in its own way--probably a more rough-and-ready way than that of British officials. The notion which has possessed most Englishmen, that Irish self-government would be another name for anarchy, is curiously erroneous. Conflicts there may be, but a vigorous rule will emerge.

Lastly, as to local government. If a popular system is established in Ireland-- one similar to that which it is proposed to establish in England--the control of its assemblies and officials will, over four-fifths of the island, fall into Nationalist hands. Their power will be enormously increased, for they will then command the machinery of administration, and the power of taxing. What with taxing landlords, aiding recalcitrant tenants, stopping the wheels of any central authority which may displease or oppose them, they will be in so strong a position that the creation of an Irish Parliament may appear to be a comparatively small further step, may even appear (as the wisest Nationalists now think it would prove) in the light of a check upon the abuse of local powers. These eventualities will unquestionably, when English opinion has realized them, make such a Parliament as the present pause before it commits rural local government to the Irish democracy. But it could not refuse to do something; and if it tried to restrain popular representative bodies by the veto of a bureaucracy in Dublin, there would arise occasions for quarrel and irritation more serious than now exist.[70] Those who once begin to repair an old and tottering building are led on, little by little, into changes they did not at starting contemplate. So it will be if once the task is undertaken of reforming the confessedly bad and indefensible system of Irish administration. We may stop at some half-way house on the way, but Home Rule stands at the end of the road.

Supposing, then, that the Nationalist party, retaining its present strength and unity, perseveres in its present demands, there is every prospect that these demands will be granted. But will it persevere? There are among the English Dissentients those who prophesy that it will break up, as such parties have broken up before--will lose hope and wither away. Or the support of the Irish peasantry may be withdrawn--a result which some English politicians expect from a final settlement of the land question in the interest of the tenants. Any of these contingencies is possible, but at present most improbable. The moment when long-cherished aims begin to seem attainable is not that at which men are disposed to abandon them.

There are, however, other reasons which suggest the likelihood of a change in English sentiment on the whole matter. The surprise with which the Bill of last April was received has worn off. The alarm is wearing off too. Those who set their teeth at what seemed to them a surrender to the Parnellites and their Irish-American allies, having relieved their temper by an emphatic No, have begun to ponder things more calmly. The English people are listening to the arguments from Irish history that are now addressed to them. They will be moved by the solid grounds of policy which that history suggests; will understand that what they have deemed insensate hatred is the natural result of long misgovernment, and will disappear with time and the removal of its causes. Many of the best minds of both nations will be at work to discover some method of reconciling Irish self-government with imperial supremacy and union free from the objections brought against the Bills of 1886. It is reasonable to expect that they may greatly improve upon these measures, which were prepared under pressure from a clamorous Opposition. What Mr. Disraeli once called the historical conscience of the country will appreciate those great underlying principles to which Mr. Gladstone's policy appeals. It has been accused of being a policy of despair; and may have commended itself to some who supported it as being simply a means of ridding England of responsibility. But to others it seemed, and more truly, a policy of faith; not, indeed, of thoughtless optimism, but of faith according to the definition which calls it "the substance of things hoped for, the evidence of things not seen." Faith, by which nations as well as men must live, means nothing less than a conviction that great principles, permanent truths of human nature, lie at the bottom of all sound politics, and ought to be boldly and consistently applied, even when temporary difficulties surround their application. Such a principle is the belief in the power of freedom and self-government to cure the faults of a nation, in the tendency of responsibility to teach wisdom, and to make men see that justice and order are the surest sources of prosperity. Such a principle is the perception that national hatreds do not live on of themselves, but will expire when oppression has ceased, as a fire burns out without fuel. Such a principle is the recognition of the force of national sentiment, and of the duty of allowing it all the satisfaction that is compatible with the maintenance of imperial unity. Such, again, is the appreciation of those natural economic laws which show that nations, when disturbing passions have ceased, follow their own permanent interests, and that an island which finds its chief market in England and draws its capital from England will prefer a connection with England to the poverty and insignificance of isolation. It is the honour of Mr. Gladstone to have built his policy of conciliation upon principles like these, as upon a rock; and already the good effects are seen in the new friendliness which has arisen between the English masses and the people of Ireland, and in the better temper with which, despite the acrimony of some prominent politicians, the relations of the two peoples are discussed. When one looks round the horizon it is still far from clear; nor can we say from which quarter fair weather will arrive. But the air is fresher, and the clouds are breaking overhead.

* * * * *

POSTSCRIPT.

What has happened since the above paragraphs were written, ten months ago, has confirmed more quickly and completely than the writer expected the forecasts they contain. Home Rule is no longer a word of terror, even to those English and Scotch voters who were opposed to it in July, 1886. Most sensible men in the Tory and Dissentient Liberal camps have come to see that it is inevitable; and, while they continue to resist it for the sake of what is called consistency, or because they do not yet see in what form it is to be granted, they are disposed to regard its speedy arrival as the best method of retreat from an indefensible position.

The repressive policy which the present Ministry are attempting in Ireland--for in the face of their failures one cannot say that they are carrying out any policy--is rendering Coercion Acts more and more detested by the English people. The actualities of Ireland, the social condition of her peasantry, the unwisdom of the dominant caste, the incompetence of the bureaucracy which affects to rule her, are being, by the full accounts we now receive, brought home to the mind of England and Scotland as they never were before, and produce their appropriate effect upon the heart and conscience of the people. The recognition by the Liberal party of the rights of Ireland, the visits of English Liberals to Ireland, the work done by Irishmen in English constituencies, are creating a feeling of unity and reciprocal interest between the masses of the people on both sides of the Channel without example in the seven hundred years that have passed since Strongbow's landing.

This was the thing most needed to make Home Rule safe and full of promise, because it affords a guarantee that in such political contests as may arise in future, the division will not be, as heretofore, between the Irish people on the one side and the power of Britain on the other, but between two parties, each of which will have adherents in both islands. We may now at last hope that national hatreds will vanish; that England will unlearn her arrogance and Ireland her suspicion; that the basis is being laid for a harmonious co-operation of both nations in promoting the welfare and greatness of a common Empire.

Many of the Irish patriots of 1798 and 1848 desired Separation, because they thought that Ireland, attached to England, could never be more than the obscure satellite of a greater State. When Ireland has been heartily welcomed by the democracy of Great Britain as an equal partner, the ground for any such desire will have disappeared, and Union will rest on a foundation firmer than has ever before existed. Ireland will feel, when those rights of self-government have been secured for which she has pleaded so long, that she owes them, not only to her own tenacity and courage, but to the magnanimity, the justice, and the freely given sympathy of the English and Scottish people.

October, 1887.

FOOTNOTES:

[Footnote 69: This article, which originally appeared in the American New Princeton Review, has been added to in a few places, in order to bring its narrative of facts up to date.]

[Footnote 70: The experience of the last few months, which has shown us rural Boards of Guardians and municipal bodies over four-fifths of Ireland displaying their zeal in the Nationalist cause, has amply confirmed this anticipation, expressed nearly a year ago.]

SOME ARGUMENTS CONSIDERED.[71]

BY JOHN MORLEY.

It is a favourite line of argument to show that we have no choice between the maintenance of the Union and the concession to Ireland of national independence. The evils of Irish independence are universally reckoned by Englishmen to be so intolerable that we shall never agree to it. The evils of Home Rule are even more intolerable still. Therefore, it is said, if we shall never willingly bring the latter upon our heads, ?fortiori we ought on no account to invite the former. The business in hand, however, is not a theorem, but a problem; it is not a thesis to be proved, but a malady to be cured; and the world will thank only the reasoner who winds up, not with Q.E.D., but with Q.E.F. To reason that a patient ought not to take a given medicine because it may possibly cause him more pain than some other medicine which he has no intention of taking, is curiously oblique logic. The question is not oblique; it is direct. Will the operation do more harm to his constitution than the slow corrosions of a disorder grown inveterate? Are the conditions of the connection between England and Ireland, as laid down in the Act of Union, incapable of improvement? Is the present working of these conditions more prosperous and hopeful, or happier for Irish order and for English institutions, than any practicable proposal that it is within the compass of statesmanship to devise, and of civic sense to accept and to work? That is the question.

Some people contend that the burden of making out a case rests on the advocate of change, and not on those who support things as they are. But who supports things as they are? Things as they are have become insupportable. If you make any of the constitutional changes that have been proposed, we are told, parliamentary government, as Englishmen now know it, is at an end; and our critic stands amazed at those "who deem it a slighter danger to innovate on the Act of Union than to remodel the procedure of the House of Commons." As if that were the alternative. Great changes in the rules may do other good things, but no single competent authority believes that in this particular they will do the thing that we want. We cannot avoid constitutional changes. It is made matter of crushing rebuke that the Irish proposals of the late Government were an innovation on the old constitution of the realm. But everybody knows that, while ancient forms have survived, the last hundred years have witnessed a long succession of silent but most profound innovations. It was shortsighted to assume that the redistribution of political power that took place in 1884-5 was the last chapter of the history of constitutional change. It ought to have been foreseen that new possessors of power, both Irish and British, would press for objects the pursuit of which would certainly involve further novelties in the methods and machinery of government. Every given innovation must be rigorously scrutinized, but in the mere change or in the fact of innovation there is no valid reproach. When one of the plans for the better government of Ireland is described as depriving parliamentary institutions of their elasticity and strength, as weakening the Executive at home, and lessening the power of the country to resist foreign attack, no careful observer of the events of the last seven years can fail to see that all this evil has already got its grip upon us. Mr. Dicey himself admits it. "Great Britain," he says, "if left to herself, could act with all the force, consistency, and energy given by unity of sentiment and community of interests. The obstruction and the uncertainty of our political aims, the feebleness and inconsistency with which they are pursued, arise in part at least from the connection with Ireland." So then, after all, it is feebleness and inconsistency, not elasticity and strength, that mark our institutions as they stand; feebleness and inconsistency, distraction and uncertainty. The supporter of things as they are is decidedly as much concerned in making out a case as the advocate of change.

The strength of the argument from Nationality is great, and full of significance; but Nationality is not the whole essence of either the argument from History or the argument from Self-government. Their force lies in considerations of political expediency as tested by practical experience.

The point of the argument from the lessons of History is that for some reason or another the international concern, whose unlucky affairs we are now trying to unravel, has always been carried on at a loss: the point of the argument from Self-government is that the loss would have been avoided if the Irish shareholders had for a certain number of the transactions been more influentially represented on the Board. That is quite apart from the sentiment of pure nationality. The failure has come about, not simply because the laws were not made by Irishmen as such, but because they were not made by the men who knew most about Ireland. The vice of the connection between the two countries has been the stupidity of governing a country without regard to the interests or customs, the peculiar objects and peculiar experiences, of the great majority of the people who live in it. It is not enough to say that the failures of England in Ireland have to a great extent flowed from causes too general to be identified with the intentional wrong-doing either of rulers or of subjects. We readily admit that, but it is not the point. It is not enough to insist that James I., in his plantations and transplantations, probably meant well to his Irish subjects. Probably he did. That is not the question. If it is "absolutely certain that his policy worked gross wrong," what is the explanation and the defence? We are quite content with Mr. Dicey's own answer. "Ignorance and want of sympathy produced all the evils of cruelty and malignity. An intended reform produced injustice, litigation, misery, and discontent. The case is noticeable, for it is a type of a thousand subsequent English attempts to reform and improve Ireland." This description would apply, with hardly a word altered, to the wrong done by the Encumbered Estates Act in the reign of Queen Victoria. That memorable measure, as Mr. Gladstone said, was due not to the action of a party, but to the action of a Parliament. Sir Robert Peel was hardly less responsible for it than Lord John Russell. "We produced it," said Mr. Gladstone, "with a general, lazy, uninformed, and irreflective good intention of taking capital to Ireland. What did we do? We sold the improvements of the tenants" (House of Commons, April 16). It is the same story, from the first chapter to the last, in education, poor law, public works, relief Acts, even in coercion Acts--lazy, uninformed, and irreflective good intention. That is the argument from history. When we are asked what good law an Irish Parliament would make that could not equally well be made by the Parliament at Westminster, this is the answer. It is not the will, it is the intelligence, that is wanting. We all know what the past has been. Why should the future be different?

"It is an inherent condition of human affairs," said Mill in a book which, in spite of some chimeras, is a wholesome corrective of the teaching of our new jurists, "that no intention, however sincere, of protecting the interests of others can make it safe or salutary to tie up their own hands. Still more obviously true is it, that by their own hands only can any positive and durable improvement of their circumstances in life be worked out" (Repres. Government, p. 57). It is these wise lessons from human experience to which the advocate of Home Rule appeals, and not the wild doctrine that any body of persons claiming to be united by a sense of nationality possesses an inherent and divine right to be treated as an independent community. It is quite true that circumstances sometimes justify a temporary dictatorship. In that there is nothing at variance with Liberalism. But the Parliamentary dictatorship in Ireland has lasted a great deal too long to be called temporary, and its stupid shambling operations are finally and decisively condemned by their consequences. That is a straightforward utilitarian argument, and has nothing whatever to do with inherent and divine rights, or any other form of political moonshine.

There are some who believe that an honest centralized administration of impartial officials, and not Local Self-Government, would best meet the real wants of the people. In other words, everything is to be for the people, nothing by the people--which has not hitherto been a Liberal principle. Something, however, may be said for this view, provided that the source of the authority of such an administration be acceptable. Austrian administration in Lombardy was good rather than bad, yet it was hated and resisted because it was Austrian and not Italian. No rational person can hold for an instant that the source of a scheme of government is immaterial to its prosperity. More than that, when people look for success in the government of Ireland to "honest centralized administration," we cannot but wonder what fault they find with the administration of Ireland to-day in respect of its honesty or its centralization. What administration ever carried either honesty or centralization to a higher pitch than the Irish administration of Mr. Forster? What could be less successful? Those who have been most directly concerned in the government of Ireland, whether English or Irish, even while alive to the perils of any other principle, habitually talk of centralization as the curse of the system. Here, again, why should we expect success in the future from a principle that has so failed in the past?

Again, how are we to get a strong centralized administration in the face of a powerful and hostile parliamentary representation? It is very easy to talk of the benefits that might have been conferred on Ireland by such humanity and justice as was practised by Turgot in his administration of the Generality of Limoges. But Turgot was not confronted by eighty-six Limousin members of an active sovereign body, all interested in making his work difficult, and trusted by a large proportion of the people of the province with that as their express commission. It is possible to have an honest centralized administration of great strength and activity in India, but there is no Parliament in India. If India, or any province of it, ever gets representative government and our parliamentary system, from that hour, if there be any considerable section of Indian feeling averse from European rule, the present administrative system will be paralyzed, as the preliminary to being revolutionized. It is conceivable, if any one chooses to think so, that a body of impartial officials could manage the national business in Ireland much better without the guidance of public opinion and common sentiment than with it. But if you intend to govern the country as you think best--and that is the plain and practical English of centralized administration--why ask the country to send a hundred men to the great tribunal of supervision to inform you how it would like to be governed? The Executive cannot set them aside as if they were a hundred dummies; in refusing to be guided, it cannot escape being harassed, by them. You may amend procedure, but that is no answer, unless you amend the Irish members out of voice and vote. They will still count. You cannot gag and muzzle them effectually, and if you could, they would still be there, and their presence would still make itself incessantly felt. Partly from a natural desire to lessen the common difficulties of government, and partly from a consciousness, due to the prevailing state of the modern political atmosphere, that there is something wrong in this total alienation of an Executive from the possessors of parliamentary power, the officials will incessantly be tempted to make tacks out of their own course; and thus they lose the coherency and continuity of absolutism without gaining the pliant strength of popular government. This is not a presumption of what would be likely to happen, but an account of what does happen, and what justified Mr. Disraeli in adding a weak Executive to the alien Church and the absentee aristocracy, as the three great curses of Ireland. Nothing has occurred since 1844 to render the Executive stronger, but much to the contrary. There is, and there can be, no weaker or less effective Government in the world than a highly centralized system working alongside of a bitterly inimical popular representation. I say nothing of the effect of the fluctuations of English parties on Irish administration. I say nothing of the tendency in an Irish government, awkwardly alternating with that to which I have just adverted, to look over the heads of the people of Ireland, and to consider mainly what will be thought by the ignorant public in England. But these sources of incessant perturbation must not be left out. The fault of Irish centralization is not that it is strong, but that it is weak. Weak it must remain until Parliament either approves of the permanent suspension of the Irish writs, or else devises constitutional means for making Irish administration responsible to Irish representatives.

If experience is decisive against the policy of the past, experience too, all over the modern world, indicates the better direction for the future. I will not use my too scanty space in repeating any of the great wise commonplaces in praise of self-government. Here they are superfluous. In the case of Ireland they have all been abundantly admitted in a long series of measures, from Catholic Emancipation down to Lord O'Hagan's Jury Law and the Franchise and Redistribution Acts of a couple of years ago. The principle of self-government has been accepted, ratified, and extended in a hundred ways. It is only a question of the form that self-government shall take. Against the form proposed by the late Ministry a case is built up that rests on a series of prophetic assumptions. These assumptions, from the nature of the case, can only be met by a counter-statement of fair and reasonable probabilities. Let us enumerate some of them.

1. It is inferred that, because the Irish leaders have used violent language and resorted to objectionable expedients against England during the last six years, they would continue in the same frame of mind after the reasons for it had disappeared. In other words, because they have been the enemies of a Government which refused to listen to a constitutional demand, therefore they would continue to be its enemies after the demand had been listened to. On this reasoning, the effect is to last indefinitely and perpetually, notwithstanding the cessation of the cause. Our position is that all the reasonable probabilities of human conduct point the other way. The surest way of justifying violent language and fostering treasonable designs, is to refuse to listen to the constitutional demand.

2. The Irish, we are told, hate the English with an irreconcilable hatred, and

would unquestionably use any Constitution as an instrument for satisfying their master passion. Irrational hatred, they say, can be treated by rational men with composure. The Czechs of Bohemia are said to be irreconcilable, yet the South Germans bear with their hatred; and if we cannot cure we might endure the antipathy of Ireland. Now, as for the illustration, I may remark that the hatred of the Czechs would be much too formidable for German composure, if the Czechs did not happen to possess a provincial charter and a special constitution of their own. If the Irish had the same, their national dislike--so far as it exists--might be expected to become as bearable as the Germans have found the feeling of the Czechs. But how deep does Irish dislike go? Is it directed against Englishmen, or against an English official system? The answers of every impartial observer to the whole group of such questions as these favour the conclusion that the imputed hatred of England in Ireland has been enormously exaggerated and overcoloured by Ascendency politicians for good reasons of their own; that with the great majority of Irishmen it has no deep roots; that it is not one of those passionate international animosities that blind men to their own interests, or lead them to sacrifice themselves for the sake of injuring their foe; and, finally, that it would not survive the amendment of the system that has given it birth.[72]

3. It is assumed that there is a universal desire for Separation. That there is a strong sentiment of nationality we of course admit; it is part of the case, and not the worst part. But the sentiment of nationality is a totally different thing from a desire for Separation. Scotland might teach our pseudo-Unionists so much as that. Nowhere in the world is the sentiment of nationality stronger, yet there is not a whisper of Separation. That there is a section of Irishmen who desire Separation is notorious, but everything that has happened since the Government of Ireland Bill was introduced, including the remarkable declarations of Mr. Parnell in accepting the Bill (June 7), and including the proceedings at Chicago, shows that the separatist section is a very small one either in Ireland or in America, and that it has become sensibly smaller since, and in consequence of, the proposed concession of a limited statutory constitution. The Irish are quite shrewd enough to know that Separation, if it were attainable--and they are well aware that it is not--would do no good to their markets; and to that knowledge, as well as to many other internal considerations, we may confidently look for the victory of strong centripetal over very weak centrifugal tendencies. Even if we suppose these centrifugal tendencies to be stronger than I would allow them to be, how shall we best

resist them--by strengthening the hands and using the services of the party which, though nationalist, is also constitutional; or by driving that party also, in despair of a constitutional solution, to swell the ranks of Extremists and Irreconcilables?

4. Whatever may be the ill-feeling towards England, it is at least undeniable that there are bitter internal animosities in Ireland, and a political constitution, our opponents argue, can neither assuage religious bigotry nor remove agrarian discontent.

It is true, no doubt, that the old feud between Protestant and Catholic might, perhaps, not instantly die down to the last smouldering embers of it all over Ireland. But we may remark that there is no perceptible bad blood between Protestant and Catholic, outside of one notorious corner. Second, the real bitterness of the feud arose from the fact that Protestantism was associated with an exclusive and hostile ascendency, which would now be brought to an end. Whatever feeling about what is called Ulster exists in the rest of Ireland, arises not from the fact that there are Protestants in Ulster, but that the Protestants are anti-National. Third, the Catholics would no longer be one compact body for persecuting, obscurantist, or any other evil purposes; the abatement of the national struggle would allow the Catholics to fall into the two natural divisions of Clerical and Liberal. What we may be quite sure of is that the feud will never die so long as sectarian pretensions are taken as good reasons for continuing bad government.

It is true, again, that a constitution would not necessarily remove agrarian discontent. But it is just as true that you will never remove agrarian discontent without a constitution. Mr. Dicey, on consideration, will easily see why. Here we come to an illustration, and a very impressive illustration it is, of the impotence of England to do for Ireland the good which Ireland might do for herself. Nobody just now is likely to forget the barbarous condition of the broad fringe of wretchedness on the west coast of Ireland. Of this Lord Dufferin truly said in 1880 that no legislation could touch it, that no alteration in the land laws could effectually ameliorate it, and that it must continue until the world's end unless something be contrived totally to change the conditions of existence in that desolate region. Parliament lavishly pours water into the sieve in the shape of Relief Acts. Even in my own short tenure of office I was responsible for one of these terribly wasteful and profoundly unsatisfactory measures. Instead of relief, what a statesman must seek is prevention of this great evil and strong root of evil; and prevention means a large, though it cannot be a very swift, displacement of the population. But among the many experts with whom I have discussed this dolorous and perplexing subject, I never found one of either political party who did not agree that a removal of the surplus population was only practicable if carried out by an Irish authority, backed by the solid weight of Irish opinion. Any exertion of compulsory power by a British Minister would raise the whole country-side in squalid insurrection, government would become impossible, and the work of transplantation would end in ghastly failure. It is misleading and untrue, then, to say that there is no possible relation between self-government and agrarian discontent, misery, and backwardness; and when Mr. Dicey and others tell us that the British Parliament is able to do all good things for Ireland, I would respectfully ask them how a British Parliament is to deal with the Congested Districts.

Nearly as much may be said of the prevention of the mischievous practice of Subdivision. Some contend that the old disposition to subdivide is dying out; others, however, assure us that it is making its appearance even among the excellent class who purchased their holdings under the Church Act. That Act did not prohibit subdivision, but it is prohibited in the Act of 1881. Still the prohibition can only be made effective, if operations take place on anything like a great scale, on condition that representative, authorities resident on the spot have the power of enforcing it, and have an interest in enforcing it. Some of the pseudo-Unionists are even against any extension of local self-government, and if it be unaccompanied by the creation of a central native authority they are right. What such people fail to see is that, in resisting political reconstruction, they are at the same time resisting the only available remedies for some of the worst of agrarian maladies.

The ruinous interplay between agrarian and political forces, each using the other for ends of its own, will never cease so long as the political demand is in every form resisted. That, we are told, is all the fault of the politicians. Be it so; then the Government must either suppress the politicians outright, or else it must interest them in getting the terms of its land settlement accepted and respected. Home Rule on our scheme was, among other things, part of an arrangement for "settling the agrarian feud." It was a means of interposing between the Irish tenant and the British State an authority interested enough and strong enough to cause the bargain to be kept. It is said that the Irish authority would have had neither interest nor strength enough to resist the forces making for repudiation. Would those forces be any less irresistible if the whole body of the Irish peasantry stood, as Land Purchase minusSelf-Government makes them to stand, directly face to face with the British State? This is a question that our opponents cannot evade, any more than they can evade that other question, which lies unnoticed at the back of all solutions of the problem by way of peasant ownership--Whether it is possible to imagine the land of Ireland handed over to Irishmen, and yet the government of Ireland kept exclusively and directly by Englishmen? Such a divorce is conceivable under a rule like that of the British in India: with popular institutions it is inconceivable and impossible.

5. It is argued that Home Rule on Mr. Gladstone's plan would not work, because it follows in some respects the colonial system, whereas the conditions at the root of the success of the system in the Colonies do not exist in Ireland. They are distant, Ireland is near; they are prosperous, Ireland is poor; they are proud of the connection with England, Ireland resents it. But the question is not whether the conditions are identical with those of any colony; it is enough if in themselves they seem to promise a certain basis for government. It might justly be contended that proximity is a more favourable condition than distance; without it there could not be that close and constant intercommunication which binds the material interests of Ireland to those of Great Britain, and so provides the surest guarantee for union. If Ireland were suddenly to find herself as far off as Canada, then indeed one might be very sorry to answer for the Union. Again, though Ireland has to bear her share of the prevailing depression in the chief branch of her production, it is a great mistake to suppose that outside of the margin of chronic wretchedness in the west and south-west, the condition not only of the manufacturing industries of the north, but of the agricultural industry in the richer parts of the middle and south, is so desperately unprosperous as to endanger a political constitution. Under our stupidily [Transcriber: sic] centralized system, Irishmen have no doubt acquired the enervating trick of attributing every misfortune, great or small, public or private, to the Government. When they learn the lessons of responsibility, they will unlearn this fatal habit, and not before.

I do not see, therefore, that the differences in condition between Ireland and the Colonies make against Home Rule. What I do see is ample material out of which would arise a strong and predominant party of order. The bulk of the nation are sons and daughters of a Church which has been hostile to revolution in every country but Ireland, and which would be hostile to it there from the day that the cause of revolution ceased to be the cause of self-government. If the peasantry were made to realize that at last the land settlement, wisely and equitably made, was what it must inexorably remain, and what no politicians could help them to alter, they would be as conservative as the peasantry under a similar condition in every other spot on the surface of the globe. There is no reason to expect that the manufacturers, merchants, and shopkeepers of Ireland would be less willing or less able to play an active and useful part in the affairs of their country than the same classes in England or Scotland. It will be said that this is mere optimist prophesying. But why is that to be flung aside under the odd name of sentimentalism, while pessimist prophesying is to be taken for gospel?

The only danger is lest we should allot new responsibilities to Irishmen with a too grudging and restrictive hand. For true responsibility there must be real power. It is easy to say that this power would be misused, and that the conditions both of Irish society and of the proposed Constitution must prevent it from being used for good. It is easy to say that separation would be a better end. Life is too short to discuss that. Separation is not the alternative either to Home Rule or to the status quo. If the people of Ireland are not to be trusted with real power over their own affairs, it would be a hundred times more just to England, and more merciful to Ireland, to take away from her that semblance of free government which torments and paralyzes one country, while it robs the other of national self-respect and of all the strongest motives and best opportunities of self-help. The status quo is drawing very near to its inevitable end. The two courses then open will be Home Rule on the one hand, and some shy bungling underhand imitation of a Crown Colony on the other. We shall have either to listen to the Irish representatives or to suppress them. Unless we have lost all nerve and all political faculty we shall, before many months are over, face these alternatives. Liberals are for the first; Tories at present incline to the second. It requires very moderate instinct for the forces at work in modern politics to foresee the path along which we shall move, in the interests alike of relief to Great Britain and of a sounder national life for Ireland. The only real question is not Whether we are to grant Home Rule, but How.

FOOTNOTES:

[Footnote 71: The following pages, with one or two slight alterations, are extracted, by the kind permission of Mr. James Knowles, from two articles which were published in the Nineteenth Century at the beginning of the present year, in reply to Professor Dicey's statement of the English case against Home Rule.]

[Footnote 72: The late J.E. Cairnes, after describing the clearances after the famine, goes on to say, "I own I cannot wonder that a thirst for revenge should spring from such calamities; that hatred, even undying hatred, for what they could not but regard as the cause and symbol of their misfortunes--English rule in Ireland--should possess the sufferers.... The disaffection now so widely diffused throughout Ireland may possibly in some degree be fed from historical traditions, and have its remote origin in the confiscations of the seventeenth century; but all that gives it energy, all that renders it dangerous, may, I believe, be traced to exasperation produced by recent transactions, and more especially to the bitter memories left by that most flagrant abuse of the rights of property and most scandalous disregard of the claims of humanity-- the wholesale clearances of the period following the famine."--Political Essays, p. 198.]

LESSONS OF IRISH HISTORY IN THE EIGHTEENTH CENTURY.

BY W.E. GLADSTONE.

Ireland for more than seven hundred years has been part of the British territory, and has been with slight exceptions held by English arms, or governed in the last resort from this side the water. Scotland was a foreign country until 1603, and possessed absolute independence until 1707. Yet, whether it was due to the standing barrier of the sea, or whatever may have been the cause, much less was known by Englishmen of Ireland than of Scotland. Witness the works of Shakespeare, whose mind, unless as to book-knowledge, was encyclop鑑ic, and yet who, while he seems at home in Scotland, may be said to tell us nothing of Ireland, unless it is that--

"The uncivil kerns of Ireland are in arms."[73]

During more recent times, the knowledge of Scotland on this side the border, which before was greatly in advance, has again increased in afar greater degree than the knowledge of Ireland.

It is to Mr. Lecky that we owe the first serious effort, both in his Leaders of Public Opinion and in his History of England in the Eighteenth Century, to produce a better state of things. He carefully and completely dovetailed the affairs of Ireland into English History, and the debt is one to be gratefully acknowledged. But such remedies, addressing themselves in the first instance to the lettered mind of the country, require much time to operate upon the mass, and upon the organs of superficial and transitory opinion, before the final stage, when they enter into our settled and familiar traditions. Meantime, since Ireland threatens to absorb into herself our Parliamentary life, there is a greatly enhanced necessity for becoming acquainted with the true state of the account between the islands that make up the United Kingdom, and with the likelihoods of the future in Ireland, so far as they are to be gathered from her past history.

That history, until the eighteenth century begins, has a dismal simplicity about it. Murder, persecution, confiscation too truly describe its general strain; and policy is on the whole subordinated to violence as the standing instrument of government. But after, say, the reign of William III., the element of representation begins to assert itself. Simplicity is by degrees exchanged for complexity; the play of human motives, singularly diversified, now becomes visible in the currents of a real public life. It has for a very long time been my habit, when consulted by young political students, to recommend them carefully to study the characters and events of the American Independence. Quite apart from the special and temporary reasons bearing upon the case, I would now add a twin recommendation to examine and ponder the lessons of Irish history during the eighteenth century. The task may not be easy, but the reward will be ample.

The mainspring of public life had, from a venerable antiquity, lain de jure within Ireland herself. The heaviest fetter upon this life was the Law of Poynings; the most ingenious device upon record for hamstringing legislative independence, because it cut off the means of resumption inherent in the nature of Parliaments such as were those of the three countries. But the Law of Poynings was an Irish Law. Its operation effectually aided on the civil side those ruder causes, under the action of which Ireland had lain for four centuries usually passive, and bleeding at every pore. The main factors of her destiny worked, in practice, from this side the water. But from the reign of Anne, or perhaps from the Revolution onwards,

"Novus s 鎔 orum nascitur ordo."

Of the three great nostrums so liberally applied by England, extirpation and persecution had entirely failed, but confiscation had done its work. The great Protestant landlordism of Ireland[74] had been strongly and effectually built up. But, like other human contrivances, while it held Ireland fast, it had also undesigned results. The repressed principle of national life, the struggles of which had theretofore been extinguished in blood, slowly sprang up anew in a form which, though extremely narrow, and extravagantly imperfect, was armed with constitutional guarantees; and, the regimen of violence once displaced, these guarantees were sure to operate. What had been transacted in England under Plantagenets and Stuarts was, to a large extent, transacted anew by the Parliament of Ireland in the eighteenth century. That Parliament, indeed, deserves almost every imaginable epithet of censure. It was corrupt, servile, selfish, cruel. But when we have said all this, and said it truly, there is more to tell. It was alive, and it was national. Even absenteeism, that obstinately clinging curse, though it enfeebled and distracted, could not, and did not, annihilate nationality. The Irish Legislation was, moreover, compressed and thwarted by a foreign executive; but even to this tremendous agent the vital principle was too strong eventually to succumb.

Mr. Lecky well observes that the Irish case supplied "one of the most striking examples upon record"[75] of an unconquerable efficacy in even the most defective Parliament. I am, however, doubtful whether in this proposition we have before us the whole case. This efficacy is not invariably found even in tolerably constructed Parliaments. Why do we find it in a Parliament of which the constitution and the environment were alike intolerable? My answer is, because that Parliament found itself faced by a British influence which was entirely anti-national, and was thus constrained to seek for strength in the principle of nationality.

Selfishness is a rooted principle of action in nations not less than in single persons. It seems to draw a certain perfume from the virtue of patriotism, which lies upon its borders. It stalks abroad with a semblance of decency, nay, even of excellence. And under this cover a paramount community readily embraces the notion, that a dependent community may be made to exist not for its own sake, but for the sake of an extraneous society of men. With this idea, the European nations, utterly benighted in comparison with the ancient Greeks, founded their transmarine dependencies. But a vast maritime distance, perhaps aided by some filtration of sound ideas, prevented the application of this theory in its nakedness and rigour to the American Colonies of England. In Ireland we had not even the title of founders to allege. Nay, we were, in point of indigenous civilization, the junior people. But the maritime severance, sufficient to prevent accurate and familiar knowledge, was not enough to bar the effective exercise of overmastering power. And power was exercised, at first from without, to support the Pale, to enlarge it, to make it include Ireland. When this had been done, power began, in the seventeenth century, to be exercised from within Ireland, within the precinct of its government and its institutions. These were carefully corrupted, from the multiplication of the Boroughs by James I. onwards, for the purpose. The struggle became civil, instead of martial; and it was mainly waged by agencies on the spot, not from beyond the Channel. When the rule of England passed over from the old violence into legal forms and doctrines, the Irish reaction against it followed the example. And the legal idea of Irish nationality took its rise in very humble surroundings; if the expression may be allowed, it was born in the slums of politics. Ireland reached the nadir of political depression when, at and after the Boyne, she had been conquered not merely by an English force, but by continental mercenaries. The ascendant Protestantism of the island had never stood so low in the aspect it presented to this country; inasmuch as the Irish Parliament, for the first time, I believe, declared itself dependent upon England,[76] and either did not desire, or did not dare, to support its champion Molyneux, when his work asserting Irish independence was burned in London. It petitioned for representation in the English Parliament, not in order to uplift the Irish people, but in order to keep them down. In its sympathies and in its aims the overwhelming mass of the population had no share. It was Swift who, by the Drapier's Letters, for the first time called into existence a public opinion flowing from and representing Ireland as a whole. He reasserted the doctrine of Molyneux, and denounced Wood's halfpence not only as a foul robbery, but as a constitutional and as a national insult. The patience of the Irish Protestants was tried very hard, and they were forced, as Sir Charles Duffy states in his vivid book, to purchase the power of oppressing their Roman Catholic fellow-countrymen at a great price.[77] Their pension list was made to provide the grants too degrading to be tolerated in England. The Presbyterians had to sit down under the Episcopal monopoly; but the enjoyment of that monopoly was not left to the Irish Episcopalians. In the time of Henry VIII. it had been necessary to import an English Archbishop Browne[78] and an English Bishop Bale, or there might not have been a single Protestant in Ireland. It was well to enrich the rolls of the Church of Ireland with the piety and learning of Ussher, and to give her in Bedell one name, at least, which carries the double crown of the hero and the saint. But, after the Restoration, by degrees the practice degenerated, and Englishmen were appointed in numbers to the Irish Episcopate in order to fortify and develop by numerical force what came to be familiarly known as the English interest. So that the Primate Boulter, during his government of Ireland, complains[79] that Englishmen are still less than one-half the whole body of Bishops, although the most important sees were to a large extent in their hands. The same practice was followed in the higher judicial offices. Fitzgibbon was the first Irishman who became Lord Chancellor.[80] The Viceroy, commonly absent, was represented by Lords Justices, who again were commonly English; and Primate Boulter, a most acute and able man, jealous of an Irish Speaker in that character, recommends that the commander of the forces should take his place.[81] When, later on, the Viceroy resided, it was a rule that the Chief Secretary should be an Englishman. On the occasion when Lord Castlereagh was by way of exception admitted to that office, an apology was found for it in his entire devotion to English policy and purposes. "His appointment," says Lord Cornwallis, "gives me great satisfaction, as he is so very unlike an Irishman!"[82] Resources were also found in the military profession, and among the voters for the Union we find the names of eight[83] English generals.

The arrangements under Poynings's Law, and the commercial proscription, drove the iron ever deeper and deeper into the souls of Irishmen. It is but small merit in the Irish Parliament of George I. and George II., if under these circumstances a temper was gradually formed in, and transmitted by, them, which might one day achieve the honours of patriotism. It was in dread of this most healthful process, that the English Government set sedulously to work for its repression. The odious policy was maintained by a variety of agencies; by the misuse of Irish revenue, a large portion of which was unhappily under their control; by maintaining the duration of the Irish House of Commons for the life of the Sovereign; and, worst of all, by extending the range of corruption within the walls, through the constant multiplication of paid offices tenable by members of Parliament without even the check of re-election on acceptance.

Thus by degrees those who sat in the Irish Houses came to feel both that they had a country, and that their country had claims upon them. The growth of a commercial interest in the Roman Catholic body must have accelerated the growth of this idea, as that interest naturally fell into line with the resistance to the English prescriptive laws. But the rate of progress was fearfully slow. It was hemmed in on every side by the obstinate unyielding pressure of selfish interests: the interest of the Established Church against the Presbyterians; the interest of the Protestant laity, or tithe-payers, against the clergy; the bold unscrupulous interest of a landlords' Parliament against the occupier of the soil; which, together with the grievance of the system of tithe-proctors, established in Ireland through the Whiteboys the fatal alliance between resistance to wrong and resistance to law, and supplied there the yet more disastrous facility of sustaining and enforcing wrong under the name of giving support to public tranquillity. Yet, forcing on its way amidst all these difficulties by a natural law, in a strange haphazard and disjointed method, and by a zigzag movement, there came into existence, and by degrees into steady operation, a sentiment native to Ireland and having Ireland for its vital basis, and yet not deserving the name of Irish patriotism, because its care was not for a nation, but for a sect. For a sect, in a stricter sense than may at first sight be supposed. The battle was not between Popery and a generalized Protestantism, though, even if it had been so, it would have been between a small minority and the vast majority of the Irish people. It was not a party of ascendency, but a party of monopoly, that ruled. It must always be borne in mind that the Roman Catholic aristocracy had been emasculated, and reduced to the lowest point of numerical and moral force by the odious action of the penal laws, and that the mass of the Roman Catholic population, clerical and lay, remained under the grinding force of many-sided oppression, and until long after the accession of George III. had scarcely a consciousness of political existence. As long as the great bulk of the nation could be equated to zero, the Episcopal monopolists had no motive for cultivating the good-will of the Presbyterians, who like the Roman Catholics maintained their religion, with the trivial exception of the Regium Donum, by their own resources, and who differed from them in being not persecuted, but only disabled. And this monopoly, which drew from the sacred name of religion its title to exist, offered through centuries an example of religious sterility to which a parallel can hardly be found among the communions of the Christian world. The sentiment, then, which animated the earlier efforts of the Parliament might be Iricism, but did not become patriotism until it had outgrown, and had learned to forswear or to forget, the conditions of its infancy. Neither did it for a long time acquire the courage of its opinions; for, when Lucas, in the middle of the century, reasserted the doctrine of Molyneux and of Swift, the Grand Jury of Dublin took part against him, and burned his book.[84] And the Parliament,[85] prompted by the Government, drove him into exile. And yet the smoke showed that there was fire. The infant, that confronted the British Government in the Parliament House, had something of the young Hercules about him. In the first exercises of strength he acquired more strength, and in acquiring more strength he burst the bonds that had confined him.

"Es machte mir zu eng, ich mussie fort."[86]

The reign of George IV. began with resolute efforts of the Parliament not to lengthen, as in England under his grandfather, but to shorten its own commission, and to become septennial. Surely this was a noble effort. It meant the greatness of their country, and it meant also personal self-sacrifice. The Parliament which then existed, elected under a youth of twenty-two, had every likelihood of giving to the bulk of its members a seat for life. This they asked to change for a maximum term of seven years. This from session to session, in spite of rejection after rejection in England, they resolutely fought to obtain. It was an English amendment which, on a doubtful pretext; changed seven years to eight. Without question some acted under the pressure of constituents; but only a minority of the members had constituents, and popular exigencies from such a quarter might have been bought off by an occasional vote, and could not have induced a war with the Executive and with England so steadily continued, unless a higher principle had been at work.

The triumph came at last; and from 1768 onwards the Commons never wholly relapsed into their former quiescence. True, this was for a Protestant House, constituency, and nation; but ere long they began to enlarge their definition of nationality. Flood and Lucas, the commanders in the real battle, did not dream of giving the Roman Catholics a political existence, but to their own constituents they performed an honourable service and gave a great boon. Those, who had insincerely supported the measure, became the dupes of their own insincerity. In the very year of this victory, a Bill for a slight relaxation of the penal laws was passed, but met its death in England.[87] Other Bills followed, and one of them became an Act in 1771. A beginning had thus been made on behalf of religious liberty, as a corollary to political emancipation. It was like a little ray of light piercing its way through the rocks into a cavern and supplying the prisoner at once with guidance and with hope. Resolute action, in withholding or shortening supply, convinced the Executive in Dublin, and the Ministry in London, that serious business was intended. And it appeared, even in this early stage, how necessary it was for a fruitful campaign on their own behalf to enlarge their basis, and enlist the sympathies of hitherto excluded fellow-subjects.

It may seem strange that the first beginnings of successful endeavour should have been made on behalf not of the "common Protestantism," but of Roman Catholics. But, as Mr. Lecky has shown, the Presbyterians had been greatly depressed and distracted, while the Roman Catholics had now a strong position in the commerce of the country, and in Dublin knocked, as it were, at the very doors of the Parliament. There may also have been an apprehension of republican sentiments among the Protestants of the north, from which the Roman Catholics were known to be free. Not many years, however, passed before the softening and harmonizing effects, which naturally flow from a struggle for liberty, warmed the sentiment of the House in favour of the Presbyterians.

A Bill was passed by the Irish Parliament in 1778, which greatly mitigated the stringency of the penal laws. Moreover, in its preamble was recited, as a ground for this legislation, that for "a long series of years" the Roman Catholics had exhibited an "uniform peaceable behaviour." In doing and saying so much, the Irish Parliament virtually bound itself to do more.[88] In this Bill was contained a clause which repealed the Sacramental Test, and thereby liberated the Presbyterians from disqualification. But the Bill had to pass the ordeal of a review in England, and there the clause was struck out. The Bill itself, though mutilated, was wisely passed by a majority of 127 to 89. Even in this form it excited the enthusiastic admiration of Burke.[89] Nor were the Presbyterians forgotten at the epoch when, in 1779-80, England, under the pressure of her growing difficulties, made large commercial concessions to Ireland. The Dublin Parliament renewed the Bill for the removal of the Sacramental Test. And it was carried by the Irish Parliament in the very year which witnessed in London the disgraceful riots of Lord George Gordon, and forty-eight years before the Imperial Parliament conceded, on this side the Channel, any similar relief. Other contemporary signs bore witness to the growth of toleration; for the Volunteers, founded in 1778, and originally a Protestant body, after a time received Roman Catholics into their ranks. These impartial proceedings are all the more honourable to Irish sentiment in general, because Lord Charlemont, its champion out of doors, and Flood, long the leader of the Independent party in the Parliament, were neither of them prepared to surrender the system of Protestant ascendency.

In order to measure the space which had at this period been covered by the forward movement of liberality and patriotism, it is necessary to look back to the early years of the Georgian period, when Whiggism had acquired a decisive ascendency, and the spirits of the great deep were let loose against Popery. But the temper of proscription in the two countries exhibited specific differences. Extravagant in both, it became in Ireland vulgar and indecent. In England, it was Tilburina,[90] gone mad in white satin; in Ireland it was Tilburina's maid, gone mad in white linen. The Lords Justices of Ireland, in 1715, recommended the Parliament to put an end to all other distinctions in Ireland "but that of Protestant and Papist."[91] And the years that followed seem to mark the lowest point of constitutional depression for the Roman Catholic population in particular, as well as for Ireland at large. The Commons, in 1715, prayed for measures to discover any Papist enlisting in the King's service, in order that he might be expelled "and punished with the utmost severity of the law."[92] When an oath of abjuration had been imposed which prevented nearly all priests from registering, a Bill was passed by the Commons in 1719 for branding the letter P on the cheek of all priests, who were unregistered, with a red-hot iron. The Privy Council "disliked" this punishment, and substituted for it the loathsome measure by which safe guardians are secured for Eastern harems. The English Government could not stomach this beastly proposal; and, says Mr. Lecky,[93] unanimously restored the punishment of branding. The Bill was finally lost in Ireland, but only owing to a clause concerning leases. It had gone to England winged with a prayer from the Commons that it might be recommended "in the most effectual manner to his Majesty," and by the assurance of the Viceroy in reply that they might depend on his due regard to what was desired.[94] In the same year passed the Act which declared the title of the British Parliament to make laws for the government of Ireland. On the accession of George II., a considerable body of Roman Catholics offered an address of congratulation. It was received by the Lords Justices with silent contempt, and no one knows whether it ever reached its destination. Finally, the acute state-craft of Primate Boulter resisted habitually the creation of an "Irish interest," and above all any capacity of the Roman Catholics to contribute to its formation; and in the first year of George II. a clause was introduced in committee into a harmless Bill[95] for the regulation of elections, which disfranchised at a single stroke all the Roman Catholic voters in Ireland who up to that period had always enjoyed the franchise.

It is painful to record the fact that the remarkable progress gradually achieved was in no way due to British influence. For nearly forty years from the arrival of Archbishop Boulter in Ireland, the government of Ireland was in the hands of the Primates. The harshness of administration was gradually tempered, especially in the brief viceroyalty of Lord Chesterfield; but the British policy was steadily opposed to the enlargement of Parliamentary privilege, or the creation of any Irish interest, however narrow its basis, while the political extinction of the mass of the people was complete. The pecuniary wants, however, of the Government, extending beyond the hereditary revenue, required a resort to the national purse. The demands which were accordingly made, and these alone, supplied the Parliament with a vantage-ground, and a principle of life. The action of this principle brought with it civilizing and humanizing influences, which had become clearly visible in the early years of George III., and which were cherished by the war of American Independence, as by a strong current of fresh air in a close and murky dungeon.

The force of principles, and the significance of political achievements, is to be estimated in no small degree by the slenderness of the means available to those who promote them. And the progress brought about in the Irish Parliament is among the most remarkable on record, because it was effected against the joint resistance of a hostile Executive and of an intolerable constitution. Of the three hundred members, about two-thirds were nominated by individual patrons and by close corporations. What was still worse, the action of the Executive was increasingly directed, as the pulse of the national life came to beat more vigorously, to the systematic corruption of the Parliament borough pensions and paid offices. In the latter part of the century, more than one-third of the members of Parliament were dismissible at pleasure from public emoluments. If the base influence of the Executive allied itself with the patriotic party, everything might be hoped. For we must bear in mind not only the direct influence of this expenditure on those who were in possession, but the enormous power of expectancy on those who were not. Conversely, when the Government were determined to do wrong, there were no means commonly available of forcing it to do right, in any matter that touched either religious bigotry or selfish interest. With so miserable an apparatus, and in the face of the ever-wakeful Executive sustained by British power, it is rather wonderful how much than how little was effected. I am not aware of a single case in which a measure on behalf of freedom was proposed by British agency, and rejected by the Irish Parliament. On the other hand, we have a long list of the achievements of that Parliament due to a courage and perseverance which faced and overcame a persistent English opposition. Among other exploits, it established periodical elections, obtained the writ of Habeas Corpus, carried the independence of the judges, repealed the Test Act, limited the abominable expenditure on pensions, subjected the acceptance of office from the crown to the condition of re-election, and achieved, doubtless with the powerful aid of the volunteers, freedom of trade with England, and the repeal of Poynings's Act, and of the British Act of 1719.[96]

All this it did without the manifestation, either within the walls or among the Roman Catholic population, of any disposition to weaken the ties which bound Ireland to the empire. All this it did; and what had the British Parliament been about during the same period, with its vastly greater means both of self-defence and of action? It had been building up the atrocious criminal code, tampering in the case of Wilkes with liberty of election, and tampering with many other liberties; driving, too, the American Colonies into rebellion, while, as to good legislation, the century is almost absolutely blank, until between 1782 and 1793 we have the establishment of Irish freedom, the economical reform of Mr. Burke, the financial reforms of Mr. Pitt, the new libel law of Mr. Fox, and the legislative constitution of Canada, in which both these great statesmen concurred.

But we have not yet reached the climax of Irish advancement. When, in 1782 and 1783, the legislative relations of the two countries were fundamentally rectified by the formal acknowledgment of Irish nationality, the beginning of a great work was accomplished; but its final consummation, though rendered practicable and even easy, depended wholly on the continuing good intention of the British Cabinet. The Acts of 1782 and 1783 required a supplemental arrangement, to obviate those secondary difficulties in the working of the two

Legislatures, which supplied Mr. Pitt with his main parliamentary plea for the Union. What was yet more important was the completion of the scheme in Ireland itself. And this under three great heads: (1) The purification of Parliament by a large measure of reform; (2) the abolition of all Roman Catholic disabilities; (3) the establishment of a proper relation between the Legislative and the Executive powers. It is often urged, with cynical disregard to justice and reason, that with the Grattan Parliament we had corruption, coercion, discontent, and finally rebellion. But the political mischiefs, which disfigure the brief life of the Grattan Parliament, and the failure to obtain the two first of the three great purposes I have named, were all in the main due to the third grand flaw in the Irish case after 1782. I mean the false position, and usually mischievous character, of the Irish Executive, which, with its army of placemen and expectants in Parliament, was commonly absolute master of the situation. Well does Mr. Swift MacNeill,[97] in his very useful work, quote the words of Mr. Fox in 1797: "The advantages, which the form of a free Government seemed to promise, have been counteracted by the influence of the Executive Government, and of the British Cabinet."

There were five Viceroys between 1782 and 1790. Then came a sixth, Lord Westmoreland, the worst of them all, whose political judgment was on a par with his knowledge of the English language.[98] The great settlement of 1782-3 was in the main worked by men who were radically adverse to its spirit and intention. But they were omnipotent in their control of the unreformed. Parliament of Ireland, more and more drenched, under their unceasing and pestilent activity, with fresh doses of corruption. Westmoreland and his myrmidons actually persuaded Pitt, in 1792, that Irish Protestantism and its Parliament were unconquerably adverse to the admission of Roman Catholics to the franchise; but when the proposal was made from the Throne in 1793, notwithstanding the latent hostility of the Castle, the Parliament passed the Bill with little delay, and "without any serious opposition."[99] The votes against it were one and three on two divisions[100] respectively. A minority of sixty-nine supported, against the Government, a clause for extending the measure to seats in Parliament. That clause, lost by a majority of ninety-four, might apparently have been carried, but for "Dublin Castle," by an even larger majority.

I shall not here examine the interesting question, whether the mission of Lord Fitzwilliam was wholly due to the action of those Whig statesmen who were friendly to the war, but disinclined to a junction with Mr. Pitt except on condition of a fundamental change in the administration of Ireland. Nor shall I dwell upon his sudden, swift, and disastrous recall. But I purpose here to invite attention to the most remarkable fact in the whole history of the Irish Parliament. When the Viceroy's doom was known, when the return to the policy and party of ascendency lay darkly lowering in the immediate future, this diminutive and tainted Irish Parliament, with a chivalry rare even in the noblest histories, made what can hardly be called less than a bold attempt to arrest the policy of retrogression adopted by the Government in London. Lord Fitzwilliam was the declared friend of Roman Catholic Emancipation, which was certain to be followed by reform; and he had struck a death-blow at bigotry and monopoly in the person of their heads, Mr. Beresford and Mr. Cooke. The Bill of Emancipation was introduced on the 12th of February,[101] with only three dissentient voices. On the 14th, when the London Cabinet had declared dissent from the proceedings of their Viceroy without recalling him, Sir L. Parsons at once moved an address, imploring him to continue among them, and only postponed it at the friendly request of Mr. Ponsonby.[102] On the 2nd of March, when the recall was a fact, the House voted that Lord Fitzwilliam merited "the thanks of that House, and the confidence of the people."[103] On the 5th the Duke of Leinster moved, and the House of Peers carried, a similar resolution.[104]

At this epoch I pause. Here there opens a new and disastrous drama of disgrace to England and misery to Ireland. This is the point at which we may best learn the second and the greatest lesson taught by the history of Ireland in the eighteenth century. It is this, that, awful as is the force of bigotry, hidden under the mask of religion, but fighting for plunder and for power with all the advantages of possession, of prescription, and of extraneous support, there is a David that can kill this Goliath. That conquering force lies in the principle of nationality.

It was the growing sense of nationality that prompted the Irish Parliament to develop its earlier struggles for privilege on the narrow ground into a genuine contest for freedom, civil and religious, on a ground as broad as Ireland, nay, as humanity at large. If there be such things as contradictions in the world of politics, they are to be found in nationality on the one side, and bigotry of all kinds on the other, but especially religious bigotry, which is of all the most baneful. Whatever is given to the first of these two is lost to the second. I speak of a reasonable and reasoning, not of a blind and headstrong nationality; of a nationality which has regard to circumstances and to traditions, and which only requires that all relations, of incorporation or of independence, shall be adjusted to them according to the laws of Nature's own enactment. Such a nationality was the growth of the last century in Ireland. As each Irishman began to feel that he had a country, to which he belonged, and which belonged to him, he was, by a true process of nature, drawn more and more into brotherhood, and into the sense of brotherhood, with those who shared the allegiance and the property, the obligation and the heritage. And this idea of country, once well conceived, presents itself as a very large idea, and as a framework for most other ideas, so as to supply the basis of a common life. Hence it was that, on the coming of Lord Fitzwilliam, the whole generous emotion of the country leapt up with one consent, and went forth to meet him. Hence it was that religious bigotry was no longer an appreciable factor in the public life of Ireland. Hence it was that on his recall, and in order to induce acquiescence in his recall, it became necessary to divide again the host that had, welcomed him--to put one part of it in array as Orangemen, who were to be pampered and inflamed; and to quicken the self-consciousness of another and larger mass by repulsion and proscription, by stripping Roman Catholics of arms in the face of licence and of cruelty, and, finally, by clothing the extreme of lawlessness with the forms of law.

Within the last twelve months we have seen, in the streets of Belfast, the painful proof that the work of Beresford and of Castlereagh has been found capable for the moment of revival. To aggravate or sustain Irish disunion, religious bigotry has been again evoked in Ireland. If the curse be an old one, there is also an old cure, recorded in the grand pharmacopoeia of history; and if the abstract force of policy and prudence are insufficient for the work, we may yet find that the evil spirit will be effectually laid by the gentle influence of a living and working Irish nationality. Quod faxit Deus.

FOOTNOTES:

[Footnote 73: 2 Henry VI., act iii. sc. 1.]

[Footnote 74: Lecky's History of England in the Eighteenth Century, chap, vii. vol. ii, p. 205.]

[Footnote 75: Lecky's History of England in the Eighteenth Century, vol. ii. p. 227.]

[Footnote 76: Duffy's Bird's-Eye View, p. 164.]

[Footnote 77: Duffy's Bird's-Eye View, p. 166.]

[Footnote 78: See Ball's History of the Church of Ireland, a valuable work, deserving of more attention than it seems to have received.]

[Footnote 79: Boulter's Letters, i. 138, et alibi.]

[Footnote 80: Lecky's History of England in the Eighteenth Century, ii.]

[Footnote 81: Boulter's Letters, vol. ii.]

[Footnote 82: Cornwallis's Correspondence, ii. 441.]

[Footnote 83: Grattan's Life and Times, v. 173.]

[Footnote 84: Lecky, ii. 430.]

[Footnote 85: Duffy, p. 177.]

[Footnote 86: Schiller's Wallenstein.]

[Footnote 87: Lecky, iv. 489.]

[Footnote 88: Lecky, iv. 477-479; Brown, Laws against Catholics, pp. 329-332.]

[Footnote 89: Lecky, pp. 499-501.]

[Footnote 90: Sheridan's Critic, act iii. sc. I.]

[Footnote 91: Plowden's History (1809), ii. 70.]

[Footnote 92: Brown, Laws against Catholics, p. 289.]

[Footnote 93: Lecky, i. 297.]

[Footnote 94: Plowden, i. 297.]

[Footnote 95: 1 Geo. II. c. ix. sect 7.]

[Footnote 96: See Lecky, vi. 521.]

[Footnote 97: The Irish Parliament, p. 64. Cassell: 1885.]

[Footnote 98: See Lecky, vi. 492, 493.]

[Footnote 99: Lecky, vi. 567.]

[Footnote 100: Plowden's Historical Review, ii. 335.]

[Footnote 101: Ibid., ii. 353.]

[Footnote 102: Plowden's Historical Review_, ii. 498.]

[Footnote 103: Ibid., ii. 357.]

[Footnote 104: Ibid., ii. 505.]